Published by **Hero Collector Books**, a division of Eaglemoss Ltd. 2020
1st Floor, Beaumont House, Kensington Village, Avonmore Road,
W14 8TS, London, UK.

BOSS Film photos by Virgil Mirano;
courtesy of Richard Edlund

ILM photos © Industrial Light & Magic. Used with permission.

Most of the contents of this book were originally published as part of
Ghostbusters: Build the Ecto-1 2019–2020

www.herocollector.com

ISBN 978-1-85875-854-1

10 9 8 7 6 5 4 3 2 1

Printed in China

GHOSTBUSTERS™
THE INSIDE STORY

STORIES FROM THE CAST AND CREW OF THE BELOVED FILMS

MATT MCALLISTER
FOREWORD BY IVAN REITMAN

CONTENTS

FOREWORD BY
IVAN REITMAN

Thirty-five years ago, no one had seen anything quite like *Ghostbusters* before. A movie populated with hilarious but charming heroes and genuinely scary ghosts. A movie that made you laugh one minute and scream the next. A big-budget comedy with elaborate special effects. This wasn't your typical summer blockbuster.

Despite the unconventional concept, we all believed we were onto something special. I felt it when I first read Dan Aykroyd's original story treatment back in '83. Dan had come up with the wild futuristic concept of interdimensional ghost-hunters that included wonderful ideas like the Ectomobile, the Stay Puft Marshmallow Man, and the apparition who would later become known as Slimer. I suggested refashioning it into a contemporary 'going into business' story set in New York City, and we brought in the brilliant, much-missed Harold Ramis to co-write the script and play Egon.

Of course, it wouldn't have been the same movie without Bill Murray. By this point I'd already worked with Bill on *Meatballs* and *Stripes* and knew what a joy it was to watch him in action. His Peter Venkman is one of cinema's great, multi-layered comic characters. Many other amazing actors were crucial to the film's success too. We were fortunate to have Ernie Hudson as Winston, who acted as kind of an explanatory voice for the audience. Joined by the wonderful Sigourney Weaver as Dana, the remarkable Rick Moranis as Louis, Annie Potts as Janine, Bill Atherton as Walter Peck… a director could not have asked for a more perfect cast.

The other characters in the movie that we needed to get right were the ghosts and ghouls. Richard Edlund and his talented team of artists at Boss Film Studios brought Slimer, Stay Puft, the Terror Dogs and all the other creatures to life with such imagination and technical expertise. The comedy and the special effects worked amazingly well together – and thankfully audiences thought so too!

This book contains stories about all of the talented people who helped make *Ghostbusters* and *Ghostbusters II* such joyful experiences. Above all, it's the fans who have kept the spirit of *Ghostbusters* alive for over three decades – and I hope for many more decades to come!

Ivan Reitman

THEY'RE HERE TO SAVE THE WORLD.

GHOSTBUSTERS™

CHAPTER 1
THE MAKING OF
GHOSTBUSTERS

IT ALL BEGAN WITH DAN AYKROYD.
The star of *Saturday Night Live* and *The Blues Brothers* had worked up a movie treatment for himself and his friend John Belushi. Entitled *Ghost Smashers*, it revolved around a team of inter-dimensional spook hunters and boasted such innovative concepts as a Cadillac Ambulance known as Ecto-1 and the Stay Puft Marshmallow Man.

Ghostbusters' director Ivan Reitman – by then a bankable filmmaker following the success of *Meatballs* and *Stripes* – loved the concept, but suggested Aykroyd revise his story to be set in present-day New York. He also recommended bringing on board another comedy giant, Harold Ramis, to write the final script with Aykroyd. Ramis would go on to co-star as the team's brainbox Egon Spengler.

Joining Reitman to facilitate the production, were his trusted colleagues Joe Medjuck (who he had worked with on *Stripes* and *Heavy Metal*) and Michael C. Gross (the former art director of *National Lampoon*) as associate producers. Meanwhile, the tragic death of John Belushi meant that the role of Venkman was filled by Bill Murray, who knew Aykroyd, Ramis, and Reitman through his work on *Saturday Night Live*, *Meatballs,* and *Stripes*.

The original script was tightly packed with quotable lines and hysterical set pieces, but it was made even funnier thanks to the furious ad-libbing of its stars during shooting. A comedy classic was gradually taking shape.

CINEMATIC LEGENDS

Of course, *Ghostbusters* wasn't a straightforward comedy. It was a comedy-horror that required extensive and elaborate special effects. These were provided by Richard Edlund, who had left ILM (where he had won Academy Awards® for his work on *Star Wars*, *The Empire Strikes Back*, and *Raiders of the Lost Ark*) and his fledgling Boss Film Studios.

Other legendary names who worked on the film included composer Elmer Bernstein (*The Magnificent Seven*), production designer John DeCuir (*Cleopatra*), cinematographer László Kovács (*Easy Rider*), and editor Sheldon Kahn (*One Flew Over the Cuckoo's Nest*). Meanwhile, the central cast expanded to include Ernie Hudson, who had worked with Reitman on *Spacehunter: Adventures in the Forbidden Zone*; Sigourney Weaver, a big star after *Alien*; *SCTV* comedy hero Rick Moranis as Louis; William Atherton (*The Sugarland Express*) as the obnoxious Walter Peck; character actor David Margulies as Mayor Lenny Clotch; and Annie Potts (*Corvette Summer*) as Janine.

The production schedule seemed impossibly tight, but its creators knew they were making something special. The result surpassed everyone's expectations. Backed by a clever marketing campaign and accompanied by Ray Parker Jr.'s unforgettable theme song, the movie was a critical and box office smash when it opened across the USA on June 8, 1984. It emerged as the second-highest grossing film of the year after *Beverly Hills Cop*, and, with a total US box office gross of $242.2 million, remains one of the most successful comedies of all time.

Yet *Ghostbusters* wasn't just a successful film. It was a bona fide sensation, one that spun off into animated series, comic books, videogames, and mountains of merchandise. Perhaps most importantly it inspired a devoted fanbase of Ghostheads who would create replica proton packs, establish their own Ghostbusters groups, and keep the spirit of the film alive for over 35 years.

DAN AYKROYD

THE
ORIGINAL
GHOSTBUSTER

Back in the early 1980s Dan Aykroyd hit upon the idea of melding madcap humor with paranormal activity. More than three decades later, *Ghostbusters* remains one of the best-loved comedies of all time.

HERE'S A FRIGHTENING THOUGHT: without Dan Aykroyd there would be no Ecto-1, no Stay Puft Marshmallow Man, no Slimer, no *Ghostbusters*. The story and structure may have evolved in later drafts, but the premise of the movie – along with its coolest ghosts and *that* car – were all in place from Aykroyd's very first treatment.

"I vividly remember when I first had the idea," Aykroyd recalls. "It was around the autumn of '81 and I was in my old ancestral farmhouse. One afternoon I was alone, and I picked up a copy of the *American Society for Psychical Research* quarterly journal, which my dad subscribed to. Other summer cottages had *Life* or *National Geographic*, but we had *Fate* and *The American Society for Psychical Research*! Anyway, there was this article on parapsychology and quantum physics. And I read a theory in there that if you build the right hardware, it might be possible to freeze, at least momentarily, the image of an apparition. I thought, 'Wow, that's neat!' It just started me wondering…"

It's no surprise that Aykroyd's dad subscribed to parapsychological journals. The Aykroyds had a long-standing interest in the supernatural. The actor's great-grandfather, Doctor Sam Aykroyd, was an Edwardian spiritualist researcher who held regular seances, while his father, Peter, wrote a book entitled *A History of Ghosts* that revealed what it was like growing up in a family that had its own medium. Spirits were simply part of everyday life for the Aykroyds.

" IT WAS MUCH DARKER, MUCH SCARIER – ALMOST LIKE A HORROR MOVIE… "

"Right up until the '40s, the family were holding their own seances," Aykroyd says. "Many entities came through. So I was really immersed in the family business, as it were, and the concept of believing in the afterlife – believing in not just life surviving, but the consciousness of an individual surviving. In trance channelling, a good medium can reach your lost aunt, your lost grandmother, your lost brother, your lost sister, your lost cat… They come through vividly to tell you things that only that lost person – or entity – would know. It's very real to me."

GHOSTBUSTERS

ABOVE Back off man, they're scientists: Dan Aykroyd (Stantz) with Bill Murray (Venkman) and Harold Ramis (Spengler).

While Aykroyd's interest in the paranormal was deadly serious, the *Saturday Night Live* star took equal inspiration from his comedy heroes. "I thought, 'Wouldn't it be great to do an old-style ghost comedy like The Bowery Boys' *Ghost Chasers* or Bob Hope's *Ghost Breakers*, or the films of Abbott and Costello?' But we could do that style of crazy comedy within the real world of paranormal research that was going on at the time – Duke University's department for paranormal research, Maimonide's Dream Laboratory, the work of Karlis Osis at the Department for Psychical Research... So then I started to write it in the autumn and winter of '81, into '82."

Aykroyd's first draft for *Ghost Smashers* – as it was originally titled – had some significant differences from the final film. "It was more inter-dimensional, touching upon theories that there are

other dimensions parallel to the four dimensions of height, length, width and time. I just thought, 'Boy, you can really bring forth a lot of havoc by extrapolating what might be going on in some of those different dimensions!'"

SUPERNATURAL EXTERMINATORS
According to Aykroyd, the Ghostbusters in this first draft were like tough sanitation workers or exterminators who constantly smoked and swore. "It was much darker, much scarier – almost like a horror movie, though with a wry humor. It was structured differently too; Stay Puft appeared in the middle of the movie rather than the end."

By this time Aykroyd was a big star thanks to his work on *Saturday Night Live* and the hit movies *The Blues Brothers* (1980) and *Neighbors* (1981). All of those projects had paired Aykroyd with his friend

John Belushi, and Belushi was lined up to star in the Peter Venkman role that eventually went to Bill Murray.

"I originally wrote it for John, Eddie Murphy and myself," Aykroyd says. "I can't remember whether Eddie turned it down or whether we never got the script to him, but Johnny was excited about it. He thought it was neat and encouraged me to do it. I remember I was working out of our office on Fifth Avenue when I got the call saying John had died… I was mid-way through writing a line for him at the time."

" I ORIGINALLY WROTE IT FOR JOHN (BELUSHI), EDDIE MURPHY AND MYSELF … "

To accompany his first draft, Aykroyd hired his old Carleton University buddy John Daveikis to draw up designs of several key concepts, including Slimer, the Ecto-1, the proton packs and uniforms, and Mr. Stay Puft. "I said I wanted Mr. Stay Puft to be a funny but menacing combination of the Michelin Man, the Pilsbury Doughboy and a Canadian product called the Angelus Marshmallow Man, who was this big, fat roasting marshmallow – a fop with a nightstick and a cap with a star on it. When John sent me the envelope with his designs, I fell off my chair with the way he had rendered Stay Puft! Because he had put that little sailor hat on him. It was just so arbitrary and so funny, I went to my knees. I remember Billy uses that line in the movie, 'So he's a sailor…' It was perfect. Everybody said, 'Oh, we gotta bring this guy to life!'"

REWRITES AND RESTRUCTURES

With his concept designs and first draft in place, Aykroyd met with director Ivan Reitman, who he knew from their time working at CITY-TV in Toronto and who was now a hot property following the success of his movies *Meatballs* (1979) and *Stripes* (1980), both starring Bill Murray. Reitman liked the film but suggested numerous changes to the story. Did Reitman suggest any changes he disagreed with?

"You know what, not really," says Aykroyd. "A first draft is never final. I knew I had some flaws in it, that I had come up with something that was maybe a little inaccessible to some people. So Ivan looked at it and said, 'What if we did this? What if we restructured it here, made it lighter, put a romance in it…'

"The first suggestion he made was to get Harold Ramis on board. I said, 'Wow, will he do it?' Because Harold, who I knew from [Canadian comedy troupe and sketch show] Second City, had written *Animal House* and *Caddyshack*… So I didn't fight it at all. I said, 'Let's go make something accessible,' which is what we went on to do once Harold got on board."

Aykroyd and Ramis's partnership was key to the success of the final script, even if they had very different perspectives on the afterlife. "Harold was not a believer in the supernatural," Aykroyd says. "But he knew all about the research. He knew about the American Society for Psychical Research and all the stuff that was being done by institutes around the world. So we were talking the same language, even though I'm a believer and he was not. But he knew exactly what I was going for in terms of marrying antic comedy with the spirit of my great-grandfather's research."

BELOW Checking the P.K.E. (PsychoKinetic Energy) meter. Ray Stantz's gear benefited from Dan Aykroyd's real-life paranormal interests.

Aykroyd and Ramis set to work thrashing out the revised story in both LA and Canada. Before long they had devised a new blueprint for the movie, with every entity in Aykroyd's original treatment making it into the new version in some form (along with some new ghouls). The duo, along with Reitman, then spent an intense three weeks refining the script at Aykroyd's house in Martha's Vineyard.

DOWN IN THE BASEMENT

"The house is on a spectacular hill overlooking the sea from a distance of several miles," Aykroyd says. "It was so beautiful looking at the trees and the view… I said, 'We can't work up here in the living room. It's too beautiful, we'll never get any work done!' So I made us go down to the basement, which was dark, moist and had this bad green wallpaper. It was like a hospital ward down there. I had bunk beds with hospital screens between them, and we sat in the corner and wrote what was the first comprehensive outline of what we were going to do. We'd work for three hours, have a nice lunch, then go back for three hours… We got a lot of work done by not looking at the view and not enjoying Martha's Vineyard like everybody else was that summer!"

Aykroyd and Ramis kept on writing right up until the film started shooting – and beyond. "All of the dialogue was just a pencil sketch," Aykroyd recalls. "We went out there with a template for the actors to springboard off using words they wanted to at the time, without being constricted. Certainly Billy [Murray]… I would say 80% of what he did was made up on the day. A lot of Rick Moranis's performance was improv. There were changes all the time. The ending… We didn't know how we were going to get rid of that guy! But all the way through we say, 'Don't cross the streams, don't cross the streams,' and that led us through to a proper ending."

The shoot itself, Aykroyd insists, went fairly smoothly – aside from the little matter of handing

BUSTED!

Rumor has it that the black Cadillac Miller-Meteor seen in *Ghostbusters* also appeared in the 1967 murder mystery *In The Heat Of The Night*. It didn't: the ambulance in that film was a 1959 Cadillac Eureka.

LEFT Dan Aykroyd on set with a plush toy of his creation Mr. Stay Puft. The Marshmallow Man, Slimer, Ecto-1, and the proton packs were all present in Aykroyd's original, much darker story treatment.

out bribes. "Back then, New York was one of the most corrupt venues in the world for any kind of activity. We had to pay people off. I won't say what entities, but money was put in paper bags and given to people. There was a lot of bureaucracy in the city and we had to deal with its rampant kickback schemes. But we did manage to do a lot by walking around without paying for permits."

Another snag was that filming Bill Murray on the streets of New York attracted wide-eyed fans, which risked prolonging the location shooting. "Billy was a huge star then because of *SNL* and the movies he'd done," Aykroyd laughs. "Crowds would gather during significant scenes and people would mob him wherever he went! But we managed to get out of New York in time to do our studio filming."

THE SWEET SLIME OF SUCCESS

On its release in June 1984, *Ghostbusters* was a box office sensation, something Aykroyd attributes to the film's "heart, honesty and warmth." For Aykroyd, the heart of the film isn't so much the relationship between the Ghostbusters themselves but the dynamic between Bill Murray's Peter Venkman,

Sigourney Weaver's Dana Barrett and Rick Moranis's Louis Tully. "That triumvirate really drives the movie along. Bill and Sigourney's chemistry, and Rick's endearing character… To me they'll always be the stars of the movie. Along with Ernie [Hudson] and Annie Potts, their performances really make it. Harold and I are kind of the least interesting characters in the movie, you know? We're more expository characters. But the Ghostbusters are all lovable… people like being around them."

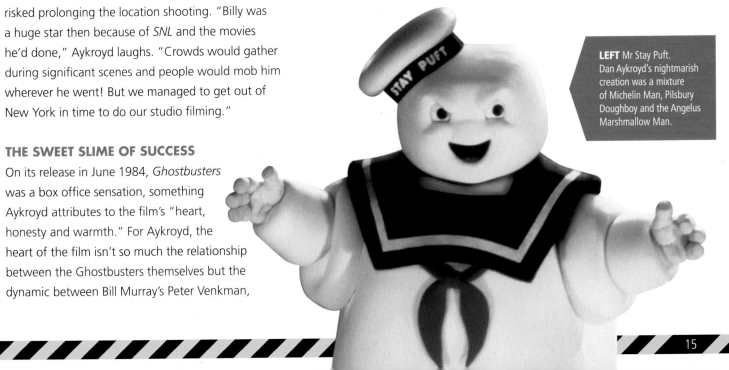

LEFT Mr Stay Puft. Dan Aykroyd's nightmarish creation was a mixture of Michelin Man, Pilsbury Doughboy and the Angelus Marshmallow Man.

BILL MURRAY

THE LEGEND OF
WILD BILL

Bill Murray's ad-libbing and manic energy were crucial to the success of *Ghostbusters* – and during the shoot, the star attracted attention wherever he went.

BILL MURRAY ALWAYS KNEW HOW TO make an entrance. When Harold Ramis and Ivan Reitman went to meet the actor at La Guardia Airport to discuss the *Ghostbusters* script a couple of weeks before production was due to start, the actor wasn't exactly inconspicuous. "Bill flew in on a private plane, an hour late, and came through the terminal with a stadium horn – one of those bullhorns that plays 80 different fight songs – and he was addressing everyone in sight with this thing and playing a song," Ramis said in the 1985 book *Making Ghostbusters*. There followed a short, positive discussion about the script at a restaurant in Queens. "I've never seen him in higher spirits," Ramis continued. "We spent an hour together, and he said maybe two words about the script. Then he took off again. But it was trust. *Ghostbusters* was the first film he'd ever committed to without fighting like crazy."

Dan Aykroyd had presented Murray with an early unfinished draft of *Ghostbusters* even before he had brought it to the attention of Ivan Reitman. Though Aykroyd had written the role of Peter Venkman for John Belushi, Murray seemed a natural choice to take on the character after Belushi's death. Murray – who had known Aykroyd, Belushi and Harold Ramis since their days at the Second City comedy troupe – responded positively to the concept and signed up.

“ [VENKMAN BECAME] HIPPER AND MORE VERBAL... A HUCKSTER ”

However, he was not involved in Aykroyd and Ramis's subsequent drastic rewrites as he was off in India (virtually unreachable, by all accounts) filming his passion project, *The Razor's Edge*. Former Columbia Pictures chairman Frank Price revealed he had a tacit understanding with Murray that he would greenlight the latter picture in return for Murray agreeing to star in *Ghostbusters*.

Aykroyd and Ramis's rewrites saw many changes to Venkman's character including, as Ramis put it in *Making Ghostbusters*, making him "hipper and more verbal than the others – more of a huckster, the salesman of the team, someone who is weaker on the technical side and probably didn't do all that well in school but is smart enough to have teamed up with guys smarter than him." Ramis also admitted that in the process some of the attitude and character of Winston (originally a bigger role) was transferred to Venkman.

Murray may not have been in the writing room, but by this stage Ramis was comfortable writing for the actor, having worked with him on the triple hits of *Meatballs*, *Caddyshack* and *Stripes*.

DR. PETER VENKMAN

Business:
110 North Moore Street
New York, NY 10012
(212) 555-6311

Residence:
14 Beecher Street
New York, NY 10019
(212) 555-8027

STAR IN TOWN

Principal photography began in Manhattan in the fall of 1983, and the presence of Bill Murray – by then, a huge star from both his movie work and *Saturday Night Live* – soon attracted much attention. "The first day we were shooting on the street in New York… everyone recognized Bill and Danny from *SNL*," Ramis told *Entertainment Weekly* in 2010. "Someone walked by and said, 'Hey! Bill Murray!' And Bill said, in a mock-angry voice, 'You son of a bitch!' And he grabbed the guy and he wrestled him to the ground. Just a passer-by. The guy was completely amazed – and laughing all the way to the ground."

"Walking around New York with Bill Murray was like walking around with the Mayor combined with whoever the star of the Giants and Knicks was," is how Murray's agent Michael Ovitz summed up the public's reaction to the actor in *Vanity Fair* in 2014.

Murray may not have contributed to the script, but like Aykroyd and Ramis he was a master of improv and was responsible for much of Venkman's glorious ad-libbed dialogue. Who could imagine *Ghostbusters*

without such lines as "Back off man, I'm a scientist," "We came, we saw, we kicked its ass," and "Yes, it's true. This man has no dick… Well, that's what I heard!" (The latter two quotes were, in fact, replaced by other Murray adlibs in the original TV cut.)

Ghostbusters proved to be Murray's biggest hit yet, with Aykroyd attributing 50% of the film's success to the actor. Yet Murray didn't entirely embrace the greater attention the movie brought him. "It was such a big phenomenon that I felt slightly radioactive," he told critic Roger Ebert in 1990. "So I just moved away for awhile. I lived in Europe for six months or so, and I was supposed to do a movie when I came back, and when I came back and I saw the script that I was supposed to do, I didn't want to do it. And that put me a whole season behind."

Murray only made a handful of movies in between *Ghostbusters* and its sequel – most notably a hilarious cameo as a dental patient in 1986's *Little Shop of Horrors* and a starring role in 1988's festive favorite *Scrooged*. He was also stung by the failure of

LEFT Bill Murray's comic energy became one of the key driving forces of the *Ghostbusters* films.

"DAN AYKROYD
ATTRIBUTED 50%
OF THE FILM'S
SUCCESS TO MURRAY"

ABOVE LEFT TO RIGHT
Murray in Venkman's beloved brown jacket; Murray and Dan Aykroyd. The two knew each other from *The Second City* and *Saturday Night Live*.

1984's *The Razor's Edge* (released four months after *Ghostbusters*), which he had co-written as well as fought to get made. Despite being one of Hollywood's biggest actors, he was reluctant to take on major roles.

Eventually, though, Murray was persuaded to reunite with the rest of the original cast for *Ghostbusters II*. "The fear with it was that we'd make a disastrous sequel just for the purposes of making money," Murray told *Good Morning America* during the sequel's publicity drive. "And it's obviously not. A lot more styling went into it than the first one even… Working with these people is close to my heart. These are people I've known my whole professional life."

However, Murray was more critical of the sequel in later years, in part explaining his reluctance to return for a third instalment. "There were a few great scenes in it, but it wasn't the same movie [as the original pitch for the film]," he told reporters at a New York press conference in 2008. "The second one was kinda disappointing… for me, anyway."

Murray ultimately did return to the *Ghostbusters* franchise again, with a cameo as ghost debunker Martin Heiss in 2016's *Ghostbusters: Answer the Call*. "I really respect those girls," he told the *Jimmy Kimmel Show* at the time of the film's release. "And then I started to feel like if I didn't do this movie, maybe somebody would write a bad review

RIGHT Venkman (Murray) in the Sedgewick Hotel with Ray (Dan Aykroyd) and Egon (Harold Ramis). Though Aykroyd and Ramis wrote the script, Murray ad-libbed many of his lines.

LEFT Murray undergoes final costume checks before filming; Peter, Ray, and Winston confront Gozer at her rooftop temple in the film's climax.

or something, thinking there was some sort of disapproval [on my part]."

Of course, Murray has enjoyed many other hits since he last played Peter Venkman, including reuniting with Harold Ramis for *Groundhog Day* (1993) and reinventing himself as a dramatic actor in films such as *Lost in Translation* (2003) and *Broken Flowers* (2005). But the manic energy of his Venkman remains a marvel to watch decades later. "It's the funniest bunch of fun you've seen in your whole life," is how Murray summed up *Ghostbusters* when he appeared on *Late Night with David Letterman* in 1984. He wasn't wrong – and a large part of that was down to Murray.

MURRAY MOMENTS

Everyone has their favorite Bill Murray story. "One day we were grumbling about the fact that we weren't included in the order for crew jackets," remembers Tim Lawrence, who puppeteered one of the Terror Dogs on *Ghostbusters*. "Meanwhile, Bill Murray had been riding a bicycle in a big circle around us. A couple of weeks later we all had jackets thanks to Bill!"

Bob Shelley, special effects foreman on the film, remembers an amusing incident that happened in the wake of Venkman being slimed. "He was a heavy smoker and he kept his cigarettes in the top pocket of the suit that he wore. Well, when we dumped slime on him, it got slime on his cigarettes. So he went across the street and asked the public, 'Has anybody got a cigarette?' Then he joked with people that he had come over to watch them for a while as they had been watching him!"

HAROLD RAMIS

MEMORIES OF EGON

Photo: Verta Maloney

Harold Ramis's daughter Violet Ramis Stiel discusses her father's comic legacy and reveals what he had in common with Egon Spengler.

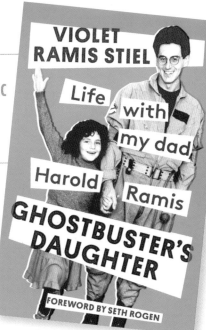

IT IS NO SURPRISE THAT SO MANY comedians, from Seth Rogen to Adam Sandler, cite Harold Ramis as a massive influence. The list of movies that Ramis wrote or directed (or both) is a roll-call of classic comedies – *National Lampoon's Animal House*, *Meatballs*, *Caddyshack*, *Stripes*, *National Lampoon's Vacation*, *Groundhog Day*, *Analyze This* – and his gift for comedy was equally apparent in front of the camera in the likes of *Stripes* and *Knocked Up*. But it is as the gadget-loving, socially awkward brainbox Egon Spengler in *Ghostbusters* for which Ramis is best remembered, and as the movie's co-writer he was responsible for helping shape the character.

For Violet Ramis Stiel, her father was a talented performer and filmmaker for as long as she can remember. But when *Ghostbusters* was released in 1984, her dad became even more well known, not least by her classmates. "He'd already had a lot of success by that point, but this was the first film he was *so* recognizable

" **MY DAD WAS THE STRAIGHT MAN TO BILL'S MANIC PERSONALITY!** "

for," says Ramis Stiel, author of *Ghostbuster's Daughter*, a heartfelt account of her father's life and career. "And it was the first one of his movies that anyone my age was allowed to see. The kids at my school were just going crazy!"

Ramis was brought on board by Ivan Reitman and Dan Aykroyd to help rewrite Aykroyd's wildly ambitious but (to quote Ivan Reitman) "unfilmable" first draft that centered around a team of futuristic, intergalactic spook-hunters. As Aykroyd told *The New Yorker* in 2004, Ramis "added the irony, the heart, the romance with Sigourney Weaver, and all the adult writing as well as the structure. And he knew which passes to throw to Bill [Murray], so Bill would look funny throughout." Although Ramis didn't share Aykroyd's belief in the paranormal, he had been an avid devourer of ghost stories in his childhood, and the duo shared comic sensibilities. With input from Ivan Reitman, their ideas swiftly coalesced into a workable and very funny script.

Once Bill Murray signed on to play Peter Venkman, Ramis, Reitman and Aykroyd's belief in the film only increased. "They were very confident at the time because they had all had a lot of success with everything," says Ramis Stiel. "They could do no wrong. And they had this great, very original idea that everyone got behind immediately, so I think they just thought, 'We've got to make this good – and if we do it's going to be incredible.'"

It helped that Ramis, Reitman and Murray were no strangers to one another, ensuring they had a close working relationship right from the get-go. "My father met Bill through Bill's older brother, Brian," remembers Ramis Stiel. "My dad and Brian were in [the sketch troupe] Second City together. I think he first met Ivan through *The National Lampoon Radio Hour*, which he did in New York for a year when Ivan was also just starting out. And then my dad, Ivan and

ABOVE Egon tinkers with the Ghostbusters' containment unit. According to Violet Ramis Stiel, Harold Ramis shared Egon's love of gadgets.

Bill did *Meatballs* and *Stripes* together. They were this amazing group of people who came up together. So they were old friends by the time of *Ghostbusters*. Even though they were different personalities, they knew each other well and knew that they worked well together. My dad and Bill complemented each other, because my dad was the straight man to Bill's manic personality. And then there was Dan, who is such a good-hearted guy with big ideas. My dad and Ivan would sort of rein him in!"

BELOW Ramis carried the most gadgets as Egon – meaning he had a greater chance of dropping props.

As Ramis refined the script with Aykroyd (the two writing separately and then rewriting each other's pages, according to Ramis Stiel), it became increasingly clear that Ramis was perfectly suited to playing Egon Spengler – a character named after Egon Donsbach, a former classmate of Ramis, and the historian Oswald Spengler. Ramis Stiel says that her father and Egon shared at least some personality traits. "He was definitely the guy who, like Egon, would say 'This is not a good plan, let's rethink it!'" she laughs. "He was also just as well read and well studied as Egon, and he was the guy with the gadgets. What separates them is that my dad was very warm and laughed a lot. He really liked connecting and engaging with people, so in that way they weren't similar."

HIGH ENERGY

Once location filming began, Ramis Stiel joined her father in New York City to watch history being made. At six years old, she was already a veteran of movie sets and had played the tongue-less Daisy Mabel in *National Lampoon's Vacation*. However, *Ghostbusters* was unlike anything she'd seen before. "It was a whole other level. It was a big special effects movie, and it was in New York! There was this high frequency of energy coming from the city

> ## [HAROLD] WAS JUST AS WELL READ AND WELL STUDIED AS EGON

itself. And people were really focused and feeling good about what they were doing."

That's not to say that filming always went perfectly on the first take. Ramis Stiel recalls how she worried that her dad had landed in trouble with Ivan Reitman while shooting the sequence in which the *Ghostbusters* flee from the library, as Reitman became increasingly frustrated that Ramis kept dropping props. "I was very protective of my dad. I wouldn't define Ivan as a screamer, but when you're a captain of a big ship like that you do need to keep everyone on track. Different gadgets would fall off as the *Ghostbusters* ran down their stairs and of course, as Egon, my dad had the most gadgets – and the most potential for screwing it up. But in the end they glued everything on, locked everything down and finally got the shot. Everyone cheered!"

SCHOOLYARD SENSATION

Unsurprisingly, there are perks to having a father in the movie business, and Ramis Stiel recalls that one of the earliest screenings of *Ghostbusters* was at her

LEFT TO RIGHT Egon and Janine (Annie Potts) share a hug in a rubble-strewn New York City; Harold Ramis and Bill Murray joke around on set; publicity still with Ramis, Potts and Rick Moranis.

school in Santa Monica in 1984. "My dad arranged the screening as a benefit for the school. All the parents and all the kids came to see it, and everyone was going crazy. It was a nice little test for them [the creators] and such a gift for us."

While the movie raised the profile of Harold Ramis – schoolboys would flock around him requesting autographs when he picked up his daughter from school – the pre-teen Ramis Stiel didn't quite feel that her father received all the kudos he deserved. "Again, I was protective of him, and I always felt like Bill and Dan got all the attention and my dad was sort of like the quiet guy, the nerd guy. I didn't

realize at the time that nerds everywhere were going nuts for this character who really spoke to them."

By the time *Ghostbusters II* had been greenlit, Ramis was very aware that the franchise was as popular with kids as it was with adults. Naturally 12-year-old Violet was recruited by her father as an on-hand script-reader. "They had so many wild ideas. He'd have me read something and stand over my shoulder waiting for a laugh," she recalls. "Every time I breathed he would be like, 'What part are you reading now?' He wanted my opinion because I was a teenager, I was their demographic. Although, I wasn't necessarily the average viewer!"

HAROLD RAMIS: THE EARLY YEARS

Ramis's movie career took off when he scripted 1978's *National Lampoon's Animal House*, but by then he'd already had many years honing his comic talents.

In the mid-1960s he wrote and performed for Washington University's college theater, before going on to join the Second City improvisational comedy troupe in his home city of Chicago and editing jokes for *Playboy* magazine. During a second stint at Second City, he met John Belushi, who eventually brought him to New York to write and perform for the seminal *The National Lampoon Radio Hour* and its *Lemmings* touring company. It was there he met the likes of Murray and Chevy Chase. Ramis went on to become head writer on the Second City spin-off *SCTV*, at one point turning down an offer to work for *Saturday Night Live*. He eventually left *SCTV* to write *Animal House* with *National Lampoon Magazine*'s Douglas Kennedy. Following its success, the movie hits kept on coming – often starring alumni from his earlier sketch-show ventures.

LASTING LEGACY

That wasn't quite the end of Harold Ramis's involvement in the franchise, as he voiced Egon in 2009's *Ghostbusters: The Video Game*. But the remainder of his career was mostly spent focusing on other projects, reaching an apex with 1993's *Groundhog Day*, which he co-wrote, directed and briefly appeared in. His final film, before his death in 2014 from complications to autoimmune inflammatory vasculitis, was 2009's caveman comedy *Year One*.

Despite her father's diverse career, Ramis Stiel insists that he never minded that *Ghostbusters* remained his most famous role three decades later. "He was always happy to talk about it and go into this effect or that effect, and he did a lot of Make-A-Wish appearances [in character]. He really loved the work that he did, so I don't think he was ever frustrated. It's great if you can contribute to pop culture in a way that leaves this legacy that lasts for so long and that really takes on a life of its own. He was proud to be part of that."

MAGICAL MEMORIES

As well as watching the location filming in New York, the six-year-old Violet Ramis Stiel also got to witness the soundstage sequences being shot in L.A., where the Ramis family lived. "I got to see the crystal staircase of Gozer and the rig that spun Dana around above the bed. As a kid you're so curious – how does it work? How do they do that? My favorite movie at the time was *The Exorcist*. So the most fascinating thing to me was that they used the same rig for Dana that they used in *The Exorcist*!"

BELOW Teamwork: Harold Ramis, Dan Aykroyd and Bill Murray. Ramis was integral to honing the script's character development.

ERNIE HUDSON

WINSTON'S WORLD

A character actor with over 200 movies and TV shows to his name, Ernie Hudson will forever be associated with Winston Zeddemore. He shares his memories of landing the role, the character's evolution, and the importance of the fans.

FOLLOWING A VISIT TO A FRIEND IN hospital, Ernie Hudson entered the elevator and was surprised to find himself standing next to Ivan Reitman. The two were not strangers, having worked together on 1983's cult sci-fi adventure *Spacehunter: Adventures in the Forbidden Zone*, which Reitman had produced and Hudson had starred in alongside Molly Ringwald, Peter Strauss and the voice of Harold Ramis. The pair quickly fell into conversation. "Ivan said he was doing a new movie with 'Danny and Billy'," Hudson remembers. "I didn't know who the hell he was talking about! I didn't watch *Saturday Night Live* – not that I had anything against it, I just didn't watch a lot of TV. Then I found out from my agent a short time afterwards that it [the project] was *Ghostbusters*. And there was a part."

Getting an audition for that part was no easy task, something Hudson attributes to his previous movie with Reitman. "I think Ivan felt I wasn't right for the part. I'm

> **"I THOUGHT THE SCRIPT WAS AMAZING. IT WAS FUNNY AS HELL!"**

pretty sure that it was because the character in *Spacehunter* was a bigger-than-life guy; I used the lower register of my voice and it was just a very different character. So I think that Ivan thought of me that way. Winston is a very different spirit. Finally – after a few months – I was able to get an audition. But the whole casting process dragged on for what felt like a month."

Hudson's persistence paid off. Eventually he received confirmation that he had landed a role in the comedy-horror – and it had all the hallmarks of a hit. "I thought the script was amazing. It was funny as hell. And then, once I met the cast – Bill, Danny and Harold… there was just something about the chemistry and the whole dynamic."

The part was, of course, Winston Zeddemore, the fourth Ghostbuster to join the spook-catching squad. Dan Aykroyd had originally written the part for Eddie Murphy (today no one can recall if Murphy actually received the script), though both script and character had evolved significantly since that point. The role was to further evolve once Hudson was on board – and it required some adjustment on his part.

"The character involvement shifted by the time we started shooting, so to start with it was hard for me to pin the character down," Hudson admits. "Originally, he was introduced a lot earlier, when they first left the university, [at] the first hotel. I felt that now I was coming in over halfway through the movie, it changed the dynamic. I felt that Winston was [now] always a little wary. So I had to dismantle preconceived notions. Now, looking back on it 35 years later, I think it's a perfect little film just the way it is, so things have a way of working out. But it took a while for me to make peace with that."

THE RELUCTANT WARRIOR

During his career, Hudson has chalked up credits for over 200 movies and TV shows, but he says that Winston is the character he has identified most with, largely due to the fact they were undergoing similar experiences. "He became an extension of my personality, the reluctant warrior!" Hudson laughs. "Winston sees himself as a Ghostbuster and fans see him very much as a Ghostbuster, but he's a little bit outside the circle. It's kind of like when you go out with three guys who are really close friends. You're all friends, but you don't have the history that those three have."

It is precisely this outsider status that many viewers have found so compelling, says Hudson. "I've met a lot of kids of all colors, but especially a lot of the black kids and Hispanic kids, who say they identify. Because I think that's a feeling that a lot of kids experience when they are in an environment or went to a school where people are nice but they feel a little bit different. I think it works for the character."

LEFT Publicity still of Hudson and his mallow-coated co-stars next to cinema's greatest movie vehicle.

HE BECAME AN EXTENSION OF MY PERSONALITY!

ABOVE Winston coated in the gooey remains of Mr. Stay Puft amid the debris of the Temple of Gozer.

Once filming began, Hudson found his co-stars' love of improvisation meant that the dialogue was often fluid. "A lot of the lines that I ended up with – great lines that fans quote to me every day – were down to the guys being willing to share. I always remember the line at the end of the movie, 'I love this town.' I don't think I can do a convention without somebody mentioning that or wanting me to sign something with that line! Because it felt to me like Winston would [otherwise] have been a little bit in limbo there [in the finale]. I think it was Danny who said, 'Hey, let's have Ernie say this line,' which I was very appreciative of. The guys were always very aware of being inclusive."

Following the success of the movie, Hudson was pleased to see how his character had connected with a young audience, with school kids everywhere playing at being Winston in playgrounds and backyards. He received frequent invitations to talk to kids, where he would make them "honorary Ghostbusters." Kids and adults alike wanted to see more of the characters, though they had to wait another five years for the sequel.

Hudson was excited to return for *Ghostbusters II*, not least because the character was an established part of the team right from the start. "He is no longer a stranger at the table or some guy off the street looking for a job… We know who Winston is now, and he actually opens the movie [following the opening titles]," Hudson says. Though proud of the sequel, Hudson admits he wishes the character played a more prominent role in the first half of the movie. "He disappears from the courtroom! And I'm always like, 'Why does he disappear?' Fans will ask too… The story works, but that [element] never made much sense to me as an actor. But then he comes back into it, and I love the writing and the scene with the train in the subway."

ABOVE LEFT TO RIGHT
Hudson with his co-stars
in New York City; filming
the Mayor's office scene;
sauntering out of the
Ectomobile; the team talk
tactics about busting Gozer.

CHARACTER ACTOR

Since the success of the first two *Ghostbusters* films, Hudson has worked solidly as a character actor in movies (including T*he Hand That Rocks the Cradle*, *The Crow* and *Congo*) and TV shows (everything from *Grace & Frankie* to *Twin Peaks)*. His distinctive voice has also lent itself to animated shows such as *Robot Chicken* and *Hot Streets.* "When I started acting years ago, I thought if I could just get in a major studio movie that was a success it would launch my career in a certain way," Hudson says. "That never happened. But I've been a steady working actor, and I'm very happy to still be working… I always felt like the guy buying the suit off the rack, you know what I mean? I gotta mold myself to that character as opposed to having the character molded to me.

RIGHT Hudson joined Harold Ramis, Dan Aykroyd and Bill Murray to become the fourth Ghostbuster. The character's slight outsider status resonated with many viewers.

I need to feel the writer's intent, trust that it's a good writer, and not make the whole thing about me. I think that is why I've been able to survive 50 years of what I love doing. My career has been a wonderful journey."

Hudson adds that even if it didn't establish him as a leading man, *Ghostbusters* had a significant impact on his career. "*Ghostbusters* didn't make the world change overnight. I was still out there auditioning and reading and trying. But it helped. I always thank Ivan Reitman. I think a lot of what's happened has been through him casting me in this film. I love the franchise and am so thankful to have been part of it."

Hudson had the chance to flesh out Winston a little further in 2009's *Ghostbusters: The Video Game*, where he returned to voice his character. "That extension of the story was really exciting. They gave him a permanency at the table." He also joined his castmates in making a brief cameo in 2016's *Ghostbusters: Answer the Call*, where he played Patty's uncle, Bill Jenkins ("I was very happy to come and be a part of it").

And then there are the conventions – including 2019's 35th anniversary Fan Fest on the Sony Pictures Studio lot – where he has met fans from all over the world and witnessed the impact that the films, and his character, have made on people's lives. "Fans really have embraced it. I see it in people and their children and their children's children," he says. "I've seen people who have turned their family cars into Ectomobiles, people with their backpacks on. And I'm just so appreciative. It's the fans who have kept this thing alive."

PARANORMAL ACTIVITY

Like his co-star Dan Aykroyd, Hudson grew up with a deep belief in spiritualism and the paranormal, something that drew him to the role. "I grew up in a family that has always believed in the paranormal. [My] grandmother, who was born in the 1800s and who raised me, is from the South, and they [the family] believed in spirits. I grew up in a culture that embraced that. There was always a strong belief in – and nervousness about – that. As you leave home and go to college, you kind of get away from that and want to dismiss all that old folk stuff. But it's always a part of you when you grow up that way. I think it's probably why I was so attracted to it, because it tapped into that."

IVAN REITMAN

PRACTICAL MAGIC

He may not have donned a proton pack and grey jumpsuit, but Ivan Reitman is definitely one of the heroes of *Ghostbusters*. The director and producer reveals some of the magic tricks behind the movie and says why working on instinct was key to its success.

WHEN IVAN REITMAN READ DAN AYKROYD'S first draft of *Ghostbusters* (or *Ghost Smashers*, as it was then titled), he knew immediately that the *Saturday Night Live* star had written something spectacular. There was just one problem: it was *too* spectacular.

"There were special effects on almost every page!" recalls Reitman. "This was before CGI, and some of the things in there would have been impossible to do. I remember his treatment was set in the future and outer space, with competing groups of Ghostbusters... But there was a great idea in there."

Excited about *Ghost Smashers*' potential, Reitman swiftly arranged a breakfast meeting with Aykroyd, who he'd known since they'd both worked on a Canadian variety show called *Greed*. "I said: 'This is a great concept, but I think it should happen on Earth, not in the future. We should have three Ghostbusters, maybe a fourth. And I think we should set it in a real environment.' I thought seeing ghosts in New York would be very cool. Seeing them in outer space would be just another sci-fi movie."

Reitman suggested that the heroes could begin the story studying at Columbia University before setting up their ghost-catching operation – a "going into business story" as Reitman describes it. Luckily Aykroyd didn't recoil with horror at Reitman's proposals. "Dan was very open to having the story reinvented, and to bringing in Harold Ramis – who I'd just worked with on *Meatballs* and *Stripes* – as another writer-slash-Ghostbuster."

" I THOUGHT SEEING GHOSTS IN NEW YORK WOULD BE VERY COOL! "

Aykroyd, Ramis and Reitman set to work on reassembling *Ghostbusters* into the version we know today. Meanwhile, the key role of Peter Venkman – originally written for Aykroyd's friend and fellow Blues Brother John Belushi – went to Bill Murray, who had also worked on *Meatballs* and *Stripes* with Reitman and Ramis. "I think the magic trick of the movie is that we did it all very quickly," says Reitman. "We wrote it quickly, we cast it quickly, we set up the animation company quickly.

From the point when I sat down with Aykroyd that morning to the point when it came out on June 8th 1984 was about 13 months! We were all working with our instincts. I'd worked with the principal cast quite a few times already, so we knew each other's strengths and weaknesses. It seemed to be going right from the beginning."

THE MAGICIAN

The fact that the production didn't run over-time and over-budget was far from inevitable. Even with some of the more outlandish elements exorcised from the original story, this was still a deeply ambitious picture for the early '80s. "This was prior to the advent of digital filmmaking, so I knew I had to do it in a live form to a great deal," Reitman says. "Everything was challenging because you had to figure out a way to shoot it."

Reitman emphasizes that this practical method of filming worked in the movie's favor, meaning it "took on a reality that you believed in." Luckily, live special effects were something he had experience in, having directed 1973's magic-themed musical show

Spellbound and co-produced its 1974 Broadway spin-off *The Magic Show*.

"I was pretty steeped in the world of magic in front of a live studio audience, so I knew what needed to be done to pull it off. That scene in Sigourney Weaver's apartment, where she starts floating and does a 360-degree turn in the air, is based on a real illusion I used on stage in *The Magic Show*. It's one of my favorite sequences in the film – this unusual, romantic scene that's both really funny and spooky – and we shot it all live. After we shot it, we realized that part of the rig under Dana's cloak was visible in the lower right-hand corner, so I had to really darken it to make it go away in the release print. But we just figured out everything step by step, and it was very much like working on *The Magic Show*."

As well as giving Reitman an opportunity to display his favourite magic tricks, *Ghostbusters* also drew on his lifelong love of horror movies – it's easy to forget just how creepy many sequences in the film actually are. "I used to go see whatever the latest horror movie was at the local matinee when I was a kid,"

Reitman remembers. "*The Thing* was my favorite scary movie from the '50s. I even had scrapbooks about horror movies. So I got the genre."

In the 1970s, Reitman produced David Cronenberg's *Shivers* (1975) and *Rabid* (1977), and he says he and his fellow Canadian filmmaker learned a lot from one another. "But it was the combination of comedy and scariness I was most taken by. One of the first movies I did was *Cannibal Girls* with Eugene Levy and Andrea Martin. It's partially really funny and there's some scary stuff in there. So I guess it's part of my nature. My work in *Ghostbusters* was certainly aided by my appreciation of that genre and knowing how to take it seriously in a humorous way."

Reitman emphasizes that the way the comedy and horror play off each other was crucial to *Ghostbusters'* success. "You get scared really early on in the film with the ghost librarian in the first five minutes. What always happened when I watched the movie with audiences is that people would scream like crazy. Then they would catch themselves and start laughing. They would continue laughing as the Ghostbusters reacted very much like regular people: being scared shitless and running out of the library. It was such an odd, goofy sequence that it became the vocabulary of the film."

ENDURING POPULARITY

Ghostbusters was, of course, a huge hit with audiences and critics alike in 1984, and its popularity has never waned. Reitman puts much of this down to its relatable characters. "What really makes *Ghostbusters* so wonderful – if I do say so myself! – is the way the characters work with each other. The camaraderie that comes from these guys is something that we recognize and identify with."

> ❝ *AUDIENCES WOULD SCREAM LIKE CRAZY – AND THEN START LAUGHING!* ❞

However, the film's success didn't entirely take him by surprise. In fact, Reitman says he always knew it would be a hit. "We were pretty cocky about ourselves and about the movie we were beginning to make," he laughs. "By this point in my career I'd produced *Animal House* and produced and directed *Meatballs* and *Stripes*, so I was feeling pretty full of myself – in a controlled manner! I just thought that *Ghostbusters* was a fabulous idea, and I thought I had the perfect cast; it turns out I did. So we were all working, I think, at the top of our game. We were at that point where we were not too young and not

BELOW LEFT TO RIGHT
Reitman directs the film's finale; the filmmaker jokes with Bill Murray and Sigourney Weaver. Reitman says there was a real sense of camaraderie on set.

ABOVE Reitman had worked with both Dan Aykroyd and Bill Murray before, meaning they had already developed a great working relationship.

too old, and fortunately it really worked out."

One thing that he didn't anticipate was just how popular the film would become with kids, a fact that led to the animated series *The Real Ghostbusters* and *Slimer!*, as well as various tie-in comics and toys. "We never thought of it as a kids' movie or even a family movie," Reitman says. "We just thought of it as a fun movie for a large, regular audience. I think what happened is that parents liked the movie so much they wanted to share it with their kids. So four or five-year-olds were being brought into the theater! But there's something about the fact that *Ghostbusters* isn't nasty. They don't have weapons – the ghosts are only trapped – and the Ghostbusters just take the ghosts away to make the world a safer place."

The film continues to thrill new generations of moviegoers – including Reitman's own four-year-old grandson. "He loved it. He was really scared at the beginning, but my daughter said he turned to her just after the sequence in the library and told her, 'It's OK – it's scary but you laugh.' That's the way he put it. And I thought, 'Oh yeah!' He got totally enamored with the film, and would sing the *Ghostbusters* theme song day in, day out in the house. It drove my daughter crazy!"

ABOVE LEFT Reitman orchestrates the action on set. The director always knew he was making a hit movie.

LEFT All smiles: Reitman with Dan Aykroyd and Rick Moranis.

ARMCHAIR THEATER

Perhaps the most memorably terrifying sequence in *Ghostbusters* is when Dana's armchair suddenly sprouts arms. This was one of many last-minute additions to the movie. "We were doing so much so quickly that a lot had to be written just before we started filming to fill in the plot holes," Reitman remembers. "I woke up at four in the morning and thought about that scene. I knew we'd be in her living room and it would be really quiet. But how was she going to become a demi-god? Then I thought how scary it would be to have arms suddenly coming out of the chair and taking her into the kitchen, which was lit up like a Spielberg science fiction movie.

"I started talking to the physical effects people to figure out how to create the illusion. We built the chair on a false platform and the puppeteers with these goofy arm units were underneath it so they could stick their arms in when the time was right. There was a track underneath the carpet that we pulled away just below frame to whip the chair back. We just figured out different ways of creating the illusions while we were filming because it was all done live."

TERROR DOG

enriquez

THOM ENRIQUEZ
CONCEPT ART

Thom Enriquez was crucial in developing the look of *Ghostbusters'* creatures in pre-production.
He shares his memories of sleepless nights, smiling ghouls, and Venkman's head lice.

THE SUSHI BAR IN BURBANK, CALIFORNIA may have been loud and crowded, but artist Thom Enriquez was glad he hadn't stayed home. Thanks to the background noise, the two strangers he'd ended up sitting next to were having to shout their conversation to one another. The pair, it seemed, were developing a new movie project – and when Enriquez heard they were looking for pre-production

artists, he couldn't help but interject. "Being an opportunist, I rudely interrupted them," he says. "I introduced myself as a concept and storyboard artist, and said that I had my portfolio in my car." The pair, it emerged, were director Ivan Reitman and associate producer Michael C. Gross. "Outside, in an alleyway, they thumbed through my work and said, 'Can you come by the studio this afternoon?'

Suffice to say, Enriquez was swiftly hired. Working from an early draft of the script ("It floored me with laughter!"), Enriquez brought his gift for creating vivid horror imagery to the film's ghosts and ghouls, along with logo ideas, poster art, crew-jacket designs and advertising art, all under the supervision of Gross.

FLOATING ONION

Working separately from other concept artists on the film such as Bernie Wrightson and Tanino Liberatore, Enriquez drew up myriad designs for the likes of the Terror Dogs, Stay Puft and Slimer. He recalls the influences on his designs of the latter. "As Michael Gross read me the script description of Slimer – then known as the 'Onionhead ghost' and sometimes 'Spud'

– I was picturing a potato-sack sized, ectoplasmic floating onion with a face on it. Then Michael said that the ghost was a homage to the late John Belushi, and for me to think of John's performance in *Animal House*. Suddenly it became John's torso with a mouth on it and an insatiable appetite to go with it."

Interestingly, Enriquez says that the character wasn't always envisioned as a performer in a suit. "I was given direction that this character would be a stop-motion puppet, so I designed Slimer with that in mind," he says. "But when the complexity and the time-consuming process of stop-motion conflicted with the schedule and the budget, it was decided Slimer would be a person in a suit. To accommodate this change, the design had to be modified. It was decided to make the

BELOW One of Thom Enriquez's early Terror Dog designs and an unused drawing of a hideous pizza delivery ghost.

LEFT Enriquez's designs for the sequence in which the Stay Puft Marshmallow Man melts. The artist had to draw many potential alternatives to the villain.

changes on a maquette that was sculpted by Kurt Conner. Kurt was instructed to fatten up the arms and make some cosmetic changes, including making the teeth larger."

Slimer was not the only ghost to go through several evolutions during the design process. "The one meeting I'll never forget is regarding the Stay Puft design. Ivan had given me a drawing of Stay Puft by [artist and Dan Aykroyd's college friend] John Deveikis to use as a starting point, and Michael felt I had nailed it. We entered Ivan's office and Michael was holding my drawing by his fingertips, rocking it back and forth in a teasing, 'look what I got' manner. In a sing-song voice, Michael chirped, 'Look what Thom did – I KNOW you're going to like this.' Ivan looked up from the script he was reading, and we watched his face transform from serious and concentrated to an ear-to-ear smile.

Beaming, he said, 'That's him! You got it! That's-the-guy!' Now, it's every artist dream to get this kind of reaction from a client, so I was beaming too, to say the least."

Unfortunately, Enriquez and Gross then watched Reitman furrow his brow and rub his chin. Not a good sign. "Ivan said, 'It's really great... but we never nail these things the first time around... Thom, can you take a few more stabs at it?'"

Enriquez spent the next five days devising two dozen new variations of the Marshmallow Man, all of which were rejected. "After I finished those other designs, Ivan started to worry that Stay Puft was too cutesy for a final villain and wanted me to design something more sinister and menacing. So, reluctantly, I came up with a tail-less pet lizard, a rabid pet-hamster, an angry shell-less pet turtle, a giant sea-monkey, a mangy parakeet, and a collective giant mass of head-lice that Venkman had as a child. Thank goodness, all were rejected for my first design."

ALL SMILES

Looking back, Enriquez has a theory as to which of his many designs were approved and which weren't. "After many failed attempts, I started to notice a pattern developing in the approved designs [compared to] the rejected ones – a smile! At first, I couldn't believe it was a possibility, so I ran some smiling test designs by them. Sure enough, they were all approved. After that

day, every character I designed was smiling, no matter how hideous or cute they looked!"

Enriquez – who would later return to design new creature concepts for *Ghostbusters II* – remembers the period as a unique blend of unbridled stress and excitement. "I worked pretty much in isolation and had my nose to the grindstone," he says. "It was a lot of work, loads of pressure, and very little sleep. But the whole concept and premise was so clever and fresh that there was no doubt in my mind I was on a hit movie. I think everyone that came onboard knew it too. It's what drove the energy throughout the production."

BELOW Enriquez worked up many different designs of Slimer causing mayhem, which would influence the final look of the ghost.

JOE MEDJUCK

THE PHANTOM PRODUCER

Ghostbusters' associate producer recalls naive studio discussions,
worried early morning phone calls and on-set magic.

I t was a proto-*Animal House* spoof about a college freshman that first brought *Ghostbusters'* associate producer Joe Medjuck and director Ivan Reitman together. "It was 1968 and I met him so he could show me [Reitman's short film] *Orientation*, which we wanted to review for *Take One*," says Medjuck, referring to the well-regarded Canadian film magazine on which he served as associate editor. Fast-forward 12 years to 1980, and Medjuck made a move into the movie industry himself after Reitman asked him to become his director of development. Medjuck took a leave of absence from his graduate teacher job – and never looked back.

In their first year, the pair collaborated on the comedy *Stripes* (where Medjuck acted as associate producer) and the animated comic fantasy *Heavy Metal* (where he was production co-ordinator). After scoring hits with both, they – along with Reitman's other trusted associate, Michael C. Gross – began searching for their next project.

> **IT WAS A THROWBACK TO THE COMEDIES THAT WE'D GROWN UP WITH**

However, this could very easily have been a project other than *Ghostbusters*.

"*Heavy Metal* had been quite successful, and Ivan said, 'We've found out a lot about making an animated movie, let's make another one'," Medjuck recalls. "So Michael and I started looking for another animated film."

After reading *The Hitch-Hiker's Guide to the Galaxy*, Medjuck thought he'd found the perfect project. "Michael and I went to meet Douglas Adams, who happened to be in Los Angeles at the time. He said he was interested in the movie but didn't want it to be animated. We began working on a live action version... Then *Ghostbusters* landed on our doorstep."

Medjuck's first thought about the script was, "That's a cool title." He agreed with Reitman's assessment that the 200-page script needed editing, but also shared his friend's enthusiasm for the project. "We loved the concept of the Ghostbusters, which was a bit of a throwback to the comedies of the '40s and '50s that we'd grown up with."

After securing the involvement of Harold Ramis, who had an office across the street on the Burbank lot, *Ghostbusters* started to take shape. However, first they had to pitch the concept to Frank Price, president of Columbia Pictures. "We pitched him the story, and he said, 'How much do you think this is going to cost?' I remember [Ivan] holding up the script as if he was weighing it and saying, '25 million dollars.' That was a lot of money in those days – and they [Columbia] didn't blink. But we hadn't budgeted or anything. I mean, Ivan was guessing at 25 million dollars; an educated guess. I think we

" WE'D NEVER MADE A MOVIE WITH SPECIAL EFFECTS BEFORE... "

budgeted in the low 30s [before production began] and my memory is that we ended up spending around 33 million dollars." Medjuck laughs at the memory of suddenly having so much money to play with. "It seemed like an extraordinary amount of money at the time. We couldn't believe we were

spending so much!"

Medjuck says that Columbia wanted the movie finished in a little over a year, leading to the film's notoriously tight schedule. Not that Medjuck or Reitman were worried at the time. "Being completely naive, we said, 'Sure, of course, that's a lot of time – it's more than a year from now! We'd never really made a movie with any special effects before. We didn't know how hard it was."

CONSTANT CHALLENGES

With Reitman focused on directing and producing the picture, Medjuck and Gross divided the other tasks on *Ghostbusters* between them. Former designer Gross remained in California to focus on the special effects and design side of things, while Medjuck helped oversee the casting, scouting and shooting, initially based in New York. Together they were a formidable team. However, Medjuck admits to being daunted at working on what was by far his biggest movie role at that point.

"I'd been on movie sets, but had never really taken the responsibility of being in charge of

things," he says. "When there were giant decisions to make, I would talk to Ivan about them, but sometimes I made the decisions so Ivan could concentrate on working on the movie. There were constant challenges. I was the guy people would phone at 6am when they were worried... There are so many things that can go wrong with a film."

One of these things was almost losing the key location of Dana's apartment block at 55 Central Park West, which was run by a housing co-operative. "They threatened to pull out at one point, and John G. Wilson, our production manager, had a big meeting with them. We'd already started

building a replica of the first couple of stories back in Burbank! I remember thinking, 'I can't believe any film ever gets finished.' And on the second day of shooting, at Columbia University, a prop man didn't have an important prop – a video recorder that the guys were carrying. So we had to borrow one from some organization at Columbia University."

Another concern was the fact that Columbia didn't yet have clearance on the title 'Ghostbusters,' thanks to Filmation's 1975 children's sitcom *The Ghost Busters*. When filming began, the studio was considering other titles. Medjuck remembers that they even shot a couple of scenes two different

CLOCKWISE FROM TOP LEFT Dana's apartment block at 55 Central Block West, which the film nearly lost; construction on the replica building; the heroes at Columbia University.

BELOW Filming in New York City, which ran ahead of schedule; Medjuck (second from right) on set with production designer John DeCuir, associate producer Michael C. Gross, and Ivan Reitman.

ways – one that referred to the Ghostbusters, and one that didn't. "But then I was standing on the street and heard 300 extras yelling 'Ghostbusters, Ghostbusters'... I called the studio, and said, 'We can't do this [consider another title]. We've got to clear that name. And they did."

THE PROFESSIONALS

Despite such challenges, Medjuck says filming largely went smoothly and remained on schedule. He puts this down to a couple of reasons. Firstly, *Ghostbusters* was not a film that suffered from much-dreaded studio interference. "The studio didn't question much," he says. "Not only did it get out of the way, but it was very helpful. They were able to jump in and help set up Richard Edlund's [effects] company, Boss Film."

Then there was the talented cast and crew. "I became aware that you're dealing with incredibly professional people. A film crew is an amazing group... You ask them for impossible things and somehow they do them. Everything was going so well in New York. We had certain cover sets that were only supposed to be in case of rain; we presumed we'd be shooting them back in LA. It never rained and we ended up using the cover sets because we were ahead of schedule in New York. We were going like crazy."

Medjuck adds that he, along with the other key players, also had great faith in the shooting script. "We didn't think it would be the biggest movie of the year; we didn't know it was going to be as big as it was. But we thought it was going to be good and we thought people were going to like it. Not everyone did [think that]. I remember hearing people saying, 'They're crazy! They're making a big-budget special effects comedy! When has that ever worked?'"

 " WE DIDN'T KNOW IT WAS GOING TO BE AS BIG AS IT WAS! "

Medjuck and Reitman's faith proved well founded when they screened the film just three weeks after completing principal photography. "We screened the film with only one special effects shot in it to an audience of outsiders, just to see how the humor worked. It went great. It was insane!"

Medjuck returned as executive producer on *Ghostbusters II* in 1989, though filming had to wait until he, Reitman and Gross had finished shooting the comedy *Twins* ("We didn't move anything, we just changed the sign from *Twins* to *Ghostbusters II* on the editing room"). He insists there was no real sense of pressure making the follow-up. "We wanted it to be good, but it felt easier in some ways."

One aspect of the second film that did pose a challenge was for the studio to strike a deal with the principal players. "Dan and Bill and Harold were obviously movie stars [before *Ghostbusters*], but after *Ghostbusters* they were *really* movie stars. And

Ivan was a star director by then, so it was an expensive film for the studio to make. But they were eager to make it because people think it's a sure thing when you're making a sequel."

DEFYING GENRES

Ghostbusters has been a recurring part of Medjuck's career, with the producer also chalking up credits on the animated shows *The Real Ghostbusters* and *Extreme Ghostbusters* and 2016's movie *Ghostbusters: Answer the Call*. He says the longevity of the franchise is largely down to its inventive premise. "The basic concept of *Ghostbusters* is its own genre," he says. "I've never seen another movie where the concept is that people catch ghosts. And the [original] movie really works. It's a little scary, it's got good music, it's got a romance. It's got something for everybody."

BILL MURRAY   DAN AYKROYD   SIGOURNEY WEAVER
HAROLD RAMIS   RICK MORANIS

An IVAN REITMAN Film

GHOSTBUSTERS II

COLUMBIA PICTURES Presents
"GHOSTBUSTERS II" · ERNIE HUDSON · ANNIE POTTS
Music BERNIE BRILLSTEIN · JOE MEDJUCK · MICHAEL C. GROSS   Music RANDY EDELMAN   Visual ILM
Screenplay HAROLD RAMIS and DAN AYKROYD   Directed Produced IVAN REITMAN
A COLUMBIA PICTURES RELEASE

OPENS JUNE 16TH AT THEATRES EVERYWHERE

LEFT Medjuck returned to produce the 1989 sequel, which he says felt easier than making the original.

THE UNGUARDED ECTOMOBILE

One of the craziest things about Ecto-1, Joe Medjuck says, is that they only had one of the cars. "We were really naive in many ways," he laughs. "If we were going to do a movie now with something like the Ectomobile, I would be saying, 'We need three or four of them.' But we had one! It did break down once, though fortunately it was a second unit shot.

"I remember walking down the street in New York and it was sitting by itself, with no one guarding it, on the side of the street. Are we out of our minds? What's going on here? What if someone stole this thing? It was crazy to me that we only had one of them. We had to ship it back from New York to shoot it in Los Angeles!"

COSTUME DRAMA

The screen-worn Ghostbusters jumpsuits can fetch thousands of dollars at auction, while many fans choose to make their own bespoke suits.

THE COTTON JUMPSUITS WORN BY THE Ghostbusters in the original two movies have become highly sought-after props. Peter Venkman's khaki suit, worn by Bill Murray in the first film, fetched a staggering £35,000 ($47,062) at Prop Store's Entertainment Memorabilia Live Auction in 2017. Meanwhile, one of the lighter hued versions worn by Murray in *Ghostbusters II*, which was made by military/aviation outfitters Flight Suits Ltd (now Gibson & Barnes), sold for an only slightly more affordable £25,000 ($32,183). One of Ray's original jumpsuits, worn by Dan Aykroyd, also fetched £25,000 in 2019. Not included were the various attached gadgets, such as the leg hoses and radios.

Of course, many cheaper replicas exist for fans who want to dress up as their heroes, and many Ghostheads choose to make bespoke suits, complete with their own name patches.

THEONI'S VISION

While the style of the suits reflected Dan Aykroyd's original vision of the team resembling sanitation workers, their precise look came from the late costume designer Theoni V. Aldredge, who also designed costumes for the rest of the cast.

Aldredge was a prolific and highly respected designer by the time of *Ghostbusters*, having won multiple Tony Awards for her work on Broadway as well as designing costumes for such movies as *The Great Gatsby* (1974), *Network* (1976), and *Annie* (1982). She continued to design costumes for dozens of theater, movie, ballet, and opera productions before her death in 2011.

All photographs courtesy of Prop Store.

ht Suits L
ON. CALIFORNIA

Bill Murray

65% POLYESTER / 35% COTTON
MACHINE WASH MEDIUM, TUMBL
MEDIUM. REMOVE IMMEDIATEL
USE WARM IRON.

ABOVE A screen-worn Venkman jumpsuit, which was auctioned on Prop Store, and Murray's autographed *Ghostbusters II* suit.

OPPOSITE PAGE Venkman's jumpsuit from *Ghostbusters II*.

LEFT Ray Stantz's jumpsuit, as worn by Dan Aykroyd. The suit fetched £25,000 at a Prop Store auction in 2019. The final costumes were designed by the Oscar-winning Theoni Aldredge.

SIGOURNEY WEAVER

ABOVE A publicity shot from the first *Ghostbusters* movie.

OPPOSITE PAGE A group shot from *Ghostbusters II* finds Weaver the center of attention.

THE GATEKEEPER

Sigourney Weaver relished the chance to show off her lighter side in *Ghostbusters*, and was directly responsible for shaping many aspects of Dana's character.

SIGOURNEY WEAVER DID something rather unusual during her audition for the role of Dana Barrett: she turned into a dog. A Terror Dog to be precise. "I remember starting to growl and bark and gnaw on the cushions and jump around," she told *Vanity Fair* in 2014. "Ivan cut the tape and said, 'Don't ever do that again.'"

In fact, Reitman loved the audition. By this point the filmmaker, along with casting director Karen Rea, had auditioned numerous actressses, including a young Julia Roberts ("I thought she was spectacular and I turned to my casting director, saying, 'She's going to be a big star,'" Reitman wrote in a 2016 *Hollywood Reporter* article). But Dana Barrett was so integral to the heart of the movie that it was crucial to have the right actress in the role. When Weaver walked in, Reitman was instantly impressed. "She was so smart about the script," he said. "She said, 'You know, I really think that Dana Barrett should be possessed. She should be like that dog on the roof.' And then she got on all fours on my coffee table, howling like a dog! She was funny and had

RIGHT Dana becomes the Gatekeeper after being possessed by Zuul.

BELOW Zuul reaches out to Dana from inside her fridge.

a regality, and having her with my Ghostbusters was like having Margaret Dumont with the Marx Brothers."

When Reitman spoke to Harold Ramis about the audition, he realized that the idea of Dana becoming possessed should be incorporated into the script. "She was barely out of my office and we were writing it already," he said.

MODEL TO MUSICIAN

Weaver's spirited audition was an attempt to prove that she could handle a lighter, comedic role. After all, she was primarily known for her more serious performances in *Alien* (1979) and *The Year of Living Dangerously* (1982). "I had to blow my own horn because I hadn't really done a film comedy, but I had done many onstage," Weaver told *Esquire* magazine in 2014. As well as influencing Dana's third-act possession, it was Weaver who suggested changing the character's job from model to musician.

The chemistry between Dana and Venkman was always going to be crucial in making the romance between these two very different characters believable; luckily when the actors first met outside the New York Public Library, they hit it off straight away. "He literally said, 'Hi, Sue' [Weaver's birth

"DANA WAS INTEGRAL TO THE HEART OF THE MOVIE"

name is Susan] and picked me up and threw me over his shoulder and walked down the street with me," Weaver told *Entertainment Weekly* for a reunion photoshoot in 2014. "Guys don't usually throw me, six feet tall, over their shoulders, and I

" THE SEQUEL BROUGHT NEW DIMENSIONS TO DANA "

just fell in love with him right then and there." Weaver and Murray both improvised much of the sweetly funny scene where Dana and Venkman first meet at Dana's apartment.

The film was, of course, another box office success for Weaver. By the time the sequel was released in 1989, Weaver had a string of other hits to her name, including *Aliens* (1986), *Gorillas in the Mist* (1988) and *Working Girl* (1989), but she was happy

to return to the role of Dana, telling *Hollywood Insider* at the time that it was "the closest character to me I've ever played."

The sequel brought new dimensions to the character, with the addition of baby Oscar and Dana switching jobs from musician to art restorer. There was also a new twist on the original romance with Venkman. However, in one early draft of the movie, Dana did not return, instead replaced by a new love interest for Venkman named Lane Walker. Luckily, Dana was back in subsequent drafts.

Weaver returned to the franchise, albeit in a different role, in a cameo as Dr. Rebecca Gorin in 2016's *Ghostbusters: Answer the Call.* "It's just a very sweet movie but also very funny and kind of crazy," she told *Harpers Bazaar* at the time of the movie's release. "I think that's a big part of what films can do – take us to another world."

SMILES AND SCARES

Ghostbusters proved that Weaver could handle lighthearted roles, and she followed it up with many more comedies in between more serious movies. Her role in 1988's *Working Girl* earned her a Best Supporting Actress nomination, while other successful comedies in Weaver's career include *Dave* (1993), *Galaxy Quest* (1999), *Heartbreakers* (2001), *Tadpole* (2002) and *Baby Mama* (2008). Of course, *Ghostbusters* is as much a horror as it is a comedy, and Weaver has also worked on plenty of other scary movies, most notably the *Alien* sequels and 1997's *Snow White: A Tale of Terror.*

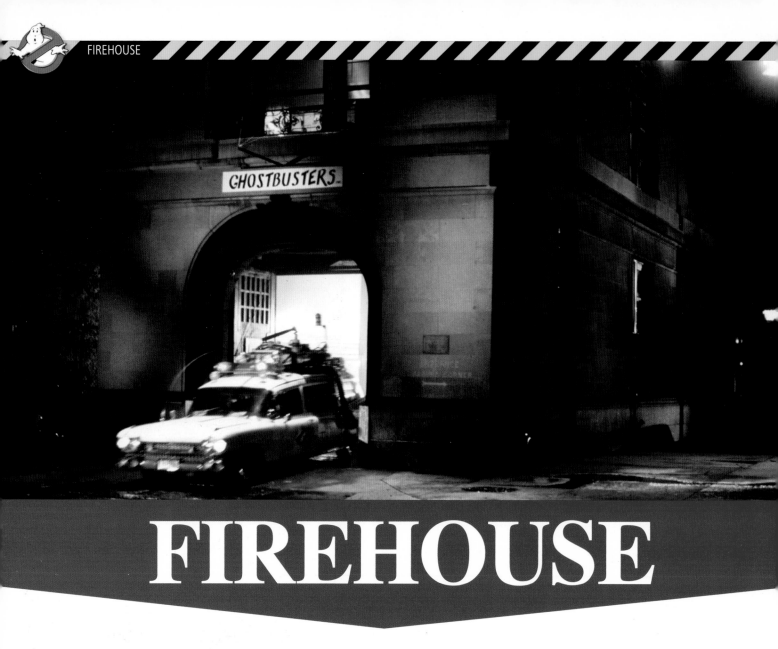

FIREHOUSE

The Ghostbusters' firehouse headquarters was shot at two stations:
New York City's Hook & Ladder Company 8 and LA's Firestation No. 23.

THE DISUSED NEW YORK CITY FIREHOUSE that acts as the Ghostbusters HQ – which may suffer from metal fatigue, substandard wiring, and an inadequate power supply, but does at least boast a great fireman's pole – was in reality two fire stations.

The first, used for the exterior shots in both films, was the Hook & Ladder Company 8 firehouse in Manhattan's Tribeca district. Associate producer Michael C. Gross first discovered the building. "I took some photos of that particular firehouse because, coincidentally, it happened to be right around the corner from where I was staying," he said in the 1985 book

Making Ghostbusters. "Curiously, that one turned out to be the perfect one." Built in 1903 in a neoclassical Beaux-Arts style, the three-story station is today both a working firehouse and a major target for tourist photos.

The interiors were, however, shot at the disused Firestation Station No. 23 in downtown Los Angeles. Constructed in 1909, the structure was once controversial for its expense and opulence. The station closed in 1960 and fell into disrepair before being hired out for movie shoots. *Ghostbusters'* production designer John DeCuir chose the location as it had a similar feel to the Hook & Ladder firehouse.

FAR LEFT The interior scenes were filmed at Firestation No. 23 in downtown LA.

LEFT The exteriors were shot at New York's Hook & Ladder Company 8.

CONTAINMENT UNIT

Every apparition that the Ghostbusters catch is transferred to their laser containment unit, located in the basement of their firehouse. The facility wasn't always envisioned as being in the Ghostbusters' HQ. In Dan Aykroyd's original script, the unit was housed at a deserted gas station in New Jersey.

While it had evolved to its current form by the shooting script, the initial intention was to offer the audience a glimpse inside. The script gives an atmospheric description: "It is a bleak repository for souls of many species. Strange lights, mists and spectral shapes waft about aimlessly... It is

a sad and frightening limbo and a most unholy makeshift asylum." Michael C. Gross discussed the unfilmed sequence in *Making Ghostbusters*. "It would have been a great shot," he said. "The inside of the storage facility was conceived as sort of a drunk tank holding cell for lost souls." According to Gross, the sequence was cut for narrative and practical reasons. "We didn't want the audience to feel too sorry for the ghosts. Another consideration was that this would have been a major special effects sequence... We just didn't have enough time left, so the shot had to go."

Jail ghost photo courtesy of Steve Neill

LEFT The slime-coated Venkman with Winston in the containment unit area.

INSET Unused 'jail ghost' sculpt by Steve Neill.

RICK MORANIS

ABOVE Louis Tully (Moranis) undergoes tests in Egon Spengler's lab. The actor replaced original choice, John Candy.

THE KEYMASTER

Rick Moranis shaped the character of lovable nerd Louis Tully and came up with much of his dialogue – including his hilarious party patter.

RICK MORANIS WAS NEVER SUPPOSED to have been in *Ghostbusters*. Fellow Canadian comedy legend John Candy was originally lined up to star as Dana's nerdy neighbour Louis Tully, but Candy and Reitman couldn't agree on the direction of the character – Reitman recalls Candy suggesting that Louis boast a German accent and own several German shepherd dogs, while associate producer Joe Medjuck says Candy wanted to base him on his *SCTV* character Johnny LaRue. After Moranis was drafted in to replace Candy, he proceeded to reshape the role and craft an unforgettable comic character.

By this point Moranis had proven his comedy credentials with performances on shows such as CBS's *90 Minutes Live* and, most famously, *SCTV* (where he replaced Harold Ramis for the third season). Moranis had gained a further following through his beer-guzzling McKenzie Brothers projects alongside Dave Thomas, an *SCTV* segment that spun off into 1982's platinum comedy album *The Great White North* and the cult movie *Strange Brew* in 1983. But it was *Ghostbusters* that kick-started Moranis's career in big-budget Hollywood productions throughout the 1980s and 1990s.

Louis was originally written as a "swinging bachelor" according to Moranis, but before accepting the role he

"MY INPUT WAS INVITED AND ENCOURAGED..."

discussed a very different take on the character with Ivan Reitman. "He asked me about this one nerdy character that I'd done in a couple of sketches on *SCTV*, and we started playing around with that and they offered me the movie," he recalled to the website *Proton Charging* in 2006.

Like Bill Murray, Dan Aykroyd and Harold Ramis, Moranis was a master of improvisation, and he devised much of Louis's dialogue and characteristics. "Right away Rick had all these wonderful ideas," Reitman told *Rolling Stone* in 2016. "I think it was his idea to play him as an accountant; he wrote that extraordinary speech when he is inviting people to a party at his house and he's walking that incoming couple through. I had the joke of throwing the coat on the dog that's in his bedroom, but that whole wonderful speech... Rick just made all of it up as he was doing it."

For his part, Moranis recalls his dialogue for the party scene as being a little less adlibbed. "The very first thing I did [after accepting the role] was sit down with Harold and start talking about taking a stab at some of the scenes," he told *Proton*

ABOVE Louis, possessed by Vinz Clortho the Keymaster, staggers out into the street outside the Ghostbuters' firehouse HQ after the shutdown of the containment unit.

Charging. "That party scene with the dog – the 'swinging bachelor' script would be very different than one with me playing the character. So I wrote the scene. I can't remember if Harold rewrote the scene or not, but my input was invited and encouraged and it was a very warm atmosphere."

The somewhat broad nature of Louis's character perfectly complemented *Ghostbusters'* delicate balance of comedy and horror. "To Ivan's credit, he knew that by having a character as broad as Louis in that mix, it almost made the other stuff a little bit more believable," the comedian pointed out to *Proton Charging*.

TULLY THE ATTORNEY

Moranis's take on Louis proved to be one of the most popular aspects of *Ghostbusters*. Lovable comedy nerds became his speciality, and the film's success was followed by roles in other comedy classics such as *Brewster's Millions, Little Shop of Horrors,* and *Spaceballs*. He also reteamed with Ramis when the latter wrote and directed *Club Paradise* in 1986.

Moranis returned as Louis for *Ghostbusters II* in 1989,

which saw the character strike up a nervy romance with Janine and mark himself out as a less-than-adept defence attorney. Several scenes in which Louis tries to capture Slimer before going on to befriend him were shot, but cut from the finished picture.

1989 was also the year of two of Moranis's other defining movies, *Honey, I Shrunk the Kids* and *Parenthood*. The film work continued after that, including playing Barney Rubble in 1994's *The Flintstones*, which topped *Ghostbusters* to become the biggest box office hit of his career.

Yet Moranis began to become disillusioned by the way his career had segued from loose-knit comedy into more straightforward acting. "I never wanted to act. I just wanted to create material, and that led to performing," he told the website *A Site Called Fred* in 2005. "I had a good time performing, but towards the end of the run of movies that I did where I was no longer writing my material and just hitting the marks and saying the lines in other people's big budget Hollywood movies... I felt much closer to work that I was responsible for the writing of, going back to the early sketches and *SCTV* and even in the films *Ghostbusters* and *Spaceballs*."

After 1997's *Honey, We Shrunk Ourselves,* Moranis took a two-decade hiatus from live action roles. The death of his wife Anne from liver cancer in 1991 had left him to raise their two young children alone, and he decided to leave acting to focus on parenthood. "For the first couple of years [following the death of his wife] I was able to make it work – doing one-and-a-half pictures a year for three months with no problem," he told *The Independent* in 2006. "But I started to really miss them [his children]... So I turned down the next pictures that came along and the break just got longer and longer."

Moranis didn't retire completely. He voiced characters in the 2003 animated role *Brother Bear* and its 2006 sequel and took on a handful of other voice roles, including reprising *Spaceballs'* Dark Helmet for an episode of *The Goldbergs*. He also made occasional live appearances, released comedy and country music albums, and appeared in *An Afternoon with SCTV*, a Martin Scorsese TV special about the show. But it wasn't until 2020 that he announced a new live action movie role in the form of a third *Honey, I Shrunk the Kids* sequel.

Moranis never regretted stepping back from his movie career for so long. "I was working with really interesting people, wonderful people – I went from that to being at home with a couple of little kids, which is a very different lifestyle," he told *The Hollywood Reporter* in 2015. "But it was important to me. I have absolutely no regrets whatsoever. My life is wonderful."

RIGHT The dishevelled Keymaster prepares to unite with the Gatekeeper before ascending to the Temple of Gozer.

THE ART OF COMEDY

Moranis has always said he considers himself a comedian and performer rather than actor, and he has often been drawn to working with others from a comic background. "Working with comedians is a different experience from working with actors and non-comedians," he told *The Independent* newspaper in a 2006 interview. "You work with Mel Brooks, or Steve Martin or Eric Idle or Bill Murray and Danny Aykroyd and Harold Ramis – that's a very different experience than working with Actor X or Actor Y. Actors are much more loyal to the script – that's their training, that's their orientation – as opposed to the comedian, who's looking for, just by instinct, a way to undermine it, destroy it, come up with something better, torture everyone along the way, make his life more interesting and yet somehow come out with a better time."

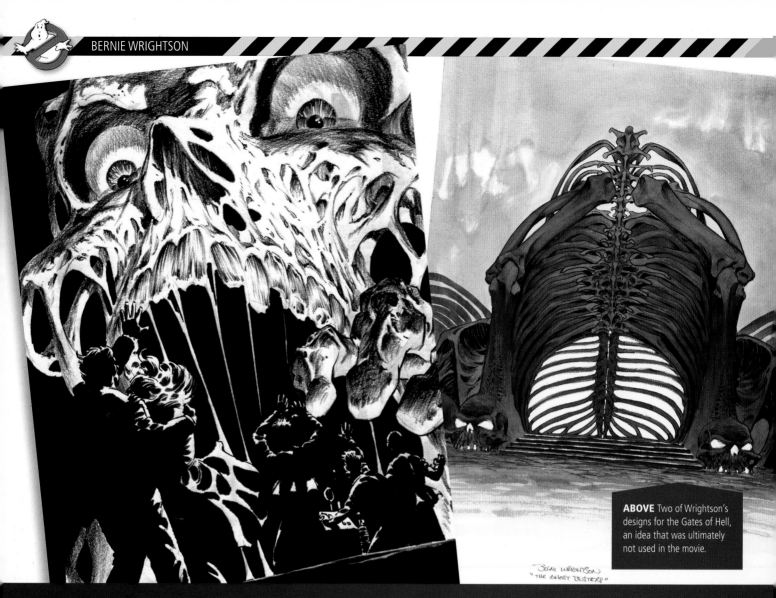

BERNIE WRIGHTSON
CONCEPT ART

The distinctive horror comics artist was brought on board as a key concept designer on the original *Ghostbusters*.

THE LATE, GREAT BERNIE WRIGHTSON WAS a perfect choice as one of *Ghostbusters*' key concept designers. The artist – who is best-known to many comics fans as the co-creator of *Swamp Thing* and for his distinctive art for DC and Marvel – had an instinctive grasp of the grotesque that was often injected with a large dose of black comedy, echoing *Ghostbusters*' perfect balance of horror and humor. He was heavily influenced by the horror comics of EC and Warren Comics, something that was also close to the heart of associate producer Michael C. Gross, who oversaw much of the film's early design work.

Gross had actually known Wrightson years earlier when Gross was art director of *National Lampoon* magazine. Wrightson's unscrupulous

LEFT Bernie Wrightson's concept sketches for the Library Ghost's transformation from little old lady to hideous demon.

character Captain Sternn had also featured in the 1981 animated fantasy *Heavy Metal*, which was associate produced by Gross and produced by Ivan Reitman.

As 'creature design consultant,' Wrightson produced 50 concept drawings during pre-production, including the library ghost, various ideas for manifestations of Gozer (including a giant skeleton figure), the containment unit ghosts, and the Terror Dogs.

Speaking about the latter to *SyFy.com* in 2016, Wrightson said, "The director would look at somebody's drawings and say, 'I like this part of it but not that part,' and they'd pass it to me and say, 'Can you redo this part of it?' It was very mix and match."

Wrightson also spoke to *SyFy.com* about working on concepts that never went beyond the development stage. "I was working from an early draft of the script which showed the Gates to Hell and the Road to Hell and all this stuff, so I did a lot of drawings of those… They never made it to the final movie."

ABOVE One of Bernie Wrightson's early design ideas for the Terror Dogs.

ABOVE A sketch showing Gozer as a towering skeletal figure.

BELOW One of Wrightson's unused specter designs and another Gates of Hell concept illustration.

ANNIE POTTS

"GHOSTBUSTERS. WHADDYA WANT?"

The actress behind *Ghostbusters'* sardonic secretary Janine Melnitz on big glasses, the anxieties of improv, and being mistaken for a genuine New Yorker.

ANNIE POTTS THOUGHT SHE STILL HAD days to prepare. Arriving in New York for costume fittings a week before shooting on her scenes was due to begin, she decided it would be fun to head downtown to watch filming on one of *Ghostbusters'* early sequences. "I was there to visit – just to visit! – but Ivan saw me and said, 'Oh, you're here! Let's put you in the scene,'" Potts laughs. Her protestation that she wasn't in costume did not, it seems, overly concern Ivan Reitman. "He said, 'Oh, you're good, let's just go with it.' So I took the very thick glasses off of the costumer who was next to me and went with those. And then I was kind of stuck with these glasses that were not my prescription and which I could barely see through. Trial by fire!"

Being thrust prematurely into a scene proved a fair indication of the spontaneous approach taken by Reitman and especially Potts's co-stars – a way of working that

was in direct contrast to Potts's own style of acting. "I didn't come from improv, I came from theater," she says. "Not that improv isn't theater, but it's a different kind of theater. I never liked improv. And I thought the script was so good. Sometimes when I saw them improvising it would be like, 'The script is so good, why don't you just say what's there? We should rehearse with that!' That kind of made me anxious."

Yet Potts soon began to appreciate Murray, Aykroyd, and Ramis's very different approach to comedy. "I came to understand that they were always looking for something funnier. The *funniest*. Harold and Danny – unlike a lot of writers – weren't particularly tied to it [the script] necessarily. They were like, 'Well, if you've got something better, let's hear it.'" Potts remembers that Bill Murray had a particularly loose approach to his lines. "It seemed to me that Bill had never actually read the script," she laughs. "He would just kind of wander into the scene and be like, 'What's going on here?'"

> " **HAROLD AND DANNY WERE NOT PARTICULARLY TIED TO THE SCRIPT...** "

THE NASHVILLIAN NEW YORKER

Though Sandra Bernhard was initially considered for the role ("She would have been wonderful at it, just different"), it's difficult to imagine Janine played by

ABOVE Potts in action as the Ghostbusters' sarcastic secretary Janine. Potts was influenced by the roles played by the actresses Eve Arden and Thelma Ritter.

anyone else. Potts was hardly an unknown when *Ghostbusters* was released – alongside her theater work, she'd starred in the hit comedy *Corvette Summer* alongside Mark Hamill, as well as appearing in the dramas *King of the Gypsies* and *Heartaches* – but *Ghostbusters* made her instantly recognizable. For a long time, the Nashville-born Potts was so synonymous with Janine that many viewers assumed she was a native New Yorker. "A lot of people thought it was my natural accent, and I think it actually stopped me being considered for other roles in the wake of it," she recalls.

While in the process of fleshing out the character, Potts drew on memories of her favorite black-and-white movies from childhood. "There were character actors who always played the B-role, always played the secretary. One was an actress named Eve Arden. The other was Thelma Ritter. They were just fantastic at playing those characters. I like to think of Janine in that way, that she was cast in that kind of role model. Of course, it's a modern piece and they were from a different period altogether, but I admired

them as actors, and that's where my mind went."

Though Potts recalls the script as "one of the funniest, most original things I had ever read," she was still surprised at just how successful – and enduring – *Ghostbusters* turned out. "[When we saw it] with all the special effects in place and everything, it was so hilarious. I thought it was executed beyond anybody's wildest expectations. You go in thinking you'll make the best movie you can but an *iconic* movie… that's kind of a bridge too far to hope for, you know?"

In between 1984's *Ghostbusters* and 1989's *Ghostbusters II*, Potts landed another one of her

BELOW The famous glasses that Janine wears in the first film were swiped from a costumer at the last minute – and were not Potts's prescription!

 **"IT WAS ONE OF THE FUNNIEST, MOST ORIGINAL THINGS I HAD EVER READ "**

RIGHT Annie Potts on set with Bill Murray, Harold Ramis, Rick Moranis, and Dan Aykroyd. Potts began shooting her scenes earlier than she'd anticipated.

best-known roles, as head designer Mary Jo Shively in the CBS sitcom *Designing Women*, which ran for a mighty seven seasons from 1986 to 1993. Did Potts ever hesitate about returning as Janine? "Oh no," she insists. "The problem was really just working it out because I was in the middle of my season shooting that [*Designing Women*], and of course it was a live audience show so it's not like they could shoot me out or include me later. Luckily, [most of *Ghostbusters II*] was actually shot on the Warner Bros lot and I shot *Designing Women* there as well, so I was running from one end of the lot to the other."

The sequel saw an expanded role for Janine, with

" I WAS PLEASED TO HAVE A LITTLE MORE CONTROL OVER WHO SHE WAS "

the love interest switching from Egon to Louis and a funky new look (including a red bob and rounded, though equally oversized, glasses). Potts says she was pleased to be given a say in updating Janine's appearance. "I had absolute input into it. I mean, people change in five years. I don't look like I did five years ago – I don't wear my hair as I did or anything. I thought it was entirely valid [to update Janine's look], and they supported me on that. I was very pleased to have a little more control [over] who she was and how she dressed. And I was able to think about it beforehand instead of, 'Hey, you're in this scene, what you've got on is fine!'"

THE PROOF IS IN THE PUDDING

Though the schedule on the second film was once again tight, Potts recalls a more relaxed atmosphere on set. "Ivan at that time was a very seasoned director and very sure comedically, and the proof was in the pudding of the first one. So all we had to do was make the best film we could. Everyone was just building on the strongest elements of the characters. I believe there was a little more time, so I think they [the cast and crew] were a little more leisurely."

Three and a half decades on from Janine's debut – during which time Potts has taken on other high-profile roles, including voicing Bo Peep in the *Toy Story* movies and appearing in *The Big Bang Theory* spin-off *Young Sheldon* – Potts is pleased to see how much life *Ghostbusters* has left in it. "More time has passed since we started shooting that film than I was old at the time! No matter how distant the first ones were, they're still very much present. These movies – and people's interest in them – keep on going."

ABOVE *Ghostbusters II* introduced a relationship between Janine and Louis, and featured expanded roles for both characters.

VANESSA THE DESK CLERK

Twenty-seven years after *Ghostbusters II*, Potts returned to the franchise, along with several of her fellow cast members, for a cameo in 2016's *Ghostbusters: Answer the Call*. Her brief role as Vanessa the desk clerk (who echoes Janine's famous line "Whaddya want?") proved a return to the spontaneous way of working that she'd experienced on the first film. "I didn't know until the day I got there what [part] it was going to be!" she laughs. "I didn't know what they were up to. But I was game. I liked Paul Feig and the girls were just wonderful and very funny. It was a fun day."

ABOVE Gozer the Destructor (Slavitza Jovan) is illuminated against an eerie fog in her temple. The lighting needed to work in tandem with the smoke.

LEADING LIGHTS

Ghostbusters' lighting technician Michael J. Schwartz on God's rays, the challenges of shooting in an old firehouse, and lighting Sigourney Weaver.

THE SEAMLESS BUT EVER-SHIFTING MOOD OF *Ghostbusters* – which can change from funny to romantic to scary within the space of a single scene – would not have been possible without the film's formidable lighting department. A small army of technicians, best boys, gaffers, and grips were responsible for setting up extensive rigs and ensuring that the lighting reflected the atmosphere Ivan Reitman and cinematographer László Kovács were trying to create. Bearing in mind the film not only danced through different genres but took in day and night shoots, interiors and exteriors, and location and studio footage, the lighting arrangements required extensive advance planning.

"I'd say 80% of lighting on movies like *Ghostbusters* is pre-planned," says Michael J. Schwartz, one of the movie's lighting technicians. "László would sit down with the director – sometimes with the gaffer and head lighting technician, perhaps the producers too – and break down the script to get a good lighting plan. But 20% of lighting would be off-the-cuff, because things can change on the day." Lighting crews would prep four to five weeks before filming and then spend at least two hours on testing on the day, he adds.

It is on-location exteriors like the sequences shot on the streets of New York that were the most unpredictable, Schwartz says, because of factors like the weather and the sun shifting in the sky. "Then at night you need to add the effects of the moon, and it takes a line of equipment to get lights up high. You use cranes and elevated platforms, so it becomes a little trickier. The size of the lights gets bigger too, and we didn't have the technology on *Ghostbusters*, like HMI lights, that we do now."

SMOKE AND MIRRORS

One of the main sequences that Schwartz worked on was lighting the interior firehouse sequences, which were shot inside the former Fire Station No. 23 in LA. Unlike studio stages, which are designed to hang lights onto, location interiors can pose their own challenges – in the case of the firehouse, says Schwartz, this included dozens of reflective windows and the fact they could not make alterations to the building. "That was the toughest part – working around the restrictions of the fire station being a historical building," he recalls. "You couldn't add anything mechanical, so you would either have to black out the window completely or take precautions to omit reflections. And it was a live location – there were a lot of civilians working in the area, so you have to be mindful when you're getting equipment in. The rigging crew would probably spend an entire day rigging some of these sets. Logistically, it was a tough set."

Other issues that the crew needed to incorporate into their lighting plans were in-car lighting and smoke effects. While the former may have been limited, there was plenty of smoke drifting through the film. "A lot of times you'll see light coming through the smoke," Schwartz says. "We call it 'God's rays.' It has both an

emotional and creative effect. We did a lot of tests with different smokes and different thickness of smoke to see how the lighting would come through best."

The amount of lighting and the type of lights used changed depending on the mood of the scene. The sequences shot in the containment unit area were infused with a sense of tension thanks to flashing red-light indicators, while more romantic moments between Venkman and Dana were shot in a softer light. Lighting Sigourney Weaver required careful preparation, Schwartz remembers – much more than the Ghostbusters themselves. "It's tougher to light the features of a woman's face than it is to light a man's," he says. "You want to expose the beauty in Sigourney Weaver. Whereas you don't mind so much what Dan Aykroyd looks like as long as you can see him!"

ABOVE Ecto-1's lights cut through the fog; Ray is bathed in bright light; mood lighting helps make the possessed Dana appear sinister but sexy; illuminated mist was key to creating an otherwordly atmosphere on the Temple of Gozer set.

WILLIAM ATHERTON

As the ill-tempered Walter Peck, William Atherton played the Ghostbusters' biggest human antagonist. He looks back on gunk, insults, and breaking free of 'sensitive leading man' roles.

"YOU WOULD HAVE TO BE A LITTLE dim creatively, intellectually and spiritually to think you could compete with them," laughs William Atherton. "I mean, I had done comedies before, but here were the funniest people in the world. I thought, 'What the hell am I going to do with this role?'"

With Atherton clear that he wasn't about to trade one-liners with the stars of *Saturday Night Live*, *Stripes* and *The Blues Brothers*, he needed a different approach for uptight EPA agent Walter Peck. The answer came courtesy of a friend who had worked with Groucho

Marx. "This friend said that Groucho had told him one of the best things that had happened to his movies was Margaret Dumont. She was the consummate straight person because she wasn't playing into a skit – she really didn't know why it was funny. So I thought, that's what I have to do. I have to play a male Margaret Dumont. I [will act like I] don't think it's funny and I'm not playing into it at all. That's the tack I took to save my ass, so to speak."

In Atherton's hands, Peck become the most objectionable and ill-tempered bureaucrat that the Ghostbusters come into conflict with; in fact, he has the honor of being the heroes' biggest foe in the human world. While Peck may not be as terrifying as a Terror Dog or as all-powerful as Gozer, his actions are directly responsible for unleashing hundreds of ghosts and ghouls into New York City after shutting down the Ghostbusters' containment unit, and he emerges as the ultimate nemesis of Venkman in particular.

"I decided to give him these narrow bureaucratic rages that people get into because the power of their profession is all they have," Atherton says. "When he felt they didn't acknowledge his power or ignored him, it really tickled him – that's how I played it."

" I THOUGHT, [I WILL ACT LIKE] I DON'T THINK IT'S FUNNY "

Of course, Peck actually works for the Environment Agency – not a natural source of movie antagonists today – and however pettily he goes about it, his concerns about the danger of the contents of the Ghostbusters' containment unit are perhaps not *entirely* unreasonable. But as Atherton points out, it was Peck's personality rather than his employer that made him such a worthy antagonist. "It's interesting that he works

for the EPA, but I didn't focus on that. It could have been the AAA [American Automobile Association] or any high bureaucracy at all. I didn't do any research into the EPA. I'll leave that to our President…"

Peck's humor-free persona meant that Atherton didn't get to nab the film's funniest lines, but the actor nevertheless improvised many of his scenes with Bill Murray, Harold Ramis and Dan Aykroyd. After all, he was well versed in bouncing around different approaches during his time working with emerging playwrights. "I think it's harder to do that [improvise] now, because financial things are so strict," Atherton says. "Movies now are kind of scheduled to the dime, and it can be more difficult to relax and riff with something. Time's become a huge constraint, and it doesn't always make for the easiest atmosphere. Back then, the movie culture was different. You just had a lot more elasticity financially than you do now."

ANTE-ROOM

Atherton looks back fondly on the *Ghostbusters* shoot, whether it was working with Ivan Reitman ("Very encouraging… he had a great depth of feeling for Dan and Bill and Harold, and I was allowed into their ante-room, which was lovely") or the beauty of shooting on

BELOW Walter Peck (Atherton) flees the Ghostbusters' firehouse headquarters as hundreds of imprisoned ghosts and ghouls are released into New York City.

ABOVE Walter Peck orders the shutdown of the Ghostbusters' containment unit – against the warnings of Egon (Harold Ramis). Peck's decision soon causes chaos throughout the city.

Central Park West ("Block after block was illuminated and it became one giant movie set... to be a fly buzzing around in the arc of those lights was really gorgeous"). He also remembers just how special it felt watching the finished movie for the first time, even if he – like most of the cast and crew – didn't foresee the phenomenon it would become. "When I first saw the film, I thought it was heaven, it was hilarious," Atherton says. "But I didn't know it was going to be a major chapter in culture. It's become like the comic *Star Wars* – and I think it deserves to be. It was one of those signature events in life where you're hit by a very special bus."

" **IT WAS ONE OF THOSE SIGNATURE EVENTS IN LIFE WHEN YOU'RE HIT BY A VERY SPECIAL BUS** "

However, Atherton did have to suffer for his art, not least having a tank of marshmallow goo dunked over him during the finale. "It was shaving cream, and I asked them how much of it there was going to be," he recalls. "They told me there was 150 pounds of it. I said, 'You're going to drop *that* on me? Can we have a little experiment to get this straight?' Because I remember from school that 150 pounds of feathers is the same as 150 pounds of lead! Finally, they got some poor stunt guy to stand under there [to be dunked], and everybody's looking at me and rolling their eyes. And it knocked the stunt guy flat! I said, 'I just wanted to make that point!' So they went back and got the weight back a little."

There was also the little matter of just how vehemently some fans took against his character, frequently yelling out Venkman's memorable insults in the street ("This man has no dick!") – something he

ABOVE Peck tussles with police officers, before he is later dunked with marshmallow goo. The actor was concerned about 150 pounds of shaving foam being dropped on him.

neither anticipated nor welcomed at the time. "It was a surprise and I probably did get a little ill-natured about it," Atherton admits. "Everybody has their vanity! So I probably over-reacted, but I got over it. Because the movie is its own engine, and that overwhelmed any minor grievance I or anyone else might have had."

TURNING POINT

The movie was something of a turning point in Atherton's career. In the 1970s, Atherton was mainly known for playing leading roles in acclaimed dramas such as Steven Spielberg's *The Sugarland Express* (1974), T*he Day of the Locust* (1975), and *Looking for Mr. Goodbar* (1977), as well as his theater work. Post-*Ghostbusters*, he tended to take on supporting roles, often playing antagonists in the likes of *Die Hard*

(1988), *Die Hard 2* (1990), and *Bio-Dome* (1996). Atherton is clear that he welcomed the change in career direction. "As a leading man, everybody has a finite time usually, and I'd been doing that for 15 years," Atherton says. "A lot of the films I did got great reviews, and *Sugarland* and those other films always made money. But they were cognoscenti things. *Ghostbusters* angled me into a different career as the funny bad guy, which I didn't really mind at all. I liked playing those kinds of parts. It gave me a lot more creative freedom – it didn't give you the worry as to whether a movie made money or not that you can have when you're a leading man. And as a leading man in the 1970s, you were often asked to stare sensitively off into the sunset, which was a huge bore! It was a lot more fun to play roles like Walter Peck."

GAME ON!

Though William Atherton didn't return for *Ghostbusters II*, he did reprise the role for 2009's *Ghostbusters: The Video Game* and more recently 2019's construction simulation game *Planet Coaster* alongside Dan Aykroyd. "That game [*Planet Coaster*] was very well written, organised and directed – I thought it was terrific," Atherton enthuses. He also joined Aykroyd and many of the other *Ghostbusters* cast and crew at 2019's huge Fan Fest convention at the Sony lot, where he got to meet fans and see close-up just how beloved the franchise remains. "That Sony convention was enormous and a great deal of fun," he says. "I didn't quite realize how all-pervasive *Ghostbusters* is! There are *Ghostbusters* clubs all over the world. The legs that *Ghostbusters* has had is interesting to me. I'm always interested in how people see it and what they like about it. I learn every time."

NO GHOST LOGO

The classic 'no ghost' logo was refined by *Ghostbusters'* associate producer and former designer Michael C. Gross, before becoming an essential part of the movie's marketing campaign.

THE *GHOSTBUSTERS* 'NO GHOST' IMAGE is one of the most recognizable movie logos of all time – simple, clever and perfectly summing up the story in one neat graphic. The logo was first described in Dan Aykroyd's original treatment for *Ghostbusters*, where it appeared on the side of Ecto-1. Aykroyd commissioned designer John Deveikis, a friend from Carleton University, to devise the first iteration (along with other concept art) to accompany his script. The basic formula – a white ghost in a red, crossed-out circle – was established. However, once the movie had been green-lit, refining the concept proved to be a somewhat lengthier process.

The task of developing the final logo fell to the late Michael

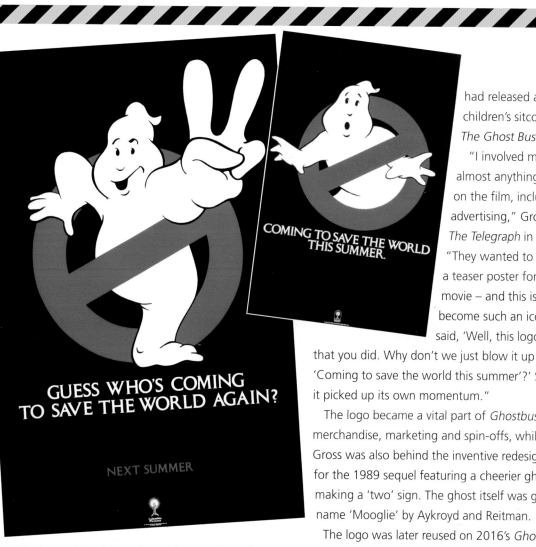

GUESS WHO'S COMING
TO SAVE THE WORLD AGAIN?

NEXT SUMMER

COMING TO SAVE THE WORLD
THIS SUMMER.

had released a 1975 children's sitcom called *The Ghost Busters*).

"I involved myself with almost anything graphic on the film, including advertising," Gross told *The Telegraph* in 2015. "They wanted to put out a teaser poster for the movie – and this is why it become such an icon. They said, 'Well, this logo's great that you did. Why don't we just blow it up and put 'Coming to save the world this summer'?' Suddenly it picked up its own momentum."

The logo became a vital part of *Ghostbusters*' merchandise, marketing and spin-offs, while Gross was also behind the inventive redesign for the 1989 sequel featuring a cheerier ghost making a 'two' sign. The ghost itself was given the name 'Mooglie' by Aykroyd and Reitman.

The logo was later reused on 2016's *Ghostbusters: Answer the Call*, and the movie even featured a sequence in which the character Rowan appeared as an incarnation of Mooglie.

C. Gross, *Ghostbusters*' associate producer and former graphic designer. He worked with talented storyboard artist Brent Boates to design as many versions of the idea as possible.

"Being a magazine art director at *National Lampoon*, I really understood what the symbol had to be," he told *SFX* magazine in 2014. "I knew it had to be simple, it needed to be clean, it had to make the point."

THE FINAL DESIGN

The pair came up with between 20 to 30 variations on the logo. Eventually Gross narrowed it down to five versions which he brought to Ivan Reitman. Together they settled on the dynamic final design, which wasn't originally envisioned to be used beyond the car and uniforms. However, the advertising department soon realized its marketability, especially as they wanted to release a title-less teaser poster (Columbia had yet to license the title *Ghostbusters* from Filmation, who

JENNIFER RUNYON

As the female student who takes part in Peter Venkman's rigged ESP test, Jennifer Runyon starred in one of the film's funniest scenes.

"I WAS SHOCKED WHEN RANDOM people came up to me and said, 'Oh my God, you're in *Ghostbusters*!'" says Jennifer Runyon. "I'm only on screen for, like, four minutes! But people still know me from it, and that's pretty cool."

Runyon may have appeared in a single scene, but it was a pivotal one. As Runyon's character, also named Jennifer, and her fellow student (Steven Tash) take part in Peter Venkman's distinctly biased ESP 'test,' the audience gets a first glimpse at Venkman's inimitable mix of amorality and charm. The sequence is also one of the film's funniest; little wonder it gave Runyon her most famous role.

By the time she'd auditioned for the part, Runyon had chalked up roles in a couple of movies (David Hess's low-budget slasher *To All a Goodnight* and rafting comedy *Up*

the Creek) as well as the daytime soap *Another World*. However, *Ghostbusters* was the biggest film she had done at that point. "And since!" she laughs.

Runyon recalls how excited she was about working on the movie after hearing the cast list. On arriving in New York for filming she was finally allowed to read the script, and her anticipation only grew. Yet she had to wait a couple more weeks before they got around to shooting her sequence. "Steven and I were brought to New York as the 'cover set' – we were like the insurance policy. If it rained, they were going to film our scene."

After a rain-free fortnight in which Runyon and Tash hung out watching other scenes being filmed ("I'd never been on a set that had so much going on"), it finally came time to shoot their sequence. Runyon headed over to the

LEFT Peter Venkman informs his student (Jennifer Runyon) that she is a "legitimate phenomenon." The early scene was important in establishing Venkman's character.

costume trailer to be fitted; what she didn't know was that she was already wearing her costume. "I walked in the make-up trailer and they went, 'Yeah, you look good, you're fine.' I'm like, '*What?*' And then the wardrobe people came in and said, 'Yeah, you look great.' If I had known that that was going to be my wardrobe, I would have worn a completely different outfit!"

Runyon recalls that filming the sequence took less than a day. "It was the fastest four or five hours ever; we didn't want it to end. We never stopped laughing! It didn't feel like we were on set, we were just having so much fun. To this day Steven and I say we wish we had three more days to work with these people. They were incredibly talented folks."

Bill Murray took the time to create a relaxed atmosphere on set and make Runyon and Tash feel comfortable. But did he engage in any of his famous improvisation? "Some of it was off-script. But it was just a word here or there that he'd play with. I had taken a bunch of improv classes, so I don't remember being surprised." Runyon adds that one of her favorite aspects of the scene is the little details. "Things like the way we

[Runyon and Murray] look at each other. It's the subtle things that make it work."

Though Runyon and Tash became good friends on the movie, they lost touch after filming ended – only to be reunited over 30 years later for the documentary *Ghostheads* (2016). "It was like no time had passed. It's so nice to rekindle a friendship with someone I hadn't seen in so long. Steven is such a wonderful human being."

In recent years Runyon has returned to acting for the first time since 1993's *Carnosaur*, popping up in 2015's low-budget *Silent Night, Bloody Night 2* ("The director made it in four days, like my uncle Roger Corman") and *Bloodsucka Jones vs. the Creeping Death* in 2017. But she says that *Ghostbusters* will always remain close to her heart. "Never in my wildest dreams would I have thought that all these years later I'd be traveling all over the world, doing conventions… You realize it doesn't matter how big your part is if it's a great part. There are some movies that become part of our film history, like *The Wizard of Oz* and *Star Wars*, and *Ghostbusters* is one of them to be sure. I count my blessings, buddy!"

John Rothman, better known to *Ghostbusters* fans as New York Public Library's Roger Delacorte, shares his memories about pigeons, street preachers, and the greatest city in the world.

JOHN ROTHMAN KNOWS A SECRET ABOUT some of his *Ghostbusters* co-stars. "Do you remember that scene where I run down the steps of the library and say, 'Did you see it?' as the pigeons take off? Those were *actor* pigeons! They were trained and hired out, and came back at the end of the shoot. They were not real New York City pigeons!"

Rothman's small but memorable role as Roger Delacorte, the buttoned-up administrator at the New York Public Library, saw him work with some pretty impressive human stars too. "I remember the call around 6.30 in the morning of the first shoot day," he says. "We were in the makeup trailer on 41st Street, and they [Bill Murray, Dan Aykroyd and Harold Ramis] were in there riffing off each other. It was fantastic to see. The movie's very funny, but it

seemed like they were even funnier when they were just kidding around with each other."

Rothman admits that when he was initially offered the role, he was far from convinced about accepting it. He had already played one library administrator in *Sophie's Choice* ("I know the American Library Association didn't like me because I was portraying librarians in an unfavorable way!"), and remembers wanting to focus his attention on larger roles. "I had had a very good part in a Woody Allen movie called *Stardust Memories*," he says. "I was on the whole picture, 24 weeks. And I thought [the library administrator] is just a bit-part, I'm not going to do it."

In the end it was an old friend who persuaded him to accept the role. "Sigourney Weaver – who I knew from Yale School of Drama – rang me up and said, 'You're crazy! You have to do it. It'll be so much fun.' I'm obviously very happy that I decided to do it."

Rothman's time on the picture – which he estimates took around two days – proved to be just as fun as Weaver had promised. In fact, the only mild hitch he can recall was when a street preacher caused commotion while they were filming on the library steps. "He was causing problems for the production with the noise, so they tried to buy him off. For me, it was sort of amusing!"

While Rothman has an impressive list of TV, movie and theater credits to his name, *Ghostbusters* remains one of the roles he is most recognized for. "It was one of the first movies that people saw many times," he says. "Over 30 years it's appeared on every platform – network TV, pay TV, airplanes, VHS, DVD... I don't think I've ever met somebody who hasn't seen *Ghostbusters*!"

One of the things Rothman says he loves most about the film today is the way it acts as a love letter to New York City, a place he has spent significant time in. "The picture uses New York City in such a good way – Columbia University, the New York Public Library, the firehouse in Tribeca. This was a time – during the late '70s and early '80s – when major movies were not really made in New York City. *Ghostbusters* has such an incredibly authentic relationship with the place. Everything about it is grounded in the specificity of New York, which everybody knows is the greatest city in the world!"

MONTAGE MADNESS

Ghostbusters boasts two memorable montages: the first sees the team become celebrity spook-hunters, while in the second escapees from the containment unit run riot in the city.

COVER STARS

The first montage featuring the now-celebrated Ghostbusters apprehending ghosts is interspersed with commentary from TV and radio hosts (including Joe Franklin and Larry King) and a succession of magazine covers featuring the heroes. The latter – which includes *TIME*, *The New York Post*, *The Globe*, and *The Atlantic* – were put together by graphic designer and artist Michael McWillie. "Michael [C. Gross, associate producer] called me in and said, 'I can't stand phony looking covers. They have to look like the magazines exactly,'" McWillie recalls. "Then he gave me a list of the covers he wanted."

In the pre-Photoshop era, McWillie painstakingly created the licensed covers using stills from the movie and manual type-setting, along with outlandish cover lines. "The politics of the next dimension: do ghosts have civil rights?" questioned the headline of *The Atlantic*, while *The Globe* talked of "The Ghostbusters' Super-Diet." There were in-jokes too, with Gross being glimpsed as a 'new poet' in *TIME* and McWillie mentioned as a "golfing champion" in *USA Today*. "There was a little pressure, because Michael was one of the best designers in the world," McWillie admits. "But it turned out very well. We had a ball."

Cover image used with permission of The Atlantic. Illustration by Randy Enos.

SUBWAY GHOST

After a triple-headed design by Brent Boates was rejected for being too expensive, it was replaced with a ghost created by artist Melody Pena and sculptor Linda Frobos. The sculpt was then cast in vinyl. "We shot that in a water tank," says Pena. "It's too bad you can't really see it, because it's so pretty!"

TAXI GHOST

The taxi driver seen in the second montage – who, unbeknown to the ill-tempered passenger, is a decomposing corpse – was created by effects artist Steve Johnson. "I designed that as part of my test for the film," Johnson recalls. "They said, 'Go to New York and shoot the zombie. If it works, we'll give you a job.' So I made it in my bedroom; I sculpted it, molded it, cast it, painted it, mechanized it. It went off really well, so they said, 'OK kid, you've got the job!'"

THE FORT DETMERRING GHOST

This dream sequence was originally part of a longer scene. As originally filmed, the scene saw Ray and Winston arriving in Fort Detmerring to investigate a haunting. We next see Ray lying in a period bedroom, dressed in an officer's uniform before a beautiful spirit (played by *Playboy* model Kym Herrin) drifts in to pleasure him. It was cut for pacing, Harold Ramis explained in the book *Making Ghostbusters*. "The plot was moving way too fast to include anything extraneous... We didn't want to let go of that [the idea], so Ivan came up with the idea of treating it as a dream and inserting into the very end of the montage."

Stuart Ziff, head of the ghost shop, recalls preparing for the sequence: "She was suspended by wires, but they had to create a cast of the front of her body for her to lie on. [Puppeteer/fabricator] Mark Wilson and Steve Johnson were gently laying these gauze bandages on her saturated in plaster, being very dainty. She said something like, 'Hey boys, this is never going to get done, go for it!' They both looked at each other, flipped their brushes in the air, and started patting her down! During filming, she wore a wispy costume with fans blowing silk streamers."

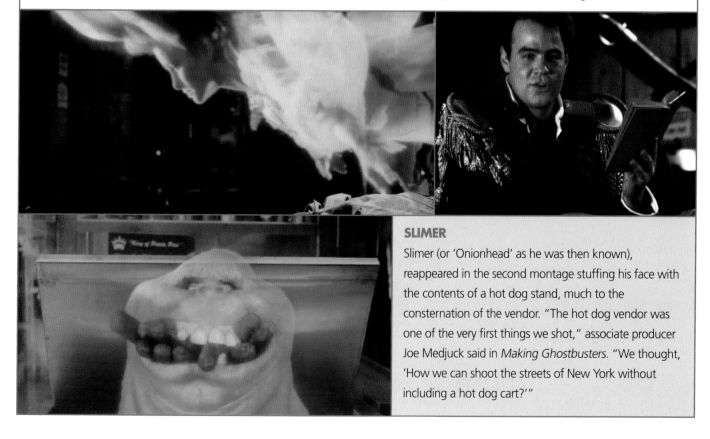

SLIMER

Slimer (or 'Onionhead' as he was then known), reappeared in the second montage stuffing his face with the contents of a hot dog stand, much to the consternation of the vendor. "The hot dog vendor was one of the very first things we shot," associate producer Joe Medjuck said in *Making Ghostbusters*. "We thought, 'How we can shoot the streets of New York without including a hot dog cart?'"

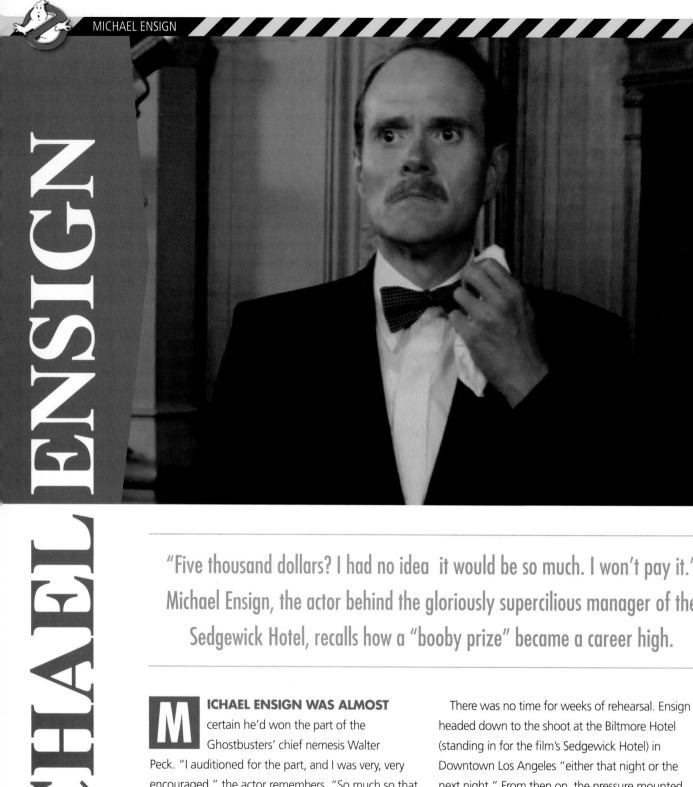

MICHAEL ENSIGN

"Five thousand dollars? I had no idea it would be so much. I won't pay it." Michael Ensign, the actor behind the gloriously supercilious manager of the Sedgewick Hotel, recalls how a "booby prize" became a career high.

MICHAEL ENSIGN WAS ALMOST certain he'd won the part of the Ghostbusters' chief nemesis Walter Peck. "I auditioned for the part, and I was very, very encouraged," the actor remembers. "So much so that my agent really thought they were going to make me an offer. But they didn't."

The part went instead to William Atherton, and Ensign resigned himself to the fact that his *Ghostbusters* experience was over before it had begun. Then he got a phone call from his agent. "They asked me if I wanted a booby prize. I asked, 'What is it?' And my agent said, 'Well, they want you to come down and play the hotel manager…'"

There was no time for weeks of rehearsal. Ensign headed down to the shoot at the Biltmore Hotel (standing in for the film's Sedgewick Hotel) in Downtown Los Angeles "either that night or the next night." From then on, the pressure mounted. "A sequence like this should take quite a long time. Probably two nights would have been sensible with the amount of work they had to do," he says. "But they wanted to get all of it finished in just one night."

Despite having had virtually no time to prepare for the role, Ensign thought he was ready for what awaited. "As a good British-trained actor, I dutifully knew my lines, knew what I was doing, knew the timing," he laughs. "And then, of course, I hit *those* guys…"

CHARACTER ACTOR

Like fellow castmates Annie Potts and David Margulies, Ensign's background was in theater. Though born in Arizona, he worked extensively within British theater, training at the London Academy of Music and Dramatic Art and joining the Royal Shakespeare Company in the mid-70s. On arriving in Hollywood in the late 1970s, he found himself thrust into a different way of working. "When I got out here, I would have to work very quickly, because that's how film and telly works [in Hollywood], with no rehearsal," he says. "But that background of having done character work through British theater gave me a computer-full of things I could pull out to use."

By the time of *Ghostbusters*, he had established himself as a dependable character actor, with roles in such classics as *Midnight Express*, *Superman*, and *WarGames*. But the freewheeling style of comedy legends Bill Murray, Dan Aykroyd and Harold Ramis was a different acting style altogether. "They weren't doing what the script said!" he remembers. "They were kind of making it up as they went along. Which was fine – I'd just wait until they stopped talking and then feed in my lines. But as we were going down the long corridor, that camera turn was very tricky. Every time we got there it was missed, because it was impossible to time it out the way they were doing it!"

With only one night to shoot the sequence, the pressure mounted. "After a couple of takes that didn't work, Ivan started getting grumpier and grumpier until he told me off, [asking] why couldn't I get it right," Ensign laughs. "I was doing my best to get it right, but you don't tell the director – in front of the stars who are messing it up – that *they're* the reason. So I humbly took my punishment. Until Dan Aykroyd spoke up and said, 'Back off Ivan, it's our fault, we're the ones doing this not him!' Anyway, he ironed it out, and we eventually got that shot."

The shoot may have been challenging, but the result was one of *Ghostbusters'* funniest sequences. Not that Ensign was fully convinced on viewing the movie for the first time. "I think I saw a cast and crew screening of *Ghostbusters* and my agent came along with me. We sort of said, 'Eh, it's alright.' Neither she nor I thought it was that great."

Ensign's ambivalence towards the film didn't last long. "I took my godsons to see it and by the time we were in queue, I'd already been recognized. Then we got into the movie theater and the audience were shouting out the lines before they [the characters] could say them. It was like *The Rocky Horror Picture Show*... So I was like, 'Oh, yet again my judgment as an actor has totally failed me!' *Ghostbusters* turned out to be this amazing thing. I really got prestige with my godsons when *MAD* magazine came out with a parody of *Ghostbusters,* and there were two drawings of me in it!"

The role remains one of the high points of Ensign's long career. "It's funny. I felt so badly about not getting that Atherton part. But the hotel manager did amazing things for me career-wise... It was so great to do!"

RON CROCI
CONCEPT ART

Artist Ron Croci looks back on creating concept illustrations for *Ghostbusters'* revered production designer John DeCuir.

BELOW Croci's study drawing of the altar, and another study showing the entire Temple of Gozer on top of the Shandor Building.

WHILE CONCEPT ARTISTS SUCH AS Thom Enriquez and Bernie Wrightson worked largely with associate producer Michael C. Gross, Ron Croci's concept art and storyboards were created for production designer John DeCuir and his son, art director John DeCuir Jr.

Croci had first met DeCuir when he walked into DeCuir's gallery in Santa Monica. "When I went in, he was painting the floor to resemble marble slabs, and I ended up helping him," Croci recalls. "On the walls and on 12-foot ceilings were famous images from mythology that he had painted freehand. He had a stage where he presented his pitches [for a movie's art direction] with performers acting out sequences."

By this point Croci was an established concept artist, with a

Study for the "altar" and scene B.G. "Ghostbusters"

STUDY FOR APPEARANCE OF MONSTERS "GHOST...

STUDY FOR MODEL COMPOSITE AND MATTE SHOT   "GHOSTBUSTERS"

CLOCKWISE Study drawing of the exploding Temple of Gozer, the sinister stone Terror Dogs, and one of the building's mascaron details.

resume that included Dan Aykroyd's earlier movie *The Blues Brothers*. When DeCuir saw Croci's name on a list of potential artists, he hired him, along with fellow artist Robert Branham. Over the next four months, Croci created concepts and design storyboards for the Stay Puft and Terror Dogs sequences, but much of his time was focused on the Temple of Gozer. His art was used as reference for matte paintings of the Temple and the subsequent explosion. "I tried to show different types of explosions on 16x20-inch paper so the effects department would have something to go by," he says.

For Croci, working with John DeCuir was one of the highlights of *Ghostbusters*. "Decuir Sr. was an amazing storyboard artist; he had this loose style where you could follow the whole movie on boards. He was probably the greatest production designer in movies. He had a technique that was very interesting. He would fly from Los Angeles to Rome and start drawing part of a scene on 8x11-inch Xerox paper on the journey. He would draw page after page. When he landed, he got to the studio and taped the pages together to form this big 4x5-foot sheet with a scene on it! One day, I said, 'John how do you do that?' He said he trained as a

violinist as a child, and he practised in a room with white square tiles on the floors. He'd stare at them for hours and would imagine things on the squares while he was practising the violin. Ain't that something?"

Croci remembers that he, Branham, and DeCuir created 2,500 panels for the storyboards, while John DeCuir Jr. used his drawings and paintings to help create elevations for the set. It was a lot of work, but at the time Croci wasn't sure it was in service of a hit movie. "When I first read the script, I thought, 'No one's going to like this!' It was a big lesson for me. After seeing everyone flipping out on the opening night, I've never assumed anything about a project."

After *Ghostbusters*, Croci went on to create concept art for movies such as Tim Burton's *Planet of the Apes* and *Flintstones: Viva Rock Vegas* ("The most fun I ever had on a show, believe it or not!"). Now retired from the movie business, Croci devotes much of his time to drawing marine art – which seems a big leap from creating concept art for *Ghostbusters*. Croci argues there is less difference than you might assume. "In concept art for films, you never want to draw the thing exactly right because people will pick it apart as they interpret it. The whole principle is to make it loose, and there is a lot of looseness when you're using markers or charcoal. You're not doing architectural illustrations, there are lines all over the plan. And in my oil paintings of marine art, I use the same technique – there's a lot of looseness and things that are suggested."

SPOOK CENTRAL

Ghostbusters' art director John DeCuir Jr. and concept artist Ron Croci
reveal the secrets behind one of the biggest sets in cinema history.

A **AT FIRST IT SEEMS AS IF THE SHANDOR**
Building – dubbed "Spook Central" by Ray – is
a typical New York City apartment block. Yet the
building houses a dark secret: Ivo Shandor, architect and
founder of the Cult of Gozer, built it as a gateway into the
spirit world. "They conducted rituals up on the roof," Egon
says, revealing the results of his research into the building to
his fellow Ghostbusters. "Bizarre rituals intended to bring
about the end of the world. And now it looks like it may
actually happen!"

Exteriors of the apartment block were shot at 55 Central

Park West, an art deco housing co-operative in the Upper
West Side of Manhattan. However, production designer John
DeCuir needed to devise a way for the structure to double
in size, something that was achieved through a combination
of design techniques. "It was felt that the existing building
needed elongating," explains DeCuir's son John DeCuir Jr.,
who was art director on the movie (and later production
designer on such films as *Top Gun* and *Inherit the Wind*).
"The design team used miniatures and matte shots to more
than double the height of the structure."

The most impressive part of Spook Central was the

stunningly ornate Temple of Gozer on the building's rooftop, which was built on Stage 16 at Burbank Studios – one of the world's largest soundstages. In fact, the set was so large it extended up to the rooftops and out to the edges of the fire escape corridors.

DeCuir worked closely with Reitman to visualize the temple, which mixed architectural styles and influences to take in everything from gargoyles to a giant pyramid and, most jawdropping of all, the underlit crystal staircase. The crystal elements were actually constructed from three-quarter-inch plexiglass – head of ghost shop Stuart Ziff remembers how the production required so much of the material that they bought virtually all of it in the states of California, Washington and Oregon.

DeCuir Jr. worked with the set designers to make his father's vision a reality, as well as drawing elevations and overseeing concept artists Ron Croci and Robert Branham. DeCuir Jr. explains that three-quarters of the temple set was surrounded by a huge cyclorama depicting the Manhattan skyline. "The lighting needs of the set were so intense that several parts of the studio had to be shut down to accommodate it," he says.

Croci remembers being in awe of the million-dollar set. "The temple was so big by the time the set designers had made the elevations... it was magnificent," he says. "There was some amazing stuff on it. There's a moment when one of the guys looks down and sees the lights below him. As this was before CGI, several basic on-stage mechanical tricks were employed in order to animate the city lights and the moving traffic."

Spook Central was further enhanced through extensive matte work and animated flourishes, while the exploding temple was created using a 20-foot miniature constructed by Mark Stetson's crew in Boss Film's model shop. The set itself was later redressed to take on a ruined, rubble-strewn appearance after Gozer is defeated.

BELOW The huge Temple of Gozer set on Stage 16 at Burbank Studios featured painstaking attention to detail.

DELETED SCENES

Several intriguing sequences were filmed during the *Ghostbusters* shoot but never made the final edit. Here are seven of the best.

THE HONEYMOONERS

One of the most famous cut sequences, available on some DVD and Blu-ray releases, involves a newlywed couple (played by Charles Levin and Wendy Goldman) at the Sedgewick Hotel. After going to bed following an argument, the wife is alarmed to witness their clock shake and shatter. The pair bicker over who broke it, before the husband glimpses Onionhead (later known as Slimer) in the bathroom and runs into the bedroom shrieking. He proceeds to ring reception, complaining about the apparition "smelling up the whole suite." It was cut to save time on adding the special effects during post-production.

PUFT HAT

In this amusing snippet, Stay Puft's hat floats down to the cheering crowd just after Walter Peck is covered in marshmallow. The eighteen-foot hat was an aluminium-reinforced construction that was lowered down into the crowd by a crane.

SUBWAY SCENE

A possessed Louis stumbles into a subway after escaping the firehouse – only to encounter a band of muggers. "Hey man, want me to stick you?" threatens one mugger. "I am the Keymaster, do you bar my way?" Louis asks, before roaring and emitting a blinding light from his mouth. The muggers flee screaming. Moranis held a lightbulb in his mouth for the shot; the real light effect would have been added in post-production.

THE BUMS

One of the most intriguing cut scenes sees Murray and Aykroyd play two bums taking a stroll through Central Park. The pair – named in Larry Milne's novelization as Harlan Bojay (Murray) and Robert Learned Coombs (Aykroyd) – debate Nicaragua and whether a martial artist could beat a heavyweight boxer. Their conversation is interrupted by Louis running through the park screaming ("All this rushing around all the time," complains Coombs). The bums were based on characters Murray and Aykroyd created for *Saturday Night Live*. Reitman cut the idea as he was worried that having the same actors in different roles would confuse audiences.

LEAVING CITY HALL

As the Ghostbusters leave the Mayor's Office to face Gozer, Janine gives Egon her lucky coin ("A souvenir from the World Fair at Flushing Meadow in 1964"), expanding on the burgeoning romance between them. "I shouldn't take it, we might not be coming back," says Egon. "Take it anyway, I have another one at home," insists Janine. The Ghostbusters proceed to head to their destination with the aid of a police motorcade.

NOBEL PRIZE

This short cut scene sees the Ghostbusters discussing winning a Nobel Prize as they walk through the Department of Psychology's Weaver Hall just before meeting with Dean Yeager. Ray argues that he and Egon deserve the prize for designing the equipment and doing all the hard research, while Peter points out he introduced the pair to one another. "And that's gotta be worth something!" Peter cries. It took 17 takes to get right, only for the scene to be cut during the editing process.

PARKING TICKET

This short sequence sees a parking inspector attempting to slap the empty Ecto-1 with a ticket. Bad idea. The inspector is made to feel uneasy as he's tracked by Ecto-1's sniffer, but eventually succeeds in his task – only for the ticket to catch alight. The scene, which hints that the car possesses uncanny powers, was deleted for slowing down the montage sequence.

CHAPTER 2
VISUAL EFFECTS OF GHOSTBUSTERS

Ghostbusters' ambitious and extensive visual effects were produced
by the fledgling Boss Film Studios, headed up by the Oscar®-winning
Richard Edlund. Hundreds of talented sculptors, fabricators, puppeteers,
painters, mechanics, and optical technicians set to work on bringing the
movie's ghosts and ghouls to life within a punishing schedule. The results
were some of the most magical effects of the entire decade.

RICHARD EDLUND

THE BIG BOSS

After founding visual effects house Boss Film Studios in 1983, Richard Edlund took on a challenging first project in the form of *Ghostbusters*. He reveals how he supervised hundreds of complex effects shots in record time while rebuilding an entire studio.

THE PHONE CALL ABOUT *GHOSTBUSTERS* came at just the right time. Having left Industrial Light and Magic – where he'd won Academy Awards® for his work on *Star Wars* and *Raiders of the Lost Ark* – to establish Boss Film Studios, Richard Edlund was all set to begin work on a fantasy movie with Ridley Scott. "He wanted to use Mickey Rooney as a troll, and I had pitched this idea of doing it *Darby O'Gill* style with forced perspective," Edlund recalls. "The project was all set up. Then all of a sudden, his producer pulled the plug and they went to London [the project was released as *Legend* in 1985]. So I was kinda without a project. And I had my crew, a bunch of people that I had brought up to ILM and had agreed to leave with me, who were all sitting on pins and needles."

To make matters worse, Edlund was then hospitalized after crushing a disk in his back while attempting to lift the roof-rack off his Land Rover. "George Lucas had set me up in

" **PART OF VISUAL EFFECTS IS THE ART OF SPENDING MONEY** "

this fancy hospital in Manheim County when I got the call from [*Cinefex* publisher] Don Shay," Edlund recalls. "He said, 'I think you need to talk to Ivan about doing this movie called *Ghostbusters*."

After undergoing surgery for his injury, Edlund flew down to meet Ivan Reitman, Dan Aykroyd and Harold Ramis in LA. His first impression on reading the screenplay? "It was really over the top! And it would have cost a lot of money to do. Gary Martin, who had taken over the President of Production position [at Columbia], said, 'You gotta do this movie for five million.' So I went through the script and said, 'I think what we need to do is pick the scenes that are the most outrageous.' Because there are good ways to spend your money and ways to waste it. Part of the art of visual effects is the art of spending money. Usually the director wants more than you can afford, so you have to talk him down from certain things and bring him to his senses."

With this in mind, Edlund worked with Ramis and Reitman on paring down the script. "We figured out what was worth pursuing and what we should drop. They originally wanted the Statue of Liberty coming out of the Hudson River, which they went on to do in *Ghostbusters II*."

REBUILDING A STUDIO

Boss Film Studios was set up in the former studio of Douglas Trumbull's Entertainment Effects Group (EEG) in Marina Del Rey. While EEG had handled major effects movies, including *Star Trek: The Motion Picture* and *Blade Runner*, the studio needed to be rapidly rebuilt to meet Edlund's requirements. "Doug did very few composites, and my approach to visual effects was completely different to Doug's," says Edlund.

Boss Film's optical department benefited from the construction of a pioneering optical printer dubbed the ZAP. "Shooting on 65mm and reducing to 35 anamorphic gave us really sharp, fantastic composites. In fact, in certain instances we had to diffuse the composites in order to get it to match the surrounding 35mm anamorphic," says Edlund. Other departments in the fledgling studio, included the model shop, the ghost shop, the machine shop and the art department, amongst many others.

The $2 million cost of building the studio was split between Columbia, the studio behind *Ghostbusters*, and MGM, the studio behind Edlund's other big start-up project, *2010* ("Literally the day after I talked with Ivan, I got the call from [*2010* director] Peter Hyams"). Yet by the time the contracts had been negotiated and the projects greenlit, there was vanishingly little time left to actually create the effects. "We had 10 months to rebuild the studio, design all

BELOW Edlund oversees the (eventually much-truncated) Detmerring Ghost effects sequence. The ghost was played by model Kym Harrin.

" WE ALL KNEW THIS WASN'T AN EIGHT-HOUR-A-DAY KIND OF JOB... "

ABOVE Richard Edlund outlines effects sequences in front of a wall of storyboards.

the effects and execute the effects," Edlund recalls. "It was a ball-buster project."

Though Edlund had between 300 and 400 people working at Boss Film at any one time, it was a significant challenge to complete work on both movies within budget and on time. Then there came a new request from Reitman: he wanted another 100 effects shots. "Everybody had blood in their shoes already! So I said, 'Ivan we've got to talk this over. We've got to make some cuts because we can't handle all that.' I met him in the parking lot with my samurai sword [and said], 'We have to do a samurai cut!' We wound up with 40 more shots."

Was Edlund ever worried about the scale of the challenge? "Of course I was daunted. I was extremely worried about it. But we all knew this was not an eight-hour-a-day kind of job. It's like, 11, 12 hours... even worse when it gets close to the end. The optical department was working 24 hours in shifts. We made every day into two days! We had to build this violin and learn how to play it. But I had an incredibly

talented team to help me do it."

While Edlund is a master of photography ("I know photographic chemistry and lenses and the intricacies of photography, which you had to know in those days in order to manipulate the processes"), he says it was his position as a "generalist" that helped him pick the right people for roles. In fact, he emphasizes that choosing the right team is one of the most important elements of overseeing a successful special effects studio. "My management style was always hire someone who is smarter than you," he laughs. "If you do that you're going to [succeed] in every different area."

Edlund dubs the heads of his various departments – many of whom he had worked with at ILM – as his "hunting band." "We had Mark Stetson in the model shop; Steve Johnson in the rubber shop; Randy Cook in charge of the stop-motion, who had an arduous task; Annick Therrien, who ran the roto department with an iron fist; Thaine Morris, the pyro guy and manager of the stage... and Mark Vargo in the optical department. Mark was a very talented guy who would

ABOVE LEFT TO RIGHT
Edlund at work at Boss Film; the subway ghost escapee; Edlund (center) discusses effects shots with Ivan Reitman, John DeCuir and László Kovács.

do these fantastically complicated wedges to get composites. It took hours to do each composite, and I'd say 85% of the composites of *Ghostbusters* are Take Ones. We just didn't have time!"

Everyone who worked at Boss Film Studio during its 14-year lifespan, from department heads down, speaks of how Edlund fostered an incredible atmosphere of trust and camaraderie. He says that much of this came from assembling a crew who he knew would work well with each other. "The chemistry of the crew needs to work. You had to give everybody as much rope as they needed to do their shots, but also [allow them to] step in and help wherever possible. If somebody was strong in one suit and weak in another, then somebody

else could help them. It was sort of like *The Blackhawks*, a great old comic about a crew of rapscallions that I remember when I was a kid."

Aside from talent and technology, the other secret to why the visual effects in *Ghostbusters* are so effective, says Edlund, is that the sequences are so well structured. "The thing about making movies is knowing how to cheat in a way that convinces the audience that they're seeing what you want them to see. You need to know where to use the lasers and where to use the animation, and how to structure scenes and compose the scenes in the most effective way. All those things came into play with *Ghostbusters*."

BELOW Slimer was one of the key effects shot at Boss Film. The sequence involved everything from sculpting to puppeteering and compositing.

MARSHMALLOW MAN OF THE MOMENT

Edlund says his favorite effects sequence in the movie – and the most technically challenging – is the Stay Puft Marshmallow Man. "I thought that was a really clever way to introduce him. First of all, the audience has no idea what's going on! You just see a little slit of the Marshmallow man, then all of a sudden you cut back and there are cabs smashing into cars. We had miniatures, a matte painting, blue screen, Bill Bryan in the costume, and a bunch of cars that were a foot long. One of them crashed into a fire hydrant, which spurted up sand to look like water. You sweeten shots with subliminal things like that in order to make it feel like it's all there. Those little things make shots work that might not have otherwise. We also had the pyro stuff when he climbs the building. Bill Neil shot that. [Matte cameraman] Neil Krepala and I were in New York with László Kovacs, the cinematographer, shooting the extras running toward the camera on Broadway. That had to be Take One as we didn't have extra cars to crash! László used every arc-light he could find in New York to light the entire of Columbus Circle. The sequence had such a fantastic feel."

RAPTUROUS RECEPTION

Despite the punishing schedule, Boss Film Studios delivered its special effects on time and only slightly over-budget. "[The schedule] was terrible, but when it was done, we had such a great feeling of accomplishment," Edlund remembers. "Though I thought, 'Now we've we pulled it off in record time, the studio's going to demand the same thing next time…'"

The results were rapturously received by both audiences and critics, earning the movie an Academy Award® nomination for its effects, although it ultimately lost out to *Indiana Jones and the Temple of Doom*. "Basically, what happened is we got nominated for *2010* and *Ghostbusters* and that split our vote… Because of that we didn't win an Oscar®. We should have! Because I think that either one of those movies was better than *Indiana Jones*, in our humble opinion."

Edlund rewatched the movie fairly recently for the first time in over a decade and remains impressed, even in the modern era of effects-saturated blockbusters. "They [the effects] hold up, you know? Well, aside from that last shot in the movie of Slimer slamming up against the screen which was done by someone else as we were tuckered out! The thing is that visual effects have gotten to the point now where you can do anything if you have the money and the time and you have thousands of people working on the show. But because everything has been done, young theater-goers are bored in a sense. Directors are scrambling to create dynamic sequences that will bring audiences in. But *Ghostbusters* was in the sweet spot of the chemical age, you know? It was a wonderful time and a really satisfying movie."

INSIDE THE
GHOST SHOP

Stuart Ziff headed up Boss Film's ghost shop, the place where all of the film's key creatures were brought to life. He explains why his role involved herding "talented cats."

"WORKING IN FILM IS TEN TIMES BETTER AND ten times worse than you can ever imagine," says Stuart Ziff. After hearing Ziff's recollections of heading up the ghost shop on *Ghostbusters*, you can see what he means. His time on the movie involved overseeing the creation of some of cinema's most memorable monsters – but it also meant being engulfed by a near-perpetual state of anxiety.

Prior to *Ghostbusters*, Ziff had worked at ILM, where he acted as creature shop engineering supervisor on *The Empire Strikes Back* and *Return of the Jedi* ("I made Admiral Ackbar's eyes!"). He also won an Academy Award for Technical Achievement for his stop-motion model-mover innovation. Yet as he points out, his background was

Slimer and Library Ghost photos: Stuart Ziff

more engineering than creature design. "I'm not Rick Baker or Stan Winston," he emphasizes. "I didn't grow up living and breathing this stuff as a teenager."

When Boss Film Studios' head honcho (and Ziff's ex-ILM colleague) Richard Edlund invited him to manage the ghost shop – the place where *Ghostbusters'* beloved creatures would be designed and built – he knew it would be a challenge. He wasn't wrong. The first thing he needed to do was hire a crack team of sculptors, mold-makers, make-up artists, puppeteers, and stop-motion animators who most definitely *did* grow up living and breathing this stuff. While Slimer sculptor Steve Johnson had already been recruited by this stage, Ziff – with the aid of special effects advisor Jon Berg – recruited many other talents for the movie, including Randy Cook (Terror Dog animator), Bill Bryan (Stay Puft fabricator and puppeteer), and Steve Neill (sculptor of the demon arms that burst from Dana's chair).

Ziff was initially informed he'd be heading up a crew of 15; by the end of the production, he was overseeing 60 people. The disparate talents he had hired meant that the likes of Slimer, Stay Puft, and the Terror Dogs all had their own distinctive look. "I feel inadvertently that this was my big contribution to the film – the fact that all the creatures had a very different look and feel," he says. "It wasn't the look of one very creative guy at the top who said, 'This is my shop and I'm going to direct everything,' but instead it was [the vision of] lots of different artists. There is also more of an individual look to things that are physically made as opposed to [created with] CGI."

PANIC STATIONS

While creature concept art by the likes of Thom Enriquez and Bernie Wrightson had been designed by the time the ghost shop was up and running, it was still a huge challenge to hone those designs and sculpt, fabricate and film the creatures within the film's notoriously tight schedule. "Looking back, the most important part of heading up the ghost shop was just making decisions," says Ziff. "On the whole wall of my office we had a pegboard with dates and little boxes that you could add notes to, and list people and projects."

It sounds like the ghost shop was a well-oiled machine, but Ziff isn't so sure. In fact, he recalls that his default setting during the production was "panic mode". He quotes effects artist Robert Blalack: "Bobby said [about setting up the ILM facility for the original *Star Wars*] it was like

ABOVE The ghost shop crew work on two of the film's key effects sequences: Slimer and the Library Ghost.

BELOW Ghost shop puppeteer/fabricator Teresa Burkett Bourgoise with Slimer.

RIGHT Stuart Ziff wearing Slimer arms. Ziff wore the costume for one day when Mark Bryan Wilson was sick – only to find that the footage was not usable.

jumping out a plane with a needle and thread in one hand and a bunch of cloth in the other, and you have to assemble the parachute on the way down.' It was exactly like that on *Ghostbusters*. There was a certain level of chaos!"

Unsurprisingly, Ziff wasn't the only one operating in panic mode. He remembers associate producer Michael C. Gross wandering in one day and being horrified at how chaotic the Terror Dogs sequence was looking. "There were a half-dozen puppeteers and, like an orchestra, they needed to rehearse to work their timing out. But when Michael walked in, it looked *horrible*. They were trying to synchronize the movements of the mouth opening, lips snarling and eyebrows raising, but weren't in sync. And, of course, Michael started to complain. But that can demoralize the puppeteers. I realized that my job was sometimes to keep certain people away from what was going on!"

He remembers having to stifle his own panic when other executives from Columbia Studios would visit the ghost shop. "It was my job to make it sound like everything was wonderful. They'd see that big calendar on the wall and it *looked* like things were well organized – and maybe it was for a day or so. But then you'd get a phone call that would upset everything. Yet you don't want the people in Production to panic, so that's the tightrope you've got to walk being a manager in that situation."

AGAINST THE CLOCK

There were, it seems, many phone calls that upset everything. Ziff recalls how the schedule was constantly changing – and never in his favor. "It's a a slow process to sculpt something out of clay, make a mold out of it, make a mechanism to go inside, and then cast the latex foam rubber. I had to allocate the resources for those things and schedule it. And then inevitably, I'd get a call saying, 'You know that thing that was supposed to shoot in two months' time? Now it's going to shoot it two weeks.' I'd go, 'You gotta be crazy! My guys are working weekends, they're burned out!' But they'd say, 'Run 'em overtime! We need it in two weeks.' We had to constantly shift things around.'"

The time pressure meant he sometimes needed to curb the creative instincts of his crew. "My job was like herding very talented and ambitious cats!" he laughs. "People aren't just working on a film like this; they're

working on getting that Academy Award®. Randy Cook gave an incredible contribution to the film, but it was my job to cajole him to move faster. And Steve Johnson went ahead on his own and sculpted this third stage to the Librarian Ghost – it's a crucial scene, but it's on screen for, what, three seconds? It's not storyboarded for 10 seconds! So I had to say, 'Steve, we can't use Version 3, we already have [enough for] the shot.'"

Yet Ziff makes clear that all the stress and panic was worth it. Not only did he get to play a part in creating movie history, he also got to work with "some of the most talented people of the period." And during his time on set, he also had the enviable opportunity of watching Bill Murray work his own brand of magic. "It was so wonderful to see Bill Murray walk in with a large boom-box, dancing and kidding around," he chuckles. "Michael Gross explained to me that when

they're doing [multiple] takes, Bill's energy goes up. He starts improvising and generating lines, and it just gets better and better with each take. Then he sort of peaks and it falls off, and that's when Ivan says, 'This set up's done, let's move onto the next one.' It was so neat to see his energy build up."

If that wasn't enough, Ziff also got to play Slimer – albeit for one day. "We were all set up to shoot, but Mark Wilson, the Slimer puppeteer, was sick," he recalls. "So I said, 'I'll go in the costume!' I ran around [in the Slimer suit] for a while. Of course, we looked at the dailies the next day and we had to throw them out. Because I didn't move like Mark Wilson at all. I guess we wasted some film, but I had fun!"

Watching Bill Murray on set and playing Slimer? Working in the film industry is at least *twenty* times better than we imagine.

ABOVE Two of the ghost shop's key personnel: fabricator and puppeteer Bill Bryan dances in the Stay Puft costume, while sculptor Steve Johnson inspects the skeletal arm of his taxi ghost.

GUNNAR FERDINANDSEN

One of Ziff's favorite memories is watching the precision work of Gunnar Ferdinandsen, the Norwegian mold-maker who worked on the film's key creatures as well as making molds for other classics such as *The Thing, Robocop,* and *Total Recall.* "If you screw up a mold, you could seriously damage the original clay sculpt – but Gunnar never screwed anything up," says Ziff. "If he was making a throwaway mold [for a proposed creature], he needed to lay a piece of string on the [clay] sculpt then add plaster on it. Then, just at the right time, he'd pull the string up and it would cut through the plaster before it hardened to make a parting line. I remember Gunnar would sit and smoke a cigarette, and he'd time it so he would pull up the string just as his cigarette was finished. If you waited too long, the string would break, but with Gunnar, it worked every time!" More recently, Ferdinandsen was the subject of the 2019 documentary *Norwegian FX.*

Gunnar Ferdinandsen photo by Lilly Christin S. Persson

ABOVE The foam latex skin of the monstrous library ghost. Underneath the skin was a set of levers that facilitated the puppeteering.

THE LIBRARY GHOST

Creating the page-flicking spectre involved mechanical ingenuity, clever puppeteering and reverse acting, explain effects artists Steve Johnson, Mark Bryan Wilson and John Bruno.

AS THE FIRST APPARITION THAT THE audience sees in *Ghostbusters*, the library ghost had to make a big impact. The preceding ESP test sequence, not to mention the presence of three of America's most popular comedians, had already established the film's comedy credentials; now Ivan Reitman wanted to let viewers know that here was a movie designed to make them scream with fear as well as laughter. To do that, the ghost needed to be a genuinely scary creation.

The two parts of the effects sequence – the first with Ruth Oliver playing the apparition in her human form, and the second with the more monstrous version of the ghost – were filmed at Boss Film Studios and optically inserted into the location footage. Visual effects supervisor John Bruno, who storyboarded the sequence, was able to incorporate some of the tricks he'd learnt from working on *Poltergeist* two years earlier. "We used the same gossamer materials in *Ghostbusters* as we did in the scene with the ghost on the stairs in *Poltergeist*, which would float using wind machines," he says. "Then, when the Ghostbusters first see her, I did what I had done on *Poltergeist* – I shot it backwards. I reversed the storyboards, shot her acting in reverse and then printed it forward. But we had to time it in a way that, in a flash, [the human form of the librarian] would convert into the monster."

Shooting in reverse had serendipitous consequences. "If you look really closely at that sequence, as she flicks a page, her hand moves to the left and the page follows it. Kinda cool!"

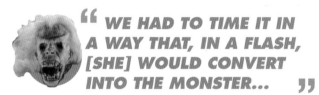

> **WE HAD TO TIME IT IN A WAY THAT, IN A FLASH, [SHE] WOULD CONVERT INTO THE MONSTER...**

THE BEAST WITHIN

Renowned horror comics artist Bernie Wrightson sketched out the initial concept art of the transformation, while it was down to the creature shop at Boss Film – led by effects artist Steve Johnson – to create the monster-ghost puppet. Johnson had already been involved in two famous monster transitions, working with Rick Baker on *An American Werewolf in London* and Rob Bottin on *The Howling*, but for this scene he was clear he wanted to do something new.

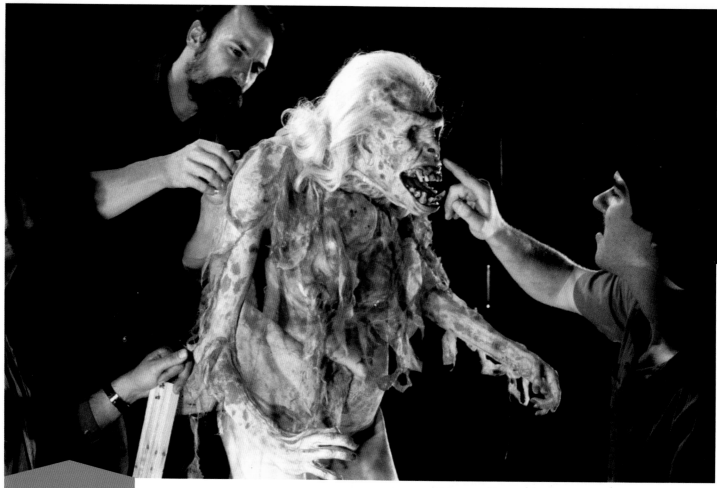

ABOVE Mechanism builder John Alberti and special effects artist Steve Johnson put the final touches to the library ghost.

"When it came time to transform this lovely old librarian actress into a demonic beast, I didn't want to fall back on the same techniques because this was my opportunity to shine," he says. "On both *The Howling* and *American Werewolf*, you saw the transformations in pieces. You saw the ears grow, the claws grow, the snout grow. It was very cinematic and made for great sequences, but I wanted to one-up both Rob and Rick. So I thought, we'll create an entire waist-up figure that will transform – and it will all happen in one shot. Her cranium will flap, her eyes will sink into their sockets, her jaw will extend, her neck will lower, her rib cage will expand, her entire torso will grow and lurch forward."

After a life-cast had been taken of Ruth Oliver

" TO RAISE HER UP, THEY USED A BALL BEARING DRAWER-SLIDE TURNED ON ITS END... "

to mold the foam latex skin, Johnson and his team worked on perfecting the puppet. Guided by Johnson, fabricator and puppeteer Mark Bryan Wilson worked on putting together a mock-up for him to approve. "I stuck things under the foam latex skin. Lumber, pieces of plastic pipe, drywall screws, hot glue," he says. "We also had a cast of gorilla teeth that we carved out a little bit to become her teeth. Steve would look at it [the mock-up] and say, 'Oh no, I want the head to come down flatter.' So I would take off the latex, I would get inside and carve it down."

However, it would take more than latex skin to pull off the librarian ghost's transformation effectively. Based on his previous experiences, Johnson was aware that the sequence posed significant technical challenges. "I knew puppeteering it could be its downfall," Johnson recalls. "If we puppeteered it the way we did on *American Werewolf* and *The Howling*, it would have taken 16, maybe 19 puppeteers to

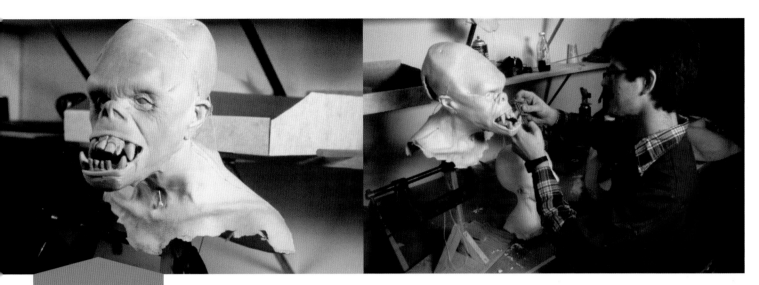

ABOVE Fabricator and puppeteer Mark Wilson works on carving out the fangs – which were taken from a cast of gorilla teeth.

make that happen because [we were using] the whole of its body. I figured there must be a way to tie all these functions to a single lever so one or two puppeteers could do it. So we hired genius engineer John Alberti to make it work."

MECHANICAL WONDERS

Alberti, working with his father Nicholas, ended up incorporating four levers into the mechanics, which could be operated by two puppeteers. These levers were attached to the 'bicycle cables' that Wilson and Johnson used to control the puppet's movements. The controls were designed to deliberately limit the number of positions that the puppet could be moved into. "I thought that was a nice achievement, because

as soon as we got on set we knew that we wouldn't have to deal with crazy timing or puppeteering mistakes," says Johnson.

Wilson was impressed as he saw the Albertis' mechanics take form. "Most of the stuff inside the librarian is wood. There were little tiny pulleys that were machined out of hard wood on sliders; they would make the arms stretch when a string was pulled. To raise her up, they used a ball bearing drawer-slide that was turned up on its end. It was pretty cool."

Once the mechanics were finished, it was Wilson's job to glue the foam latex skin on to the armature and add details. "If you tried to push up the ribs as she raised up, there was no definition," Wilson

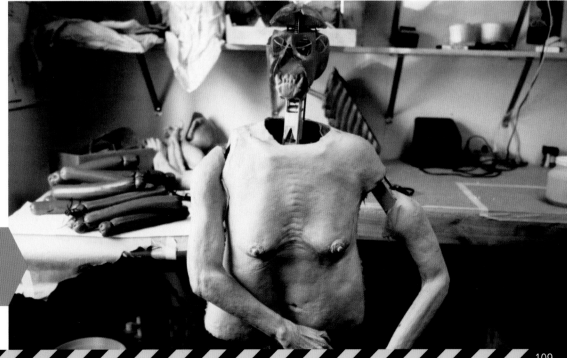

RIGHT The ingenious armature underneath the latex skin. The mechanics were created by Jon and Nicholas Alberti.

SILENCE!

In the working script, the apparition hissed 'QUIET!' at the end of the sequence, based on one of Bernie Wrightson's sketches. In the end this was exorcised in favour of a roaring sound – something that Ivan Reitman thought would give audiences more of a shock. John Bruno's suggestion that the ghost make a 'Shhh!' sound did, however, make it into the movie.

recalls. "I had to go into the creases of the ribs and glue in these buttons that I had custom-made, which I could tie back on a line to hold securely. So now when the ribs pushed up, at a certain point the skin would not move anymore but the ribs would continue to push up. There was a lot of developing. I

had built puppets and marionettes, mechanical heads and simple mechanisms in my early puppet-building, so it was basically taking what I knew step by step until everything did what we wanted it to."

Several copies of the skin were initially cast, before Johnson and Wilson settled on the final "hero skin"

BELOW The unpainted head of the library ghost stares out; the final ghost, complete with shredded fabric and armature.

RUTH OLIVER

Philadelphia-born astrologer Ruth Oliver (sometimes known as Ruth Hale Oliver) played the *sssh!*-ing library ghost and provided the life-cast for the demonic puppet. As well as teaching astrology and writing books and articles on the subject, she was known for giving astrology readings throughout Hollywood. Oliver's only other dramatic screen credit was in an episode of the *M*A*S*H* spin-off *Trapper John, M.D.* in 1983. Her daughter Susan Oliver was also an actress, perhaps best known for playing Vina in the *Star Trek* pilot 'The Cage.' Ruth Oliver died in 1988.

– the one that "had the least amount of bubbles, the best integrity and the best stretch" according to Wilson. Now all the model needed were the the final paints, hand-punched hair, and some flourishes of shredded fabric, which gave the ghost a burst of terrifying energy once they were blown by air jets.

While it took around eight weeks to create the puppet, filming took less than two days. Thanks to the preparation, it went as smoothly as Johnson had hoped. However, Johnson had originally harbored even greater ambitions for the scene. He remembers he had created another, more demonic sculpt that he'd planned for the first puppet to morph into in a further stage of transformation. "We were going to lap dissolve it and match-control it into the second sculpture so it all happened in one shot," he says. "However, everybody saw the first one and said, 'That's enough! It's fine, we don't need anything more.' I was so disappointed!"

However, the sculpture that Johnson and his team created for the second stage of transformation did not go to waste, and was incorporated into the next movie Johnson worked on at Boss Film Studios. "We pulled it out and dusted it off later," Johnson says. "It ended up as the final Jerry Dandridge puppet when he deteriorates in *Fright Night*." The elongated demon arms that Wilson sculpted for the librarian were also used in the scene in *Fright Night* where Evil Ed has been staked through the heart and is painfully returning back to human form.

ABOVE Special effects artist Steve Johnson designed and sculpted Slimer. He created up to 12 versions over three months, eventually devising the iconic final design.

THE STORY OF SLIMER

Effects artists Steve Johnson, John Bruno, and Mark Bryan Wilson reveal how the ghost formerly known as Onionhead was brought to the screen.

GHOSTBUSTERS **IS PACKED WITH** memorable ghosts, but one remains the film's signature spook. Slimer may not have had a huge amount of screen time, but he made quite an impression. He swiftly became one of the movie's most popular characters, securing a prominent role in *The Real Ghostbusters* and returning in both the sequel and 2016 update. He even gained his own 1988 spin-off animated series, not to mention having his face plastered over mountains of merchandise.

Few working on the film predicted the gluttonous apparition's longevity. "I had no idea," says Steve Johnson, veteran special effects artist and the man who designed and sculpted Slimer. "You never do when you're working on something. And now, over 30 years later, it's still the most famous thing I've worked on. He's become a Christmas decoration, a refrigerator magnet, a fruit drink, a toothpaste… I mean, talk about iconic!"

The entity that became Slimer was present in Dan Aykroyd's early drafts of the script but was a nameless "vaporous phantasm" at that point. On set the character earned the name 'Onionhead' thanks to his fetid aroma (something more apparent in a cut scene in which his stench freaks out a couple of squabbling newlyweds). He

only gained the moniker 'Slimer' in *The Real Ghostbusters* two years later, though everyone refers to him by that name today.

The first-unit footage of the actors and sets was filmed first, with Slimer added in post-production at Boss Film Studios. While scenes in the Sedgewick Hotel ballroom were shot in the real ballroom of the Biltmore Hotel, the hallway sequences were shot separately on a soundstage set. Visual effects art director John Bruno was on set prior to and during principal shooting to ensure these scenes would blend into what Boss Film had planned. "We figured out the color of the beams and how [the effects] would best read with the paint of the hallway," he remembers. "[Production designer] John DeCuir would then design the hallway in a color that would work best for the visual effects."

Once principal photography was over, it was up to Boss Film to blend the slimy star in with the footage.

SLIME TIME

While concept artist Thom Enriquez created initial designs for Slimer, it fell to Steve Johnson to make him a reality. It was Johnson's job to create the full-size clay sculpt that the foam rubber Slimer costume would be cast from. This

costume would then be worn by performer Mark Bryan Wilson, with additional puppeteers operating Slimer's expressions.

Johnson was only 22 at the time but, having proven his creature-sculpting abilities working for Rob Bottin on *The Howling* and Rick Baker on *An American Werewolf in London*, he was hired to co-supervise the department. Keen to prove his talents, Johnson's sculpts evolved significantly from the original concept designs during the process. "I was young and cocksure and wanted to make history," he recalls. "This was my first opportunity to do something without working underneath another special effects artist. Enriquez's design looks like Slimer's cousin. It has the same general anatomy but doesn't look a whole lot like Slimer in the film."

After creating a series of maquettes, Johnson set to work creating a full-size clay sculpt for design

approval. Fabricator Wilson, who shared a design room with Johnson and had studied puppetry and mime, was tasked with wearing the suit, both in test fittings and during filming. For Wilson it was an exciting development. "I always wanted to be a living cartoon character!" he enthuses.

The full-size sculpt was created on a plaster life-cast of Wilson's torso, arms and head so it would closely fit his shape and size. Wilson also wore a custom-fit fiberglass helmet that was affixed to a fiberglass shell for Slimer's skull, while mechanics that operated the eyebrows and eyeballs were attached to the skull. Most of the lower section was reinforced by Wilson with thin spring steel strapping, bits of foam, and fabric. Wilson says this lower section resembled a Victorian hoop skirt. "That way his body could be pulled, or compressed, to create usual shapes, but it would maintain the basic form," he explains. "This would also keep his bulges from buckling, or creasing in the wrong place."

Once Johnson received comments back from the studio on his initial full-size design, he incorporated them into another full-size sculpt. However, approval was not forthcoming. In fact, Johnson recalls how he ended up sculpting up to 12 versions over a 12-week period, each design failing to meet with everyone's satisfaction. "I just about lost my mind!" he remembers. "Everyone wanted input. 'Make the eyes bigger.' So I made the eyes bigger – and they're too big. 'Put ears on him. Take the ears off. The nose is too small. The nose is too big. Give him more pathos. Give him more humor. Make him wilder. Make him calmer. Make him crazier. Make him more intelligent…' It was insane!"

" WORD CAME DOWN THAT THEY WANTED IT TO LOOK MORE LIKE JOHN BELUSHI … "

The ever-increasing design sculpts varied wildly. "I tried everything. Different expressions, different looks. I tried long puppet arms, really skinny with long fingers. I started sculpting smaller and smaller versions as we weren't close to approval. Twelve-inch versions, four-inch versions… If it had been going on any longer, I'd have sculpted one-inch versions!"

The night before what was supposed to be the final big approval meeting, there was a new twist. "Word came down from the studio that they wanted it to be like John Belushi. I was like, 'Why didn't anyone mention this three months ago when I started the process?' But Ramis and Aykroyd wanted it to be a homage to their deceased friend, based on Belushi's character Bluto from *Animal House*. So I stayed up all night to meet the deadline and make it look more like John Belushi."

Johnson's all-nighter paid off. The next day, word came through that Onionhead was finally approved.

BICYCLE CABLES AND TONGUE SLEEVES
Aside from securing approval, another challenge Johnson faced was how to imbue Slimer with his larger-than-life attributes. "What I'd learnt from Rob Bottin and Greg Cannom was to use what was basically a bicycle cable [to puppeteer it], but that doesn't give you a whole lot of movement and we needed him to deform and change shape," says Johnson. "I wanted the movement to be very cartoony, very Tex Avery. The way I came up with to solve that was shooting him against a black screen and compositing it with double exposure, so he'd be transparent. I also realised that I could have puppeteers in black leotards who'd stick their hands inside the puppet and muscle it into different positions. They would strongarm the expressions by hand and make it change shape in really broad ways. We basically used old-school green screen – everything black, including the performers' legs, went away instead of everything green." Other shots, according to John Bruno, were shot against a blue screen and the blue was later removed in a similar way.

In addition to Wilson inside the suit, other puppeteers were in charge of manipulating Slimer's expressions using a mixture of "umbilical bicycle cables" that were attached to the character's facial mechanisms and operated by joystick, and hand-puppeteering. In fact it was Johnson's arms that were inserted into the puppet's cheeks to make Slimer chew. "Even the tongue was someone standing behind him with a tongue-sleeve on, who would reach in and lick his chops!" adds Bruno.

BELOW While Mark Bryan Wilson was inside the suit, additional puppeteers manipulated Slimer's facial expressions using cables and joysticks.

ABOVE Steve Johnson and his team in Boss Film Studio's creature shop created multiple Onionhead models with different expressions.

In a pre-digital age, as much as possible had to be done in-camera. This included, says Bruno, using oversized props to make the hefty Slimer suit feel smaller than the people he interacts with. During certain sequences, the camera was locked off and the Slimer puppeteers were moved towards it – not the simplest maneuver. "The creature had to move in from a wall on our left and stop facing us," says Bruno. "So we would move all these puppeteers on this cart, and then that would be optically composited." For other sequences, adds Wilson, it was the camera that moved rather than Slimer and the puppeteers would have to generate the illusion of moving forward while staying in one place.

The puppeteers worked closely from the storyboards, and Wilson says part of the challenge was figuring out how big Slimer was in frame at any moment and how much to exaggerate their movements in order to be funny. "A lot of times a plate shot from the first unit would be stuck into the camera," he explains. "It helped us see that, 'OK, when we put it together Slimer's going to be about this big, he's going to move down the hall there.'"

The role gave Wilson ample opportunities to draw on his love of mime and physical comedy. "For me

a lot of the role was imagining in space – 'hey I'm moving, I'm flying, I'm digging in the air, I'm pulling myself forward…' There was a lot of counting and timing. Like, 'We'll start on 1, then the eyes will blink on 2, then the eyebrows will go up on 3, then I'll begin to move on 4, then I'll be flying.' Watching cartoons as a kid definitely helped."

Wilson says that the experience was a lot fun – but not always easy. Aside from enduring food sliding down his neck and shirt after it was hurled into Slimer's mouth, the puppeteering was physically exhausting. "Working inside a rubber suit is hard work. It's like taking all of your limbs and rubber-banding them to your body. Then you're pulling against that tension to make the suit move and stretch. But we would only work for an hour, maybe a couple of hours so I could rest. And I was 26 – still young and fit!"

Aside from puppeteering, another technique used to give Slimer his ghostly appearance was altering the frame rate. "We shot him between four and six frames a second," says Bruno. "All the actions were a little bit deliberately overdone, over-animated and over-quick. And we shot a lot of different experiments." The dailies were shown each day at

Boss Film's screening room for the visual effects team to give their input. "Everyone chipped in and gave suggestions, giving us a much better chance of getting it right when we redid a shot," says Wilson.

As well as the full-size Slimer, a miniature 'speeding bullet' version sculpted by Mark Siegel was used for the moment Slimer shoots down the corridor ("It looked like a screaming egg with a face on one end," says Wilson), while another miniature was used for the sequence in which Slimer spins around the chandelier. Once the effects had been finished, it was just left to add Slimer's burbling vocals, courtesy of Ivan Reitman. The months of hard work paid off – the team had created a riotously funny, visually incredible character that everyone was happy with.

SLIMER'S LEGACY

Unfortunately the principal Slimer suit isn't today housed in a museum – or anywhere. While Wilson has kept hold of the dental acrylic fingercaps from the original arms ("the latex is still clinging to a few of them"), the suit itself has long turned to dust. "We went back to the storage room when we were working on *Fright Night*," Wilson recalls. "He should have been crated up and protected to the nth degree, but instead he was put on a stand and stuck in a storage room. Other crates were pushed against the original costume and squashed it out of shape. Within a year it was unserviceable. That was an amazing suit. When you figure out the hours it took to get the foam work right, to get him painted, get him assembled, get him shot... It would be so great to see that in person now. Sadly it's long gone."

Still, even if the suit didn't have a long post-movie afterlife, the character most definitely did, and the team who brought him to screen remain proud of their achievements. "He's such a great, funny character," Wilson says. "And I got to be the first Slimer!"

MARK BRYAN WILSON

The man in the Slimer costume, and the lead fabricator on the character, Mark Bryan Wilson remembers how thrilled he was to be working on his first big Hollywood movie. "I'd worked on *Monster in the Closet* and *One Dark Night*, and we'd done some cool stuff on a low budget. But now, all of a sudden, there was this large crew and really cool designs." Wilson remembers he got the job after meeting Steve Johnson a few months earlier and showing him his portfolio as Boss Film Studios started building their effects shop. "To go from those low budget films to be working with Steve Johnson and Randy Cook in one of the highest-grossing movies within a couple of years was pretty phenomenal."

In addition to working on Slimer, Wilson helped build and puppeteer the Librarian Ghost and the Terror Dogs, the latter filmed on the Gozer's Temple set. "After I saw the storyboards I saw what we were going to be bringing to life and knew we would have a chance to do some really great stuff.".

Since then, Wilson has worked as fabricator and puppeteer on dozens of genre movies, including *Big Trouble in Little China*, *Beetlejuice*, *Species*, and *Team America: World Police*. But Slimer remains close to his heart. "I actually collect Slimer merchandise," he says. "Anything where Slimer has been a spokesperson for the product."

ATTACK OF THE
TERROR DOGS

Stop-motion animator Randy Cook and puppeteers Mark Wilson and
Tim Lawrence reveal how they brought the snarling Terror Dogs to life.

RENOWNED STOP-MOTION ANIMATOR Randy Cook has a confession. "I never found stop-motion creatures to be scary," he admits. "When they were good, I always found them to be thrilling, but not scary. Of course, I didn't tell anyone at the top that…"

It was probably a wise decision. Cook – who oversaw Boss Film Studio's creature shop with Steve Johnson – was explicitly told to make the demonic Terror Dogs "straight and scary." He had initially hoped to animate either Slimer of Stay Puft ("Though considering how well they both turned out in other hands, I can't really object"), but once it became clear that his domain was going to be Gozer's canine demi-god acolytes, he set to work trying to find a way to make them as effective as possible.

Groundwork on the design had begun before Cook started. "They showed me a bunch of sketches by a number of artists – Bernie Wrightson, Thom Enriquez.

They were fishing around for an idea. Thom Enriquez especially did about 50 different designs. He eventually did a very simple sketch of what became the Terror Dog. But it was much like the *Forbidden Planet* monster. It was suggestive of a creature, but it was a concept design rather than a creature design. It was subject to interpretation in any number of ways… I said to [associate producer] Michael Gross, let me do something that's animatable, that's got some kind of organic quality so you can move the legs and make it lope across the street."

Cook worked quickly on creating a maquette, which he positioned on top of a wooden platform. Not entirely happy with his work, he remembers his trepidation in showing the model to his fellow crew-members. "As I was sculpting it, it got top-heavy and too big for the stand. It was sort of moving forward and I had it grip the front of the platform because that was the way it evolved. I went to show it to [production designer] John DeCuir, but was a little embarrassed by it. John DeCuir did *Cleopatra* for Pete's sake! But he said, 'Oh, this is great, I love it!' He was very complimentary,

which was a huge thrill for me. He said, 'We've got to have some static statues on a plinth. Is it OK with you if I take this idea?' Sometimes the mistakes lead you in the right direction!"

Visual effects supervisor Richard Edlund felt that the model needed to be bigger, so a larger quarter-scale version was made. Cook says that the larger model had certain disadvantages. "Something this big can be hard to move and you have to move it in a more mechanical fashion… What happens is you require more stage space, and problems can become exponentially larger when you're dealing with something this huge. It was the biggest puppet I ever worked with!"

The foam rubber model was fitted to a metal armature made by experienced animator and machinist Doug Beswick. This model was also used as

a guide for the full-size Terror Dogs, which were shot on location prior to the stop-motion sequences.

The two full-size versions, which were sculpted by Linda Frobos and Michael Hosch, were four times the size of the stop-motion Terror Dogs at around six feet. Cook oversaw their construction, and it was his responsibility to ensure that the two versions matched one another. "I basically just kept taking pictures of the two of them with a Polaroid camera – close up of the small one, close up on the big one. When I couldn't tell the difference between the two, I knew it was time to stop."

Though the full-size models had cables that allowed puppeteers to operate them, there wasn't time to finish the mechanics before shooting. However, Cook says this didn't matter for the initial footage.

"Work hadn't progressed far enough to have

the fully articulated dogs up – they didn't have any moving parts. But because they were going to be in a wide shot, you wouldn't necessarily see them. We did the inserts [with a third model] later when the mechanics were finished." This articulated third model was completed near the end of shooting and used for the shot in Dana's kitchen.

STAIRCASE TO THE TERROR DOGS

The full-size Terror Dogs were operated by various puppeteers, including Harrison Ray, Mark Bryan Wilson, Tim Lawrence and Terri Harden. Holes were cut into the back of the puppets, allowing the puppeteers to operate them from beneath the floor. "We could push down on the head to make it lean forward, backward and side to side, and we had a pole we could lean on to make the Terror Dog spread its legs," Wilson remembers. "There were tiny Watchman monitors inside the Terror Dogs which allowed us to react to what was happening in front of camera."

For the climactic sequence at the Temple of Gozer, the Terror Dogs were fastened to rigs constructed by mechanism builder Larz Anderson. Wilson recalls how much he enjoyed the experience of climbing into the Terror Dogs. "It was phenomenal! We were on the tallest stage on Warner Bros, pretty high up. We would go through the back of the staircase and climb up ladders to get inside of the Terror Dog. It was super-exciting."

Tim Lawrence also has vivid memories of clambering inside the Terror Dogs. "It was like climbing into a kids' treehouse with all the chains, rigging and crossbars," he says. "We wore these special safety harnesses to clip us into the armature. So if there was an earthquake or something, we wouldn't just fall out. But it turned out that since we were fastened to the puppet with those, we could use them to move the puppet to give it more animation. Mark was the front half of the long-horn [Vinz Clortho] and I did the eyes, which you almost never see in close-up. The pupils were lights behind glass orbs; they moved and had direction."

Anything that required the Terror Dogs to jump or

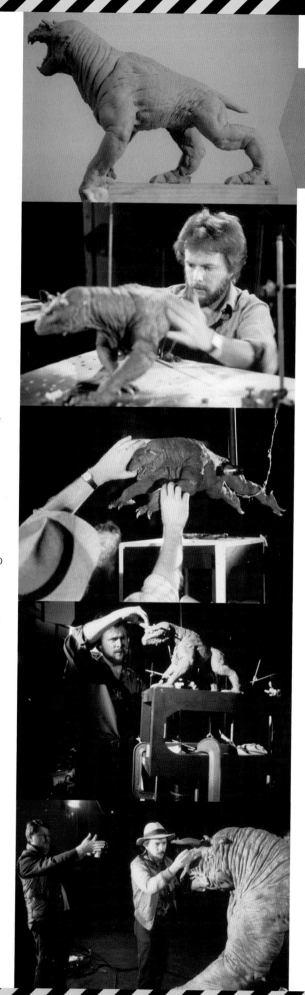

TOP TO BOTTOM Randy Cook's original maquette; Cook moves his Terror Dog model into a new position; the puppet on the motion-mover; stop-motion work on the model; Cook inspects the full-size model.

LEFT TO RIGHT The full-size model, complete with glowing eyes; the Terror Dog in Louis's apartment, which was operated from beneath the floor; the armature inside the full-size Terror Dog.

BELOW Linda Frobos and Michael Hosch sculpt the head and tail while Gunnar Ferdinandsen makes the mold of one of the front feet.

run was created using stop-motion in post-production. Cook shot the animation with cameraman Jim Aupperle and computer technician Mike Hoover. To give the creature a sense of movement, the puppet was attached to a programmable model-mover rig and shot with a motion control camera to generate motion blur. "It was stop-motion fed into a computer," says Cook. "It was the early days of those computers, and we were kind of making it up as we went along."

Cook recalls numerous challenges. Firstly, the sequence where the Terror Dog leaps across the street had to match the location footage – but no measurements of the street had been taken during first-unit filming. "We had to send someone back to New York to take all the measurements, and Hoover and Aupperle matched it frame by frame," Cook says. Another problem soon arose. "It almost worked – except that it was changing scale as it went across the street. I finally realized, the street's got to have a camber in it! A little higher in the centre so the water can flow down. We figured out what the camber was and I redid the move. Then it all came together."

The schedule was so punishing that Cook estimates they worked for around 28 hours straight over Easter Sunday on the sequence. "This was a big deal scene on a motion control rig which required us to make a 30-foot move on the stage, more or less. The thing took a long time to set up and we were up against it."

When the dailies came back, Cook was largely happy with their work except for one issue. "After we made the model touch down [on the street] for the first time, we moved it [into position for] the next frame – but the model-mover started to tear the model apart [because it was moving so quickly]. So we turned off the model-mover when it touched down. But because the motion of the camera wasn't canceled out by the moving model, the model blurred during

the touchdowns. If I had been able to do it over, I would have shot it without blurring. But when I came back, the whole set-up had been struck. The camera was gone and the blue screen was down for [creating effects on] 2010."

The stop-motion segments of the sequence inside Louis's apartment were also not without challenges. "There was a shot where I had him hit the wall and his head compressed, then his body went way up to the wall and flopped down. It was my favorite shot in the picture. Ivan Reitman saw it and said, "It's funny. But we don't want it to be funny…" So we wound

up taking out the armature in the creature's neck and having it accordion a bit as it fell backwards."

Despite these difficulties, the Terror Dogs became one of *Ghostbusters'* key ingredients, with the screams of cinema-goers proving that stop-motion – as well as puppetry – could most definitely be scary. "Menacingly cute" is how Wilson sums up the creatures. "I think that the Terror Dogs are so memorable after all these years, because of their strong character design," he says. "A lot can be seen in their brows. You'd really like to pat them on the head – but you might not have a hand there when you pull it back."

BROKEN TOES

The shot of the Terror Dogs' toes bursting out of the marble statues did not go to plan first time, says Randy Cook. "It was a big elaborate shot, Ivan was shooting with a big crane, and I was underneath the set with levers to break the toes out of the plaster. We got to where the final position was, Ivan said 'break!'… and nothing happened. I said, 'Sorry, it's not working.' So we tried again and the same thing happened. Supposedly, the outer shell was cast in snow plaster which crumbles very easily, so what was going on? A big burly grip came down and said, 'OK, kid, I'll do it.' And this guy groaned like this [makes elaborate groaning noise]… and broke one of the cables! Turns out they cast this thing in hard plaster, like concrete. They had to break and score the plaster so the toes would finally break out!"

THE CANDYMAN

As well as donning the famous Stay Puft suit, Bill Bryan was lead sculptor on one of cinema's most bizarre monsters. He recalls his experience of sculpting, sweating, and stomping.

Stay Puft illustrations by Ron Croci

ONE OF THE FIRST THINGS THAT AN excited Bill Bryan did upon landing a role in *Ghostbusters* was to call his mother. "I said, 'Hey Mom, I got a part in a big-time movie!'" he remembers. "She replied, 'That's wonderful! Who are you going to play?' 'Uh… I'm going to be a Marshmallow Man.' 'Well, er, that's nice honey…erm…'"

Of course, Bryan's mom – or, in fact, anyone – could hardly be blamed for not foreseeing how famous the Stay Puft Marshmallow Man would become. Bryan didn't predict it either, but he knew he loved the script. "I had no idea it was going to be as important to the world as it turned out to be, but I laughed all the way through it. I read every line in Bill Murray's voice as I couldn't remember what anyone else sounded like!"

Bryan first heard about *Ghostbusters* through sculptor Linda Frobos, who he'd worked with creating stillsuits for *Dune* and was now based at Boss Film Studios. "Linda said, 'How would you go about building a Marshmallow Man suit?' I started describing how to do it as a favor, and then she said, 'Well, would you like to do it?'"

Stay Puft – conceived by Dan Aykroyd as a mischievous twist on the Michelin Man, the Pillsbury Doughboy and Canada's Angelus Marshmallow Man – had been part of *Ghostbusters* right from Aykroyd's original treatment, and

designer John Daveikis had created concept drawings, complete with sailor hat, to accompany that first script. The look of the character was further developed in concept illustrations by Thom Enriquez. Yet realizing the outlandish concept involved some element of trial and error.

Once Bryan got the job – hiring many of his other *Dune* colleagues in the process – he created a series of maquettes and began experimenting with different materials. Although Bryan sculpted an early version of the head, it was Frobos who created the final head and hat, while Bryan concentrated on sculpting the suit from the neck down. "I tried carving marshmallows out of solid polyfoam, but it's tough to get the texture smooth enough. Eventually we built a big Marshmallow Man out of soft foam and did a test with it. Unfortunately, the crotch kind of collapsed. I figured that was probably not the look they were going for!"

HERO IN A HALF-SHELL

To solve the problem of the collapsing crotch, ghost shop advisor Jon Berg suggested that the area should be rigid with a fiberglass shell fitted inside the soft foam. "I carved the shape and Mike Hosch fiberglassed it, and we ended up with this solid thing that I certainly didn't want to wear!" Bryan laughs. "I mean, if you put your legs down through

ABOVE Chief effects cameraman Bill Neil conducts a light reading on the suit. Also pictured is sculptor Linda Frobos.

holes of fiberglass, you're going to regret it. So I cut it in half, sort of as a sabotage effort. Jon Berg said, 'I think you've got an earwax problem! That's not what I said to do!' Oops…"

With the fiberglass shell abandoned, Bryan and his team instead constructed an inner shell of L200 foam. "L200 is about the density of boogie board or pool-noodle foam, but it's tighter with a smaller pore structure," Bryan explains. "It's stiff enough to absorb shock and not collapse inwards round the crotch!" Bryan compares the inner shell of the Marshmallow Man to the staves of a barrel. "There were thin strips as side sections, and then a cylinder that went around."

The final layer of foam was fitted over the top of the shell by several of Bryan's crew stretching the foam ("like firemen holding onto a fireman's net") before another crew member attached it with spray glue. One of the biggest challenges was hiding the wrinkles and seams. "We made long needles out of welding rod that passed through the foam with a string, which would

gather [excess] foam around the arms," Bryan explains. "All the wrinkles were pushed over the horizon, hidden behind the arms, under the legs, under the bib."

The sculpted foam arms, legs and head – all of which were two layers thick – were then attached to the body. The foam itself wasn't painted, says Bryan, but was uncoated Scot Foam. "It was kind of yellow, like your regular mattress foam. It looked so good and moved so well. Once you coat it with anything, you'll see surface wrinkles."

Meanwhile, the use of multiple suits helped disguise the seams – the front-view suit had seams on the back, the back-view suit had seams on the front, and so forth. The front-view suit was the one most frequently worn by Bryan, while the others were largely reserved for the sequence in which a flaming Stay Puft climbs Dana's apartment block. "[Stuntman] Tony Cecere did the burns. My wife told me she'd divorce me if I put on a burning suit," Bryan says. "She did divorce me, but not over that…"

THE HEAT IS ON

The Stay Puft sequence was shot on a miniature slice of Central Park West – complete with 1:18 scale cars – constructed by Mark Stetson and his team in the model shop. It was shot against blue screen and illuminated with high UV bulbs ("I heard some people were getting eyeburn, but I was protected... I think the sun protection factor of the Stay Puft suit is pretty high!"), before the sequence was composited with footage shot at Columbus Circle.

Wearing the suit during filming posed several challenges. The first, inevitably, was the heat. "It was hollow and flexible, so when I moved my arms up and down, it acted like bellows and I got fresh air through the mouth," Bryan recalls. "But it was very hot, very sweaty, and it quickly started to stink. There's a picture of me after I'd taken the head off, with the crew turned toward the camera holding their noses!"

Bryan's vision through Stay Puft's mouth was also impaired thanks to a black scrim over his eyes, though he says this in itself didn't pose a major problem. More challenging was the restricted hearing due to the layers of insulation. "A fiberglass shell with a layer of foam over it is going to deaden sound. They did get me a headset, but it quickly shorted out because of the sweat. It couldn't take the moisture. What can I say? I'm a sweater!"

Although several Stay Puft heads were constructed, only one was worn by Bryan. He says that the head he wore was modified to reflect Stay Puft's swing from cheery to ferocious simply by "adding a prosthetic eyebrow, which was sculpted and glued over the face." Meanwhile, puppeteers operated the character's mouth and eye movements. "If you look closely at pictures of the model, there's a cable going down into the road at ankle level. The road was made out of neoprene – which is soft, like wet suit material. It would close up behind it so you wouldn't see a crack. Underneath the platform with the road was a little cart with puppeteers on it. They had a monitor so they could follow my walk, along with controllers that pulled cables [to operate] the mouth and eyes."

TOP TO BOTTOM
Linda Frobos in the sculpting workshop; the fiberglass inner head; Bill Bryan testing out Stay Puft's foam bands; a suited-up Bryan is prepped for filming; the Stay Puft sequence is shot against blue screen.

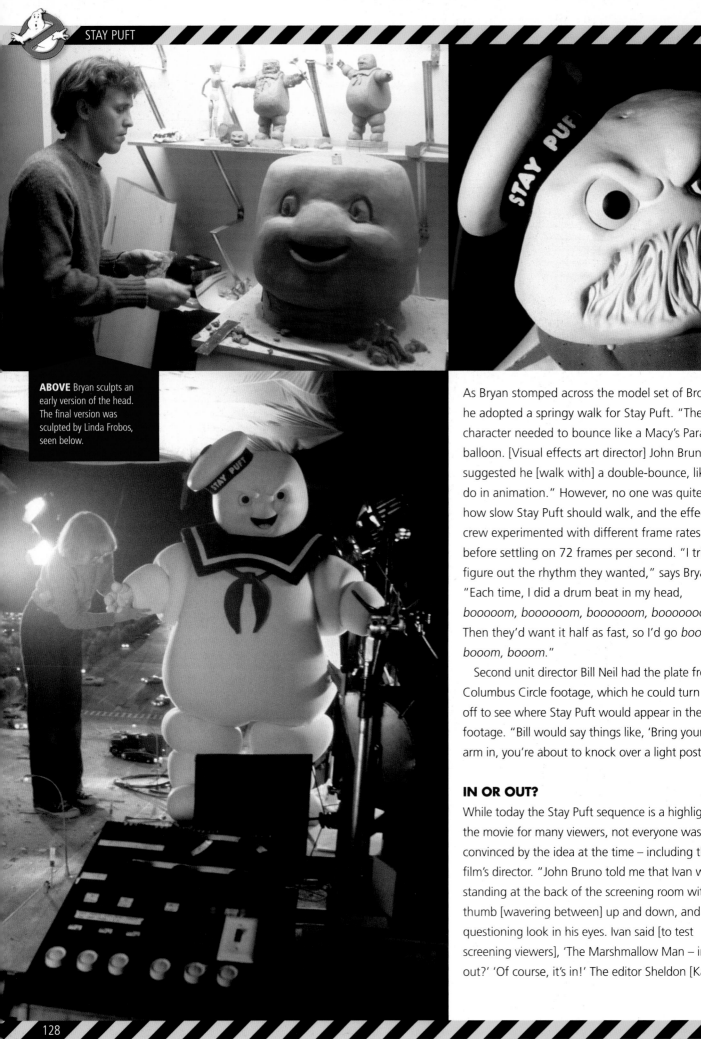

ABOVE Bryan sculpts an early version of the head. The final version was sculpted by Linda Frobos, seen below.

As Bryan stomped across the model set of Broadway, he adopted a springy walk for Stay Puft. "The character needed to bounce like a Macy's Parade balloon. [Visual effects art director] John Bruno suggested he [walk with] a double-bounce, like they do in animation." However, no one was quite sure how slow Stay Puft should walk, and the effects crew experimented with different frame rates before settling on 72 frames per second. "I tried to figure out the rhythm they wanted," says Bryan. "Each time, I did a drum beat in my head, *booooom, boooooom, boooooom, boooooooom*. Then they'd want it half as fast, so I'd go *booom, booom, booom*."

Second unit director Bill Neil had the plate from the Columbus Circle footage, which he could turn on and off to see where Stay Puft would appear in the final footage. "Bill would say things like, 'Bring your right arm in, you're about to knock over a light post!'"

IN OR OUT?

While today the Stay Puft sequence is a highlight of the movie for many viewers, not everyone was convinced by the idea at the time – including the film's director. "John Bruno told me that Ivan was standing at the back of the screening room with his thumb [wavering between] up and down, and a questioning look in his eyes. Ivan said [to test screening viewers], 'The Marshmallow Man – in or out?' 'Of course, it's in!' The editor Sheldon [Kahn]

had doubts too apparently. But Ivan kept it in, and I think we've proven it was the right thing to do."

Bryan has fabricated and puppeteered all kinds of crazy on-screen creatures since *Ghostbusters*, including operating Chucky for *Child's Play* and creating an alien plant for Reitman's *Evolution*. But he has kept Stay Puft alive through convention appearances, as well as revisiting his own designs. In fact, in 2011 he resculpted the hands, while in 2016 he repurposed a

wrinkled Halloween version of the suit ("Stay Puft 30 years later!") for a *Ghostbusters* edition of the *Jimmy Kimmel Show*, with Kimmel's sidekick Guillermo inside the suit. "They dragged him up on their laps and really challenged that suit!"

Bryan is certain he knows the reason why Stay Puft remains so well loved after all these years. "It's because his head is shaped like our mother: the TV screen! That's my philosophy anyway."

ABOVE LEFT TO RIGHT
The version of the head used in the 'melting' sequence; Stay Puft stomps down a miniature recreation of Central Park West, and Bryan in the suit minus its head.

DRESSING DOWN

While few cinema-goers noticed it at the time, there is a blooper in the Stay Puft scene that is forever burned on Billy Bryan's memory. "Did you ever notice that the first time the Ghostbusters hit Stay Puft and he backs away from them, it's revealed he's not wearing his tie?" Bryan laughs. "I remember the day it happened. [Pyrotechnics supervisor] Joe Viskocil was putting flash-bulbs into the bib. The tie was on the table as he was afraid he would lean on it and mess it up. And of course, I didn't put it back on after that. I remember waking up at two in the morning, bolt upright. My wife says, 'What's up?' I said, 'He wasn't wearing his tie!' The next day after everyone filed out after watching dailies, I walked up to [associate producer] Michael Gross and said, 'Michael, I don't want to tell you this, but he wasn't wearing his tie.' He replied, 'Ohhh. I didn't notice. Well, it's such a complicated shot that I don't think anyone will notice. But if they do notice, to whom should I charge the $35,000 reshoot?' I pointed in both directions and said, '*That person!*' As it turned out, it wasn't until years later that someone came up to me in a bar and said, 'You're in my book of bloopers!'"

ABOVE Ronald B. Moore on a line-up bench in the optical department during the making of *Ghostbusters*. Years later he would become VFX supervisor of multiple *Star Trek* series.

OPTICAL ILLUSIONS

The optical department was key to assembling *Ghostbusters'* complex special effects. VFX veterans Ronald B. Moore and Bruno George explain the magic behind the process.

BACK IN THE EARLY 1980S, THE LANDSCAPE of visual effects was very different. Not only did everything from monsters and spaceships have to be created practically rather than on computers, but the job of assembling the various elements involved in effects shots was done on optical printers. These machines, which boasted a projector at one end and a camera on the other, had been in operation since the early days of cinema, and worked by duplicating the original footage with visual effects sliced in. While optical printers have long since been phased out, they – and their highly skilled operators – were vital in making movies like *Ghostbusters* look as spectacular as they did.

It was the optical department at Boss Film Studios, headed up by Mark Vargo, that seamlessly blended the likes of Slimer and Stay Puft into real-life environments, effects that still hold up today.

Visual effects veteran Bruno George was optical printer operator on the movie. He had the job of making sure the various elements were correct before they reached fellow operator Chuck Cowles, who created the final composites. "Oh boy. How to explain what an optical printer operator does in this day and age!" George laughs. "To put it simply, you operated a camera that was designed for rephotographing film, and you would combine different strips of film, called mattes, into layers."

"It was an organizational job," adds Ronald B. Moore, who was optical line-up technician on the film years before he became visual effects supervisor on multiple *Star Trek* series. "When shots were designed, it was up to us to put all the pieces together."

Optical printing was the forerunner of digital compositing that is created today using packages such as After Effects, and the process wasn't entirely dissimilar. Firstly a key visual effects element, such as Slimer, would be shot against a blue (sometimes black) screen, creating a clear outline. This element was known as the 'foreground matte.' Anything extraneous (like puppeteers or rigs) could be removed by rephotographing the sequence in the optical printer, using 'masks' to block out unwanted objects. Through further rephotographing, the foreground matte could be aligned with the background matte (such as the ballroom in the Slimer sequence). The process was more complicated when foreground mattes, like Slimer or Stay Puft, were moving, or when there were multiple elements, and it took real precision to avoid misaligning the mattes. Luckily, the optical department on *Ghostbusters* was up to the task.

DEPARTMENT OF MAGIC

George recalls that in the years before *Ghostbusters*, people didn't always view optical departments fondly. "People had a pretty low opinion of it, because a lot of times there seemed to be compromises when it went through the opticals. I was dead set on making sure that my role and my department was not going to be seen as a place to compromise. It was going to be seen as a place where magic was breathed into the movie."

One of the sequences where this magic happened was in the sequence featuring Slimer (or Onionhead, as he was known at the time). "We shot most of him against black, but they also shot a couple of him

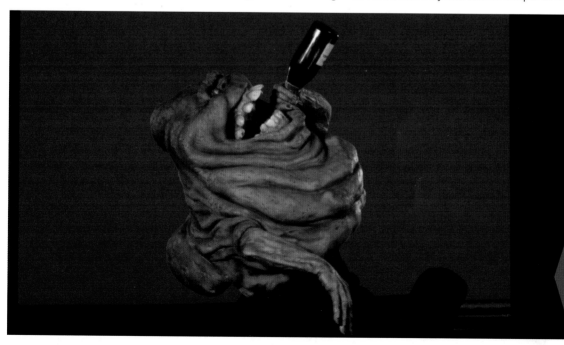

LEFT Elements for optical effects, such as Slimer, were shot against a black or blue screen to create a clear outline. They were then spliced together with the background matte using an optical printer.

ABOVE Some of the talented optical team. Back row (left to right): Dan Kuhn, Mary Mason, Mark Vargo, Chris Regan. Middle row: Pat Repola, Chuck Cowles, Brad Kuehn. Front row: Alan Harding, Ed Jones, Mary Walter.

admits. "You'd think, 'Are you kidding me? They want to change it *again*?'. So many people are involved in every single shot in a movie like this, and no one cares if a change sets you back by three weeks – but you shouldn't either. This is your job. Yes, it could be frustrating when we were under the gun, but as [fellow optical line-up technician] Phil Barberio said, you know that [if there was an imperfection] you'd end up watching the movie one day and saying to yourself, 'If only I'd have stayed 10 minutes longer, that wouldn't have happened!'"

The nature of the work, combined with an extremely tight schedule and the high cost of film effects, inevitably meant incredibly long working days. "It was always on the agenda to do things as quickly as possible," says Moore. "And we were kind of the last people in line – once our work was done, the film just went back to the director and the studio for approval. As a consequence, the hours we worked were exceptionally intense. If you left before you'd done 18 hours, you felt guilty!"

However, Moore emphasizes that these hours of hard work more than paid off. "When you see what they did... *Wow!* They added people in each of the windows in the buildings [during the Stay Puft sequence]. Inside one window you can see someone playing pool; over there you have a family eating dinner. And adding that water tower in the background gave it so much depth. When I see the movie, there's such a pride that I was a part of that team and that we were able to add so much to it. That sequence has a lot of meaning for me."

Both Moore and George went on to become heavy-hitters in the effects world in the years that followed. Amongst other projects, Moore became visual effects supervisor on *Star Trek: The Next Generation*, *Voyager* and *Enterprise*, winning five Emmys in the process, while George became one of the first digital department managers at ILM and visual effects supervisor on the likes of *In the Line of Fire*, *Hook* and *The Nutty Professor*. Though clearly fans of optical effects, both men embraced the transition to digital. "When I was at Boss Film, someone mentioned that doing things optically was

against a blue screen, which is a different technique for making a matted element," says George. "So I had to do as much as I could to make sure that those two photographic techniques matched visually when it was composited on the screen. Consistency is the name of the game."

The Stay Puft Marshmallow sequence was also extremely complex, according to Moore, not least because it featured so many layers. "The first shot I did was of the Stay Puft Marshmallow Man walking behind the building," he says. "I remember thinking, 'I'd like to get this shot done, then I'll be ready for anything else.' So much for that plan! That shot was one of the last ones I finished. It was a complicated visual effect because so much was added once we started."

UNDER THE GUN
Working on the same shot over and over to take in changes could sometimes be exasperating, Moore

going to go away one day," remembers George. "It stuck in the back of my head, so I kind of decided well, dammit, maybe I should be the one who helps make it go away! So I started focusing a lot of my early supervisory work into doing things digitally."

The industry may have changed drastically, but *Ghostbusters* – and the positive, collaborative atmosphere that Richard Edlund fostered at Boss Film Studios – remains close to both men's hearts. While neither knew what to expect when they signed up to work on the film 35 years ago ("*2010* was the one we were all looking forward to," Moore admits, referring to the other movie that Boss Film took on alongside *Ghostbusters*), Moore remembers when it first dawned on him that they were working on a potential classic. "There was a day when Dan Aykroyd and Harold Ramis came in and we saw a piece of the film. And we realised, 'Holy mackerel. This is something special!' It came out so well."

"I think as a department we did a beautiful job," agrees George. "I take pride in knowing everybody who was in that team and I was proud to say I worked with those people. I look very fondly at the optical work we did on *Ghostbusters*."

ABOVE It took many hours to complete the optical effects for the Stay Puft Marshmallow Man, with frequent changes and additions along the way. It paid off, though, with the sequence featuring incredible attention to detail.

POPS, ZAPS AND DUPES

On some pre-digital effects films, you may be able detect what Moore calls a "pop" in the quality of an effects shot as it moves from the original negative to a 'dupe' (ie, the duplicated piece of film with the visual effect sliced in). However, in *Ghostbusters*, the opposite was true.

"The majority of *Ghostbusters* was shot in 35mm, but our work was done in 70mm, which Richard Edlund's ZAP printer would eventually reduce down to 35mm," explains Moore. "So even though we were dealing with a dupe, the quality of the dupe was pristine. In fact, the producers were concerned because when they cut the effects in, they would 'pop' because they were sharper and better quality [than the rest of the film]! So Richard went back and tweaked the printer to make it a better match. The quality of what we were doing was incredible and it was a thrill to work with."

SMALL WORLD

Model shop supervisor Mark Stetson and model makers Adam Gelbart and Leslie Ekker reveal how they recreated Central Park West and the intricate Temple of Gozer in miniature.

GHOSTBUSTERS IS A MOVIE OF GIANTS, BOTH on screen in the form of the lumbering, car-squashing Stay Puft and behind the scenes, with the full-size Temple of Gozer standing as one of the largest indoor sets ever built. But miniatures were key to the success of both sequences – thanks largely to the work of the model shop at Boss Film Studios.

Supervised by *Blade Runner*'s chief model maker Mark Stetson, the model shop was responsible for creating the scale replica of the Shandor Building that the flaming Stay Puft climbs up; it was this model that exploded so spectacularly in the film's climax. In addition, the model shop recreated a large chunk of Central Park West for the Marshmallow Man to stomp on. Working over eight months, Stetson's team of carpenters, sculptors, mold-makers, and artists had to construct miniatures that would blend seamlessly into the live action footage.

ABOVE Scale model cars are arranged on the replica Central Park West set, while Mark Stetson helps Kento Gabe prepare the Gozer Temple for detonation.

When it came to constructing a miniature of the upper floors of the Shandor Building – including the ornate Temple of Gozer that adorns its rooftop – the model shop was given a head-start by production designer John DeCuir, who supplied them with construction drawings. "That was the first time I remember a production department ever doing that, and it was great that we could build from them," says Stetson.

These drawings were passed on to the talented carpenter Milius Romyn, the main fabricator of the miniature. Model maker Adam Gelbart – whose work on *Ghostbusters* marked the start of a long career in the industry – has fond memories of Romyn. "He was a Scandinavian cabinet maker, and you could have eaten off the things he made for the film. It was so beautiful. It was a shame we had to clad them [the wooden parts] and mess them up, as we needed to make them look like they'd been around forever."

The replica was built at 1/18th scale of the actual set, but was still an imposing construction at 20 feet high on top of an eight-foot riser. It also required incredibly decorative detailing, and Stetson points to the importance of Tom Silveroli, who sculpted the crucial door panels. Stetson's *Blade Runner* colleague Leslie Ekker (who would later be nominated for an Oscar for his model work on *Apollo 13*) was another artist who worked on the building. "It was a large model, especially towards the bottom, and we needed to sculpt many ornate, vintage architectural details like cornices and caryatids," he recalls.

While the model needed to look ornate, it also needed to be hardy enough to withstand being moved around on stage. "We made things like windows and fire escapes out of acid-etched brass," explains Stetson. "Brass is good as it's pretty durable and malleable – you can bend it into kits. That technology was later replaced by laser-cut materials."

PRIMED TO EXPLODE

After pyrotechnics supervisor Thaine Morris briefed Stetson on the cruciform-shaped explosion he wanted to achieve, Stetson oversaw the construction of a metal framework and blast plate inside the model. Once the model was primed with explosives, it detonated in four directions, exactly as Morris had specified.

One of Gelbart's roles on the movie was casting molds for chief mold-maker Daveed Shwartz. "We needed hundreds and hundreds of parts for Gozer's Temple as it was blown up repeatedly," he says. "You'd have 50 new parts [after each explosion], so we'd have hundreds of bricks, finials, and other details to mold. They only wanted certain key areas blown off – it wasn't about the [whole] building blowing up, it was about how beautiful the explosions were. There had to be something left, but what was left was pretty charred. So you'd have to go in and tear off the burnt bits and glue new bits on. But you had to wear gloves as the building was covered in naphthalene – mothballs. That stuff's gross!"

The model was blown up in a parking lot at Boss Film over two nights, according to Gelbart. "We'd do it three

times each night to get different angles and try different techniques. They were big explosions – though it looks much bigger on screen. It was controlled mayhem!"

WALKING SMALL

The other key sequence that the Model Shop worked on was Stay Puft's destructive stomp through the streets of New York City. Stetson and his team again worked to a 1/18th scale, based on specifitions from Ivan Reitman that Stay Puft was 112½ feet tall.

"We had to bear in mind certain constraints as it wasn't shot on a large stage," says Stetson. "To fit it in, we created a forced perspective for the background." Ekker elaborates on how this forced perspective worked: "In the foreground, the perspective was normal; the street was parallel and flat. But we shot on a platform that ramped upwards and tapered in width. We reduced the scale of the models towards the background, so the furthest objects were in a smaller scale than the foreground objects. From the perspective of the camera, it looked like a normal street. The perspectives aligned and everything fell into place, but it looked many times longer than it really was."

Because of the forced perspective, the larger models at the front were much more detailed than those at the back. "We found a model car that was an appropriate scale for the Marshmallow Man [in the foreground]," remembers Stetson. "We went to all the Toys R Us stores in Southern California and cleared out all their stock! We turned them into fire chief cars, taxis, police cars, and normal cars. We also scratch-built some cars, such as the fire engine. For the background cars, we used smaller 24th scale cars – they're a lot more

common and easier to find. As we were shooting, we would roll them down the tilt-plane of the background of the street. We also wire-pulled some of the cars in the foreground."

"We would repaint the cars and add details like a flat tire, a broken windshield and bumper stickers, adds Ekker. "We'd gunge up the paint a bit to make them look more real and lived in."

When it came to creating the multitude of cars for the background, it was all hands on deck, according to Gelbart. "The best two were made by the guy who was answering the phones at the front desk. He made a police car with a crime scene inside it, which you'd never get to see on screen. He also made a pick-up truck that looked like it came from *Invasion of the Body Snatchers*. It was peeled away and had what looked like corn husks in there. It was brilliant! But he could afford to take the time to do that in between answering phones. We had to just crank out cars for the background and couldn't take the time to for that."

The trees in Central Park also required producing on mass. "That was not trivial to do in miniature," says Stetson. "We came up with the concept of finding twigs of local trees that would represent the trunks and branches, and then using material like hemp to create their bodies. For branch-like foliage, Daveed Shwartz came up with the idea of using a household blender to grind up foam, dying it green and then spray-gluing it to the body of the model trees."

The buildings surrounding Central Park and Times Square in the sequence were, according to Stetson, a mixture of plates that matte department supervisor Neil Krepala had shot in New York City and approximations

of real buildings. "We recycled some of the model buildings from *Blade Runner* for that moment when Stay Puft is revealed behind that skyline, though we had to make them appear more conventional first," he adds. "We also added in some water towers for the tops of buildings for that first reveal shot."

Another trick that Stetson's crew concocted was the jet of water created as Stay Puft kicks a fire hydrant, which Pete Gerard created using air-blasted silica sand. It is attention to detail like this that is so vital in model building, Stetson emphasizes. "I hate to hear a director or producer say, 'Oh, they'll never notice.' Audiences have become much more critical than they were in 1983, especially if you don't have a script as strong as *Ghostbusters* did."

Expanding on this, Ekker recalls the approach of *Blade Runner*'s effects supervisor Doug Trumbull. "Doug had a theory he called 'subliminal detail.' Some of the details we're talking about would not register on film, but Doug always felt that the eye would feel those details if they were there. He has a point: [the details] change a particular piece of film grain – the way something is hit by light in a different way. So on *Ghostbusters* we went all-out, the whole hog, on the models we built. You really have to focus on the tiny details."

ABOVE A costumed Bill Bryan, fabricator Diana Hamann, VFX art director John Bruno, and DoP Bill Neill get ready to film on the tilt platform.

BELOW Patrick McClung operates an R/C transmitter while Pete Gerard prepares to operate the fire hydrant gag.

TREE SURGERY

Constructing trees for the Central Park set turned into something of a competition for the model team, according to Adam Gelbart. "We had a bet: who could make a tree the fastest. I painted my tennis shoe green, and it went into the back of the set! It was out of focus; it just had to be something green. So we took some liberties. But Mark kept a careful eye to make sure nothing too outrageous got through. It wouldn't have looked bad on camera, but if anyone important came by they might have asked, 'What's that doing there? We're paying for this?!'

LEFT A disgusted Venkman recovers after being gunked by Slimer. The slime was actually a thickening agent called methylcellulose.

SLIME TIME!

The ectoplasm generated by *Ghostbusters'* apparitions was made using the thickening agent methylcellulose, explains special effects foreman Bob Shelley.

CTOPLASM – THE GREEN, SLIMY RESIDUE generated by ghosts and ghouls – can be found everywhere in *Ghostbusters*. On the book shelves of the New York Library, in the hallways of the Sedgewick Hotel – and eventually all over Peter Venkman thanks to that most ectoplasmic of ghosts, Slimer.

Ectoplasm is a term derived from the early days of spiritualism. It was invented by the psychical researcher Charles Richet in 1894 to explain the substance that was said to manifest during a medium's contact with spirits. This psychic force could appear from the medium's mouth, ears or nose, and was also emitted by spirits as they

made contact with the physical world. Unsurprisingly, Dan Aykroyd – an expert in all things paranormal and long-time reader of the *Journal of the Society for Psychical Research* – ensured it found its way into the *Ghostbusters* script.

The special effects team had to figure out the best way to convincingly – and safely – replicate the ectoplasm. "It was suggested that we use the same kind of slime as they used in [1956 horror movie] *The Blob*," recalls special effects foreman Bob Shelley. "But we found out that was caustic and we couldn't use it anymore! Then a product came up called methylcellulose and separator."

The methylcellulose – a thickening agent used in food products, lubricants, and laxatives – was mixed with water and various food colorings. "As the foremen, we set up 55-gallon drums of stainless steel and mixers to mix up the different colors of slime that Ivan wanted," Shelley adds. "Ivan decided that he liked the green color, so that became Slimer's color."

As well as the regular 'bulk slime,' special effects supremo George Giordano provided the variant 'mouth safe' slime for sequences in which performers risked swallowing the substance. Giordano earned the enviable job title of 'Slime Supply' on the movie.

The sequel involved even more slime, thanks largely to the appearance of the magnificent River of Slime.

Marshmallow Gunk!

In addition to mixing up slime, foreman Bob Shelley was part of the team responsible for creating the Marshmallow Man's white goop after he explodes – which, of course, ends up all over Walter Peck. "There was a type of whipped cream that we were going to dump over him, but that didn't work," Shelley remembers. "By the time we filled up a dump tank and weighed it, it was too heavy to drop from 15 feet! By hook and crook we came up with a solution using Barbasol shaving cream. It was the lightest weight material that we could use. It almost floated. We got the materials from Barbasol to make the creams – minus the additives that would have hurt somebody, because all this stuff had to be approved by the FDA and Screen Actors Guild. The cream was shaken, pumped into the dump tank and dropped on him [William Atherton]. He survived of course!"

THE ARMCHAIR

Steve Neill sculpted the demon hands that grab Dana, as well as puppeteering one of them. He looks back on the chair-bursting sequence.

IT WAS ONE OF *GHOSTBUSTERS'* MOST PERFECTLY orchestrated horror sequences. Dana has just finished a phonecall to her mom when an eerie light emanates from the doorway. Shapes push against the door. All of a sudden, demon arms burst out of Dana's armchair and grab her, before the chair slides towards a waiting Terror Dog. Audiences were almost as shocked as Dana.

The scene was the brainchild of Ivan Reitman, who devised it as a narrative bridge into Dana's possession by Zuul as well as a way to inject an extra dose of horror into the movie. The effects team who helped realize his idea included mechanism designer Don Carner, who sliced up the chair and treated it with acid to help it break away easily, and Steve Neill, who sculpted the demon arms.

The three demon arm sculpts were all based on Neill's own limbs and were created with the assistance of mold-maker Gunnar Ferdinandsen, fabricator Rob Berman, and make-up artist Craig

 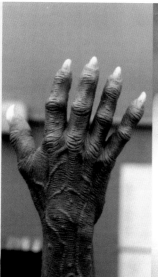 

Caton. "Two of the [humanoid] hands were from the same sculpt but painted different colours, and the other one had three big claws," Neill explains. "There was another hand that had octopus fingers too. It was really well done, but they rejected it for not being scary enough."

Neill puppeteered one of the demon arms during filming, alongside Mike Hoover and Mike Jones. The stage was built four feet off the stage floor to allow more space for the puppeteers to hide beneath the chair, although as Neill explains, three different chairs were actually used in the sequence. "Besides being stuffed into the arm of an oversized armchair [for the arm-bursting sequence], there was another chair for the shot where it's tight on Sigourney Weaver so you can't see us. And then there was the one they used for the shot where you see it being pulled along – those arms didn't have anyone in them, they were just positioned up against her. We spent a few days on that sequence because there were many parts to it."

THE GENTLE TOUCH

It took some time to get a shot of the hands grabbing Dana that everyone was happy with, Neill remembers. "Because the fabric of the chair had been [treated with] a material that made it very weak, it was easy for me to break through and grab her in the face. But I was trying to be very careful so I didn't poke an eye out or scratch her in the face

with the claws. They should have been latex, though there still would have been danger in that. We did several takes and Ivan wasn't getting what he wanted – he wanted it to look like it was more realistic rather than Dana just throwing her head back."

Weaver encouraged Neill and the other puppeteers not to hold back. "I said, 'I can't do that, I'll make you black and blue!'" Neill says. "But Sigourney told us, 'I can't act as well unless you do it [push her head back harder] – it will look better if you do that.' So that's what we did, and they got the shot. Between the three different set-ups, they achieved a very good effect."

ABOVE LEFT TO RIGHT Close-ups of two demon hands; test of the arms bursting through the chair; the hands grab Dana.

OPPOSITE PAGE Steve Neill, Mike Hoover, and Mike Jones on set with Weaver.

BELOW A demon arm sculpted and puppeteered by Steve Neill emerges through the arm-rest.

FIRESTARTER!

As mechanical effects supervisor, pyrotechnics expert Thaine Morris was responsible for detonating the Temple of Gozer, amongst other fiery effects. He reveals how to make things go 'BOOM!' without anyone getting hurt.

"**I**F YOU'RE NOT AFRAID OF FIRE, YOU SHOULD** not be in this business," cautions seasoned pyrotechnician Thaine Morris. "You need to think of all the bad things that can happen and try to mitigate for that before you start putting bombs inside whatever you're trying to blow up."

Morris has made a lot of things blow up in his 40-odd years in the business. He has worked as pyrotechnics supervisor and special effects foreman on dozens of blockbusters, including *The Empire Strikes Back*, *Raiders of the Lost Ark*, *Die Hard*, and *The Fifth Element*, and is co-owner of MP Associates, the largest manufacturer of motion picture pyrotechnics in the world. As *Ghostbusters'* mechanical effects supervisor, he was also the man who made Gozer's Palace detonate and, along with fellow

LEFT Pyrotechnics expert Joe Viskocil prepares to light up Stay Puft. The scene in which the flaming character climbs Dana's apartment took two stuntmen, three suits and thousands of dollars.

pyrotechnics specialist Joe Viskocil, he toasted the Marshmallow Man.

Morris, who doubled up as stage manager, was part of the talented visual effects crew at Boss Film Studios, where he worked closely with the studio's model shop. The shop had created a detailed miniature of Dana's apartment block, and Morris needed to work out how the upper stories beneath the Temple of Gozer could detonate in a cruciform pattern, while the rest of the building remained standing. To ensure that the entire miniature wouldn't simply collapse, Morris asked model shop supervisor Mark Stetson to construct a steel framework. "Mark made the outside of the building out of high-temperature epoxy, very thin so it would fracture easily," recalls Morris. "For the actual shot, there was about one pound of black powder in it. Then there were a lot of other chemicals put in it to make the color and the fire."

The explosion itself was shot in a parking lot beside one of the buildings at Boss Film. "We didn't have a whole lot of room," says Morris. "The explosion itself had arms on it of about 15 to 20 feet long. I was tucked up underneath the scaffold where we had put some lighting equipment. I was probably, oh, 25 feet from that building under the platform when it went off."

As usual, Morris protected himself from the blast with his trademark gear – "a leather jacket and a motorcycle helmet to protect my face." While the blast looked intense, Morris insists that the sequence was not particularly dangerous or loud as far as explosions go. "It went 'BOOM!' but it wasn't totally deafening. If you make things terribly loud, you're using up energy in sound. You want to use as much energy as you can in taking whatever it is apart. And it was not terribly dangerous. The nice thing about working with miniatures is that the explosions are relatively small. With that being said, they can also put you in hospital…"

The detonation of Gozer's temple, which was shot in slow motion at 360 frames per second, went so smoothly that only one take was required. However, the lighting up of the Stay Puft Marshmallow Man proved a trickier proposition.

TOASTING MARSHMALLOWS

Though Stay Puft was played by Billy Bryan, the flaming sequence required a stuntman to take over the role in a fire-retardant version of the suit covered in flammable liquid. Once the stuntman had been set alight, his job was to approach the Temple, step up onto an apple box, slap the top of the miniature building, and then lay down so the fire could be extinguished.

"Because the foam rubber we were using [in the flaming suit] would create a toxic gas, I had rigged up a supplied air system for the stunt guy," Morris

ABOVE The Marshmallow Man's head was melted by a heater that caused the gelatine to melt and flow. Unfortunately, the heater also melted part of the pioneering camera!

says. "He was breathing through a scuba thing with a hose that went down one of his legs. It had a nose plug and glasses to protect his eyes, and he could look through the mouth of the Stay Puft [suit]." The stuntman was also protected by an inner layer of pyrothane and a flame-resistant Nomex suit.

The sequence was safe and appeared relatively straightforward. The main worry was the fact that there were only three suits, each costing around $20,000 – meaning there were only three chances to get it right. "Day one, we light him up, he walks towards it [the building]... and lays down for us to put him out [before he gets there]. There goes the suit!" recalls Morris. "Day two, same thing. In discussing it with the young man [inside the suit], he admitted he was afraid of fire and had never done burns."

Rather than risk destroying the final suit, Morris and Viskocil turned to stuntman Tony Cecere who, says Morris, "made his living by setting himself on fire in movies." As Cecere was much smaller than the Stay Puft Marshmallow Man suit, he wore lift shoes to make him the right height. However, while Cecere was comfortable around fire, Morris says the stuntman had another concern.

"An argument ensued about the supplied air," Morris remembers. "He said that it took all the challenge out of it! I explained that there were two challenges – for him to come up from under the stage [on fire] and for us to get the shot. So he agreed to the supplied air."

Cecere successfully squatted down next to the building and then, after being set alight, stepped onto the apple box and slapped the top of the building – a move Morris says he repeated three or four times while wearing the flaming suit. "It seemed like a week and a half that he was on fire! Then we yelled 'Cut!', put him out and got him out of the suit. He said, 'I could have gone on quite a bit longer!' But it wouldn't have made any difference – the pink skull of the Stay Puft guy was already showing. It had completely burned away. He [Cecere] was quite a guy!'

The melting of the Stay Puft head required a separate effect, and Morris was able to bring his prior experience to the sequence. "I'd done it before on *Raiders of the Lost Ark*," he remembers. "For this we used a gelatine head on a fiberglass skull. The head was mounted sideways against black with the camera mounted up close to it. We put a

BELOW Tony Cecere was brought in to play Stay Puft during the 'fire burn' sequence after things didn't work out with the original stuntman.

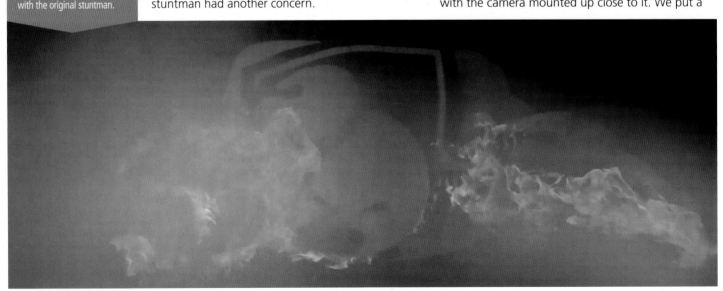

heater on it that would cause the gelatine to melt and flow when shot at very low film rate."

Unfortunately, the melting effect proved *too* effective. "We were using the first ever 65mm mirror-reflex camera, which we had just finished making. And the heater melted the lab box off the camera! I got in quite a bit of trouble for that. I didn't think I was responsible for the camera, but it was quickly explained to me that as stage manager I was responsible for *everything*. From then on I watched out for camera guys putting them [cameras] too close to things…"

Despite such minor hiccups, Morris stresses there were no scary or dangerous incidents on the film, and the pyrotechnics were more straightforward than some effects he has been involved with (he cites the famous rooftop helicopter explosion in *Die Hard* as being one of the trickiest).

Even in the digital age, pyrotechnics remains big business today, with many filmmakers favoring the realism offered by practical explosions (though Morris adds that CGI has "added an eraser to our pencil" by allowing them to wipe out detonation wires). In fact, Morris's company supplies two to three thousand pounds of explosives for entertainment purposes per day.

So, what's the key to a successful career in pyrotechnics? "I studied to be a chemist – never actually worked as one – so I understand the chemical formulation for pyrotechnics. That makes it a little easier for me than a lot of other people. And you've always got to be careful when you're dealing with energetic materials; it's not a case of 'if' it goes off when you don't want it to, it's 'when'. But the thing about working in the motion picture business is you're *simulating* explosions rather than doing them [for real]. It looks a whole lot whole worse than it is."

RIDDLE OF THE SANDS

In addition to supervising the movie's pyrotechnics, Morris had a variety of other roles on *Ghostbusters*, including aiding the stop-motion team and drawing on his former job as a television engineer to flip screens on TV sets so the Slimer puppeteers could see what they were doing. He also assisted in some of the film's other "gimmicks," including the moment where Stay Puft kicks over the fire hydrant and water blows everywhere – a sequence that was not easy to pull off convincingly. "One of the more difficult things to do was getting that water to look correct in miniature, because the fire hydrant was only about three inches tall," he remembers. "The model shop came up with the idea of using sand and blowing it out with water. It worked great! It looked exactly like water coming out of that thing when filmed at high speed."

THE BURNING MAN

Veteran stuntman Tony Cecere played Stay Puft during the sequence where the Marshmallow Man was set alight. He reveals more about fireproof costumes, climbing the crumbling building, and how he remains calm while on fire.

TONY CECERE MAY NOT BE A HOUSEHOLD NAME, but most movie fans will have seen him on screen multiple times. Now retired, Cecere spent over 35 years doing stunts in Hollywood movies – which more often than not involved setting himself alight. His resume includes dozens of iconic monsters and villains, from a flaming Freddy Krueger tumbling down a stairway to the Terminator staggering through the flames of an exploding truck. He is also the stuntman who played the burning Marshmallow Man.

While Stay Puft was played in the main by Billy Bryan, Cecere took over for the fire-burn sequence after another stuntman was let go for being uncomfortable around fire. He vividly remembers receiving the call about the job. "They said, 'We want you to do a fire-burn on this little low budget show down here in Culver City. Would you come down and do it for us cheaply? I looked it up and found out it was a 20 million dollar show, so I said, 'I'll do it but I won't do it cheaply!'"

Before filming began, Cecere, as always, insisted on taking his own safety precautions, including bringing his regular two "safeties" with him ("One to help me get dressed, the other to put me out when I give a hand

signal") and donning his own protective gear underneath the Stay Puft costume. "I wore a tight-fitting white Nomex suit with special gel on it," he says. "In fact, I usually wear two layers of Nomex. It's a fire retardant and fire resistant material that stunt guys still use. I also had goggles, and a hood and gloves with gel on them that stops fire penetrating."

In the event, Cecere's insistence on wearing his own safety gear proved to be a wise move. "On the first or second burn, the head of the Stay Puft costume split open and the inside of the head caught on fire! Only the outside of the Stay Puft suit had been fireproofed, not the inside. I was glad I had my Nomex suit and goggles on!"

IN THE LINE OF FIRE

While some fire-burn jobs involve fire that builds slowly over a victim, the fuel on Stay Puft was strategically placed so it would ignite all at once. Cecere and the pyrotechnics team ensured that the flames would lay low to Stay Puft's body so that the fire wouldn't dwarf Stay Puft. If these techniques were fairly standard, the fact Cecere had to do it while climbing the replica of Dana's apartment block posed more of a challenge. "It was kind of tough climbing that building on fire," he recalls. "I had to grab on to these special handholds while wearing the suit. I only had to climb a couple of feet, but some of the building was made out of a soft porous stone that would crumble whenever I put my hands on it. There's that one shot that you see where my hand comes in and crushes the whole corner of that building."

However, the climb did allow Cecere a glimpse into the model shop's attention to detail. "The effects people had created these itty-bitty people inside the building that no one would ever see except for me!" he says. Cecere also enjoyed working with Stay Puft's puppeteers, who controlled Stay Puft's facial expressions. "I said to them, 'Why do you have four people? Can't you do it on just one board?' They said, 'This way all four of us get royalties instead of one!'"

Of course, it's difficult for anyone who hasn't set themselves on fire to imagine how the experience can be anything other than completely terrifying. Cecere emphasizes that safety – both before and during the stunt – is the number one priority. "If you start feeling any heat, you have to know when to give the signal to be put out. Because if you wait until the heat is too extreme, by the time you get put out you'll be burnt."

The other important factor, he says, is mental preparation. "Before I do any fire-burn, I go off to a corner and sit down and relax. I even say a little prayer. It calms me so I don't have anything on my mind when I'm doing a fire-burn. I have to be aware of everything that's going on around me, and I try not to let the adrenaline build."

Like most stunt jobs, Cecere was only given a breakdown of the scene rather than a full script, so he had no idea what the Stay Puft sequence would look like in the finished movie. On seeing *Ghostbusters* for the first time, he marveled at how everything had come together. "I was very impressed as I didn't even know what the movie was about," he says. "I had no idea he was going to walk around stepping on stuff!"

ABOVE Cecere clad in his tight-fitting Nomex suit, goggles, hood, and gloves; filming on the fire-burn stunt; the costume is carefully pulled off after the burn sequence.

OPPOSITE PAGE Tony Cecere inside the Stay Puft suit during the fire-burn sequence.

CHAPTER 3
GHOSTBUSTING TECH

The Ghostbusters boast some nifty tools of the trade, including proton packs, ghost traps, and PKE meters — not to mention Ecto-1, perhaps the coolest car in cinema history. The gadgets were the result of Dan Aykroyd's original concepts, and were realized with the help of Stephen Dane's concept art and Chuck Gasper's clever mechanical effects. Today, original props fetch significant sums at auction, while many Ghostheads enjoy constructing their own innovative props.

THE WALLOWER

From the moment he invented Ecto-1, Dan Aykroyd knew it was going to be a 1959 Cadillac Ambulance. He reveals how his vision was realized on screen and why the car was such fun to drive.

A HUGE FAN OF CLASSIC CARS, DAN AYKROYD always knew that the Ecto-1 would be a 1959 Cadillac Ambulance – not least because of its size. "They're huge!" he enthuses. "If it was half an inch wider, it would by law have required clearance lights either side like a truck. It could fit four Ghostbusters who had to ride in the same car, and had a place for the equipment. And the 1950s and '60s Cadillac was the coolest car ever built! There were two wonderful designers in the 1950s, Harley Earl at General Motors and Virgil Exner at Chrysler – those guys brought rocket fins on automobiles into the American consciousness. It was either the Miller-Meteor Corporation or Hess & Eisenhardt who

ECTO-1 FACTS!

Miller-Meteor was an Ohio-based company that took the basic Cadillac chassis and made specialized versions, in particular hearses and ambulances. They dominated this business in the 1950s and 1960s.

[first] stretched out Earl's design into hearses and ambulances. Keeping the fins on them was so great. So I always knew it would be this car!"

IONIZERS AND CANISTERS

In the first draft, the Cadillac was already outfitted as the Ghostbusters' car, but as the script evolved its first appearance came to be as a black, beaten-up hearse. "The conceit in the movie was it was a hearse converted to an ambulance, but in real life it was an ambulance that we converted to a hearse and then converted to an ambulance!" Aykroyd laughs. "The hearse just has a pallet to put the coffin in the back, but the ambulance has things like stretcher bars. And inside, next to the side door where we put our packs, there was a little seat where patients could be attended to. There's no way a hearse would have a seat there for anyone to attend to a passenger!"

When he first saw his vision for the Ghostbusters' car realized by the set designers, Aykroyd was ecstatic. "I was just so pleased. They put stuff on there that I never imagined. All those scrubbers on top, those ionizers, those canisters. You would assume with four portable accelerator packs at the back there's going to be a lot of leaky stuff, so you want to continually bathe the vehicle in ion washes and anti-polarizing stuff to keep it clean. I was so tickled when I saw what they'd done."

Ecto-1 also turned out to be a pleasure to drive. "That car is a wallower," Aykroyd says. "It's got beautiful power steering but it's wide and handles like a boat. It's got a really good, big motor in it, it's comfortable to sit in... It's a little difficult to drive around corners because of its width and bars underneath, but then a Cadillac of that vintage isn't going to handle like a Porsche. There was one with a normal motor for pulling away and interior shots, and another one with a fast motor for getting away quickly. And, boy, it was fast. It was fun to drive it in New York with all its pot holes!"

Unsurprisingly, Ecto-1 soon gained attention from curious onlookers in the city. "As we drove by in New York, people didn't know what it was," Aykroyd recalls. "It produced such a great reaction wherever it went!"

LEFT Aykroyd has always loved cars and knew straight away that he wanted the Ghostbusters to use a converted Cadillac. The car they used in the movie was originally an ambulance but they dressed it up as a hearse because it was a better joke.

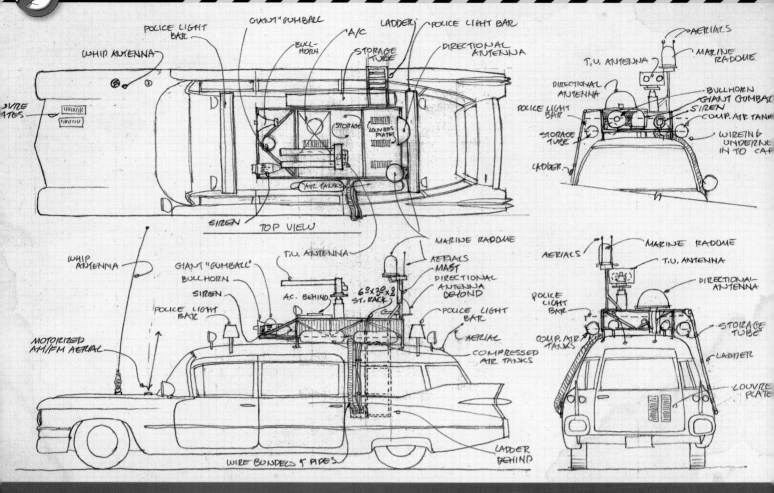

STEPHEN DANE'S
ECTO-1 DESIGNS

Concept artist and hardware consultant Stephen Dane was
key to designing the final look of the iconic Ectomobile.

D **ESIGN CONSULTANT STEPHEN DANE WAS**
integral to Ecto-1's journey to screen – but he came
to the movie late in the process. The Ectomobile had
featured in Dan Aykroyd's very first treatment for the movie,
though the car originally differed in some aspects (see boxout).
Aykroyd went on to commission his friend, artist John Deveikis, to
draw preliminary sketches of the vehicle. But around six weeks
before filming was due to start, the final design for the car (along

with many key props) had not been completed. It was at this
point that Dane – the assistant art director on *Blade Runner* and
Brainstorm – was called in.

"It turns out the prop man thought the decorator was making
the prop and vice versa, and two weeks before the shoot, they
discovered they didn't have the vehicle!" the late artist told the
website *Beyond the Marquee* in 2014.

The unconverted Cadillac Miller-Meteor ambulance had at least

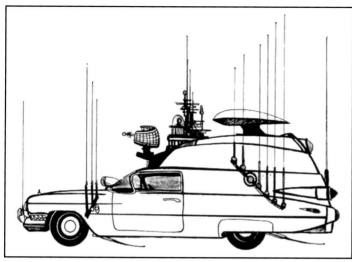

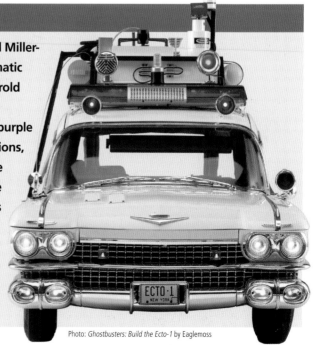

been purchased by the time Dane started work, along with a rented back-up that was never converted into the Ecto-1 (though it was used as the pre-converted hearse Ray purchases early in the film). After Ivan Reitman briefed Dane on what he wanted, the artist paid a visit to the car at the Burbank Studios backlot. "I took reference photos and measured it, and then brought that information home to draw up isometrics and its various views and elevations," Dane told *Beyond the Marquee*.

Dane's concept art refined Deveikis's early drawings to give the Ecto-1 its final iconic appearance, including adding the assorted gadgets on the roof rack. "I'd seen the roof rack on fire trucks and things like that," Dane explained in the 2015 book *Ghostbusters: A Visual History*. "I put a TV antenna on it, a directional antenna,

an air-conditioning unit, storage boxes, a radome – I just filled it up with bullshit."

Once Reitman had approved the designs, they were given to the prop masters and painters to apply the paint scheme and logos, and fit the equipment. Dane supervised the build and helped procure parts. He revealed to *Beyond the Marquee* that a few aspects of the car in the movie subtly differed from his designs. "If you look at my sketch for the proton pack gurney in the Ecto-1, you'll see that I designed the packs to lay sideways. The guys who built the car changed that and what you see in the movie are the packs positioned upright and at a slight angle. There were also parts on the roof rack that changed position from my drawings. Everything is still there, but some of the parts may be on top of each other or facing in a different direction."

THE ORIGINAL ECTO-1

Though Dan Aykroyd always knew he wanted Ecto-1 to be a converted Miller-Meteor ambulance, the vehicle in his original treatment had some dramatic differences. For a start, it boasted paranormal powers. According to Harold Ramis in the 1985 book *Making Ghostbusters*, the car could originally "dematerialize," and it had a more sinister air with flashing white-and-purple strobe lights. It was also originally black. "For more practical considerations, we had to get away from the idea of an all-black Ectomobile," associate producer Joe Medjuck told *Making Ghostbusters*. "In going through the script, László [Kovács, cinematographer] noted that every shot of it was at night. If it had been black, you wouldn't have been able to see it though most of the movie… So keeping that in mind, we decided we better go with a white ambulance trimmed in red." In early versions of the script, the car was also described as a 1975 Cadillac Miller-Meteor rather than the 1959 version seen in the film.

Photo: *Ghostbusters: Build the Ecto-1* by Eaglemoss

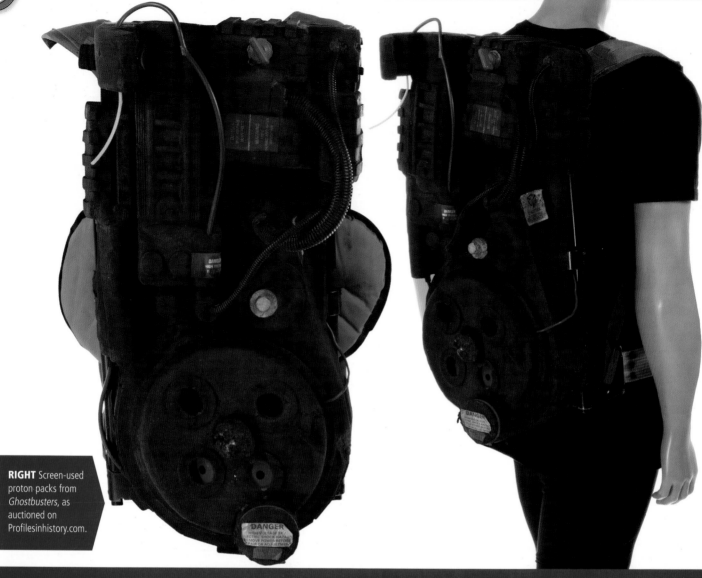

RIGHT Screen-used proton packs from *Ghostbusters*, as auctioned on Profilesinhistory.com.

PROTON PACKS

The iconic portable nuclear particle accelerator was inspired by military hardware and waste management equipment, while retaining a 'do it yourself' quality.

THE PROTON PACK IS THE MOST IMPORTANT piece of equipment deployed in the capture of apparitions. It is also one of the most recognizable movie props of all time, and its iconic status has inspired hundreds of *Ghostbusters* fans to construct their own impressively faithful replicas.

The device is essentially a portable nuclear particle accelerator that emits a proton stream from an attached neutrona wand. This has the effect of neutralizing a ghost's negatively-charged energy, holding the spook in stasis before it can be directed into a ghost trap. The key component of the proton pack is a circular cyclotron, a particle accelerator that sends charged particles spiraling outwards. Other elements include the motherboard,

distributor generator, lightbar and valves, with the pieces all connected to an ALICE (all-purpose lightweight individual carrying equipment) pack frame – an apparatus-carrying system first used by the US military during the Vietnam War.

In *Ghostbusters*, all proton packs are built by Egon Spengler. In real life, proton packs were a feature of Dan Aykroyd's original treatment for the movie, inspired by the sort of equipment waste management workers might use.

The subsequent design of the pack fell to the late concept designer and hardware consultant Stephen Dane, who worked under Ivan Reitman's guidance. Dane designed several variations, including one that featured control handles, before he and Reitman settled on the final design. One of Reitman's key requirements for both the packs and the Ecto-1 (which Dane also worked on as concept designer) was that they had a "do it yourself" quality to them, but at the same time Dane ensured that they also felt like genuine hardware.

"The backpacks were always in play script-wise," Dane told the website *Beyond the Marquee* in 2014. "Ivan and I had an early conversation and he told me what he wanted. I then drew up some rough sketches based off flamethrowers I had seen in a few military magazines. Once I had a basic idea and shape, I went out and got a pack frame from California Surplus on Santa Monica and Vine in Hollywood."

BALSA WOOD AND CARDBOARD
Dane built the first proton pack prototypes out of balsa wood, cardboard and the aforementioned pack frames, and went on to purchase parts and offer guidance for the prop fabricators. The movie props themselves were constructed by mechanical effects supervisor Chuck Gasper and his team. According to Don Shay's 1985

book *Making Ghostbusters*, the shape was sculpted in foam and molded in rubber, which was then used to create the fiberglass shells. These shells were attached to the aluminium motherboard backplate and a military surplus ALICE frame. "They were then finished with various surplus 1960s resistors, pneumatic fittings, hoses and ribbon cable, as well as surplus warning labels and custom-made metal fittings," explained Shay. The weight of the packs was a hefty 50 pounds including batteries, Harold Ramis told *Cinefex* magazine in 1989. However, during stunts these 'hero packs' were substituted with lighter foam rubber versions.

"The finished proton packs seen on screen had a rough surface on close-up inspection since there wasn't enough time to make them perfect and smooth," Dane revealed to *Beyond the Marquee*. "The prop builders did a great job of building the screen-used proton packs considering they had to build several packs and wands in such a short amount of time."

The packs returned in *Ghostbusters II* – in fact, it was in the sequel that we heard the term "proton pack" for the first time. We also learnt that the nuclear energy cells of the packs have a "half-life of 5,000 years." Dane helped redress the props for the sequel, which had minor upgrades such as black (rather than gray) crank knobs and additional padding. The sequel also featured lighter stunt packs and 'semi-hero' packs (a combination of the other two versions) for wide-shots. All proton pack props from both movies have become highly sought after collectibles.

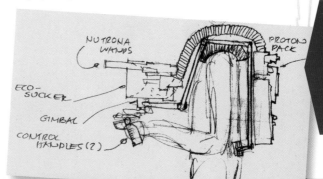

NEUTRONA WANDS

ABOVE A close-up of a neutrona wand in Judge Wexler's courtroom. The wand features a number of switches to vary the intensity of the plasma stream.

The device used to direct proton beams at apparitions was enhanced with rubbery light effects, a digital pitch device, and tiny lights.

ALSO KNOWN AS A PARTICLE thrower and positron collider, the neutrona wand is the device used to direct proton streams (or 'capture streams') at spirits before they are pulled into a ghost trap. The wand is connected to the proton pack via a hose, and features several switches to vary the intensity of the plasma stream.

Like much of the film's other tech, the idea and name of the neutrona wand was present in Dan Aykroyd's first treatment – though according to Don Shay's book *Making Ghostbusters*, it was originally described as

looking less like a firearm. "The hi-tech ghost-herding devices of Dan Aykroyd's original concept were indeed wand-like," explained Shay. "Attached via thick black flex-cords to a back-mounted proton power source, the wands were strapped in place at the wrist… and extended out along the palm to a point six inches beyond the fingertips. When fired – by means of an elbow toggle switch on the backpack – phosphorescent beams of red and green light issued forth."

The wands – designed by Stephen Dane and constructed by Chuck Gasper – were made largely of

aluminium. Small, flashing lights and fluorescent bargraphs were built into their tips as a marker to assist the animation team at Boss Film Studios, who added the proton streams in post-production. "I told the guys we're not going to do lasers," visual effects supervisor Richard Edlund told *Build the Ecto-1*. "This is a comedy, so we had this rubbery, multi-colored light."

The animation itself was supervised by Terry Windell and Garry Waller. "What we had to create was basically a 'rubberized' laser with a secondary source of energy," Windell told *Starlog* in 1984. "There had to be a stream of power shooting out of the gun and a counter action-something pulling back into the gun." Meanwhile, the gushing sound that accompanied the trigger of the neutrona wand being pulled was created by sound designer Richard Beggs, who experimented with a digital pitch device.

As Ivan Reitman explained in *Making Ghostbusters*, when we first see the Ghostbusters clutching their neutrona wands in the Sedgewick Hotel, they have far from mastered how to operate their equipment. "I knew that when they blew the maid away with their neutrona wands, we'd get a big laugh," he said. "It's the first time you see the equipment work – and you get the sense that it's the first time they've seen the equipment work. Too often in movies, you have characters using equipment they've never even seen before and suddenly they acquire instant expertise. I thought it would be funnier if the guys were trigger-happy and nervous – like rookie cops with loaded weapons."

By the end of *Ghostbusters*, the heroes have much greater experience in directing proton streams. They eventually realize that the only way to defeat Gozer is by breaking the cardinal rule of 'don't cross the streams.' This leads to 'total protonic reversal,' causing molecules in the vicinity to explode at the speed of light and closing the door to Gozer's world.

ABOVE The Ghostbusters break the key rule of 'don't cross the streams' to defeat Gozer, leading to total protonic reversal. Thankfully, the plan is a success.

LEFT Ray and the other Ghostbusters take time to become experts in using their spirit-catching equipment.

Replica photo courtesy of Mattel

PKE METER

This handheld instrument, used to locate ghosts by tracking their psychokinetic energy, was built using a redressed shoe polisher.

THE PSYCHOKINETIC ENERGY (PKE) meter is a nifty handheld device used to track down apparitions by reading their spectral energy. As the ghost-hunter approaches the location of an apparition, the arms will extend and the machine's lights will flash increasingly rapidly. Other features of the device include an LED readout screen and level adjustment buttons.

In the *Ghostbusters* universe, the device was built by Egon, but behind the scenes it was Stephen Dane who drew the concept sketches and helped design the prop. The prop itself was built using a redressed Iona SP-1 portable shoe polisher with added electronics. "It's all just this weird stuff, but it's credible enough," is how Dane summed up the device in the 2015 book *Ghostbusters: The Visual History.*

One of Dane's original sketches showed a larger instrument that resembled a minesweeper. This iteration incorporated a computer monitor, sling, hydraulic extending arm, and sensing ring, and was given the title of a giga electron voltmeter (GEV meter). It was decided that a handheld, dowsing rod-style device would be more practical for the Ghostbusters. A device called the giga meter did appear in *Ghostbusters II* along with the PKE meter, though this was a different looking instrument that was used to measure psychomagnotheric energy.

The PKE meter prop was later rented out and re-used in various movies and shows, including as a communicator in John Carpenter's *They Live* (1988) and as a homing device in the Hulk Hogan comedy *Suburban Commando* (1991).

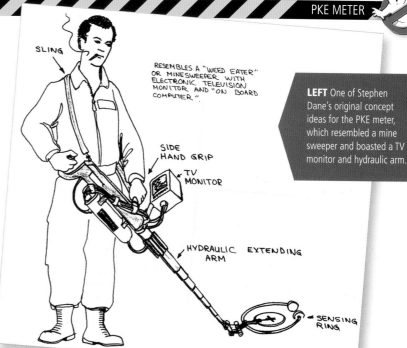

SLING

RESEMBLES A "WEED EATER" OR MINESWEEPER WITH ELECTRONIC TELEVISION MONITOR AND "ON BOARD COMPUTER"

SIDE HAND GRIP

TV MONITOR

HYDRAULIC EXTENDING ARM

SENSING RING

LEFT One of Stephen Dane's original concept ideas for the PKE meter, which resembled a mine sweeper and boasted a TV monitor and hydraulic arm.

STEPHEN DANE

Photo and quotes copyright: Kevin Stern — Beyond the Marquee

Ghostbusters' hardware consultant Stephen Dane was responsible for drawing up concept designs for Ecto-1 and the majority of the Ghostbusters' other tech across both films, as well as creating prototype props. While his designs had significant input from Dan Aykroyd (who came up with the original concepts), John Daveikis (who drew the initial Ecto-1 illustrations), and Ivan Reitman (who provided guidance on what he wanted), Dane was integral to the look and feel of the Ghostbusters' technology. "I would go home about four or five miles away from the studio, draw up the ideas then go back to Ivan pretty much the next day," Dane told Kevin Stern at the website *Beyond the Marquee* in 2014. "It was a very fluid relationship allowing us to pin down the design of the various props."

Movies were always a big part of Dane's life. His mother was an Oscar®-winning costume designer, while his father was a publicity agent for 20th Century Fox. In his childhood he even had a small role in the 1954 comedy *Her Twelve Men*. After working for years as an architect, including doing period architectural design at Universal Studios' theme park, Dane landed the job of assistant art director on *More American Graffiti* in 1979. Roles as assistant art

director on *Blade Runner* (1982) and *Brainstorm* (1983) and art director on *The Adventures of Buckaroo Banzai Across the 8th Dimension* (1984) followed. His work attracted the attention of Reitman as he was prepping *Ghostbusters*. "It was wonderful to work with Ivan," Dane told *Beyond the Marquee*. "He would discuss what he wanted and I'd sketch it up. He was very accessible at all points from concept through fabrication. He would tell me his ideas and I'd draw them out for him, get his approval, go out and gather parts and then make up some of the rough mock-ups of props and oversee the build on the Ecto-1. I worked with Ivan very closely throughout the entire design process."

Aside from returning on 1989's *Ghostbusters II*, where he helped design new tech such as the slime-scooper and the giga-meter, Dane's post-*Ghostbusters* career included roles as the visual effects art director of *Spaceballs* (1987), assistant art director on the Richard Edlund-produced *Solar Crisis* (1990), and set designer of *Home Alone II* (1992). He died in 2016.

GHOST TRAPS

The metal trap used to capture, store and transport ghosts was designed by concept artist Stephen Dane and manufactured by effects supervisor Chuck Gasper.

AS SOON AS THE GHOSTBUSTERS have an apparition locked in their proton stream, one of the team will activate the ghost trap using the attached hydraulic foot pedal. The spirit is then sucked safely into the trap's containment chamber, at which point the trap will snap shut and an indicator light will begin flashing. All that's left is for the steaming trap to be taken back to the firehouse where the ghost is transferred into the Ghostbusters' containment unit.

As with the proton packs, the ghost trap was featured in Dan Aykroyd's original treatment for *Ghost Smashers* (as it was then titled) and designed by concept artist Stephen Dane.

"I did some early sketches that [Ivan Reitman] liked and went home and perfected the design," Dane told the website *Beyond the Marquee*. "It became a reverse bomb-bay – instead of something coming out of the open bomb-bay doors, something got sucked in."

TRICKS OF THE TRAP

Like the proton pack, the ghost trap was manufactured by special effects supervisor Chuck Gasper and his team. According to a letter that associate producer Michael C. Gross wrote to accompany an auction at Prop Store, four traps were built for the film, with at least one of them reused in *Ghostbusters II* (albeit with additional animated effects). A remote control box was also constructed but never seen on screen.

The trap is seen several times in the *Ghostbusters* movies, including during the capture of Slimer, the Scoleri brothers, and the ghost jogger. The latter is a rare occurrence of the trap being used without a proton pack. Other features of the trap include a set of wheels for ease of movement and a selection of calibration knobs. The book *Haynes Ectomobile Workshop Manual* suggests that the latter includes a NRADS Absorption Wheel to adjust the level of radiation and a PKE Condenser knob to compact the ghost into a transferrable state. The trap has sometimes been called the 'muon trap' in the expanded *Ghostbusters* universe, after the negatively charged particles that apparitions are made from.

In the first film, Ray exclaims "Don't look directly into the trap!" as he dons his Ecto-goggles. However, this rule appears unnecessary: Egon proceeds to look directly into the trap without any lasting damage.

BELOW A spirit is sucked into the device in an explosion of light, and one of Stephen Dane's ghost trap concept drawings.

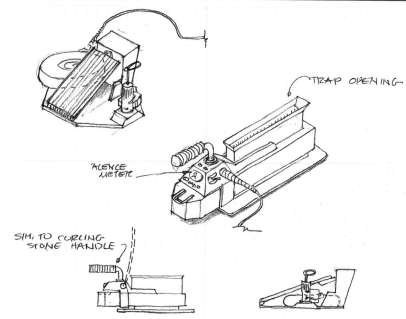

CHUCK GASPER

Ghostbusters' special effects supervisor Chuck Gasper was responsible for overseeing the film's dazzling on-set (rather than post-production) mechanical effects. This included everything from the construction of the proton pack and ghost trap props to making Dana's eggs leap from their box and organizing the destruction in the Sedgewick Hotel's ballroom. He also oversaw the team who produced the film's slime and gunk, with the aid of special effects foreman Joe Day. Gasper's first special effects work was on Hitchcock's *The Birds* in 1963, and over the subsequent 35 years he worked on dozens of Hollywood movies, including *Lethal Weapon*, *Beetlejuice*, and *Batman Returns*. He also resumed his role as mechanical effects supervisor on 1989's *Ghostbusters II*. Gasper died in 2009, and received a posthumous Oscar® for technical achievement in 2014.

CHAPTER 4
GHOSTLY SOUNDS

Ghostbusters isn't just remembered for its visuals.
The film boasts a classic, tonally varied score courtesy
of the legendary Elmer Bernstein, while the phenomenally
successful theme song by Ray Parker Jr. still receives heavy
airplay to this day. Then there is the movie's innovative
array of zaps, crunches and wails, courtesy of *Apocalypse
Now*'s sound designer Richard Beggs.

STRANGE NOISES

Ghostbusters' sound designer Richard Beggs reveals how he created the film's weird and wonderful wails, zaps and crunches.

Interview: Daniel Wallace

THE SPUTTER OF AN ION STREAM, THE GROAN of the Ectomobile's siren, and the whump of Stay Puft's heavy footfalls. What do all these things have in common? Sound designer Richard Beggs.

Ghostbusters wowed audiences with its visual effects, but the audio innovations that Beggs spearheaded were just as critical for anchoring the otherworldly action within a real world context. After winning an Academy Award® for his work on Francis Ford Coppola's *Apocalypse Now*, Beggs planted roots in San Francisco and continued his Coppola partnership. It was then that he got an offer to work on Ivan Reitman's new horror-comedy in Hollywood.

"I was called in almost like a hitman to deal with certain [audio] aspects," says Beggs, who explains that director Reitman had specific sound needs that were tied to the film's high-tech hardware and its ectoplasmic specters. "I really hadn't done many Hollywood pictures. When they called me up I was excited, but this was going to be a first for me."

Though required to fly down to the Columbia offices once or twice a week to attend meetings, he found that most of his sound work could be completed at his San Francisco sound studio. At the outset Beggs didn't quite know what to expect from *Ghostbusters*, but as soon as footage started rolling in he connected with the film's breezy wit. "I'd be sitting alone up in my little cave [studio] and I'd just be laughing," he says. "I'd laugh at the same scene every time I watched it, and most scenes I had to watch 60 or 100 times!"

Reitman immediately began doling out audio tasks to his new sound designer, and Beggs tackled the checklist with stubborn skill and old-school tech.

SONIC EXPERIMENTS

"My process was somewhat eccentric," Beggs admits. "I had a 24-track recorder synched to a video tape, and I composed my sequences using 22 tracks – one

" I WAS CALLED IN LIKE A HITMAN TO DEAL WITH CERTAIN AUDIO ASPECTS "

track reserved for time codes and a guard track to prevent bleeding into an adjacent track. I had hot-rodded an Ampex two-track machine by removing a heavy flywheel idler, so when I punched it, it started instantaneously. But I still had to punch it! You couldn't synch visually the way you can today by checking waveforms. Everything was purely by eye."

With those 22 tracks Beggs wove layered, evocative sonic moments. He steered away from stock sound effects as much as possible, preferring original recordings instead. "I have a penchant for organic sounds based in reality that are then altered," he says. "80% of the sounds on *Ghostbusters* were organically made in my own studio."

Such was the case with the noise of the energy gushes that accompanied each squeeze of a neutrona wand's trigger. "I used a digital pitch [device] and fed it back into itself, using the pitch control knob to arrive

BELOW Ecto-1's wail was actually the sound of a leopard cry which had been cleverly manipulated.

LEFT The crunch of Stay Puft's footsteps was created by rubbing a thumb over leather and slowing it down.

llıılıı SOUND DESIGN GLOSSARY ıılıılı

ADR: Dialog re-recorded in post-production to improve quality

CONTRAPUNCTUAL SOUND: Sound that deliberately contrasts with the visuals or tone.

DIEGETIC SOUND: Sound inside the universe of the movie.

DOUBLE-SYSTEM RECORDING: Sound for a scene that is recorded on a separate device from the camera.

FOLEY SOUNDS: Everyday sounds (such as creaking doors or breaking glass) recreated and synched to the movie in post to enhance the impact.

HYPER-REAL SOUND: Exaggerated, rather than realistic, sound.

NATURAL SOUND: Background noise while filming, such as birds chirping, cars driving past etc. Useful for establishing a sense of realism.

NON-DIEGETIC SOUND: Sounds added outside of the universe of the movie, including the music soundtrack.

PARALLEL SOUND: Sound that matches the visuals or tone.

SOUND FX: Sounds created/enhanced and then added to the movie, such as the blast of an explosion. Unlike foley, they are not recorded to sync directly.

SUBJECTIVE SOUND: Sounds only heard (or imagined) by a character.

TIME CODES: Used to sync video and audio tracks.

WALLA: Sound effect imitating background murmur of a crowd.

at those sounds," says Beggs. "I must have spent a week at it. But I got this weird liquid quality that was more interesting than conventional sci-fi zaps."

SURGES AND PULSATIONS

The technology of the early '80s offered no way to save sound settings as presets, so Beggs had to go all-in when inspiration struck. "I knew if I came back the next day and tried to replicate it I'd never get it again," he explains. "So I recorded as many variations as possible, building a library so Ivan would have a choice. I was betting he'd be happy with at least one of them."

Beggs's sonic variations for the ion streams included many surges and pulsations, which proved useful for scenes where the ghostbusting crew blasted tables and dragged ion streams across walls. "It had a surging quality, and when it hit things it had more of a splash," he says. "Back then I was at a disadvantage because it was very hard to cut sounds to correspond with quick shifts on screen. But the looseness of the sound made it easier. At any time there was a chance

that something would hit just right, and I could pop my track on that spot to emphasize it. If you've been around a fire hose and seen how it works, that registers. That kind of familiarity with the physical world makes it easier to connect with the moment."

There's no better example of Beggs' organic philosophy than the siren of the Ecto-1. Its bleating wail is both familiar and bizarre, and its distinctiveness stems from its designer's strange choice of an audio backbone. "It was a leopard cry," Beggs explains. "I didn't have access to leopards, so I got [the sound] from the private collection of a colleague. I manipulated it to get that *err-reearr-err-reearr* by slowing it down, playing it backwards, and filtering it until I got it to where it was almost impossible [for someone else] to reverse-engineer. It sounds a little unrealistic but it doesn't sound implausible. The audience is willing to go with it and not dismiss it."

To create the sound of Stay Puft's colossal footsteps, Beggs found inspiration close to home. "I was looking around my studio for surfaces and there were these chairs in the studio where the seat was this stretched piece of leather," he says. "Not as tight as a drumhead, but taut. I impulsively licked my thumb and rubbed it on the seat and got this dull crunch sound. I pitched it down by slowing the tape, and I re-recorded it until I got it where I wanted."

Because Beggs wasn't embedded in the Hollywood studio culture, Reitman viewed him almost as a neutral everyman. During production, the director approached Beggs for a sanity check on the film's climax, which he feared was veering into outrageousness. "[I sometimes felt like] a voyeur looking from the outside," says Beggs. "[One day] we were in the Columbia studio in Burbank and Ivan asked, 'What do you think of Stay Puft? Will people think it's over the top?' I told him 'No' with a kind of 'Are you crazy?' slant on it. But at the time Ivan was worried he might have been pushing the whole thing too far." It was a conversation that Beggs has kept in mind over the years. "It taught me something about making movies," he sums up. "Sometimes it can be hard to see what you've actually got."

BELOW Beggs created the sound of the neutrona wands being squeezed using a digital pitch device.

" I GOT THIS STRANGE LIQUID QUALITY THAT WAS MORE INTERESTING THAN SCI-FI ZAPS "

Photo: Petermbernstein.com

THE PERFECT SCORE

Ghostbusters' orchestrator Peter Bernstein looks back on working with his father, legendary composer Elmer Bernstein, on one of the greatest scores of the 1980s.

COMPOSING THE MUSIC TO *GHOSTBUSTERS* was a trickier prospect than any of the four scores that Elmer Bernstein had previously written for Ivan Reitman. Reitman required a score that echoed the film's unusual balance of comedy, horror and romance, and while Bernstein had composed music for all of those genres, he hadn't had to blend them together quite like this.

"The music had to walk a fine line between all of those things without tipping too far one way or another," says Elmer's son Peter Bernstein, who orchestrated the score with David Spear. "The ghost story had to be scary enough, but then there was the comedy and the love story which had to be believable – plus the end of the world was in there somewhere. All of that meant he had to make a lot of choices along the way."

While the final score couldn't be composed until principal filming had finished, Elmer and Peter Bernstein got a feel for the story by reading the script and taking a tour of the sets during filming. "It looked funny and interesting, but making a movie – especially when you're as well-prepared as Ivan – is very workmanlike," says Peter Bernstein. "It was difficult to get a complete picture of what was going to happen. Though I do remember that Ivan had a golf cart with the *Ghostbusters* logo, which I thought was very impressive at the time!"

While composing the score for such a tonally varied film was a challenge, it helped that Elmer Bernstein and his orchestrators had a long-established working relationship. "By that time I had been working for him on and off for about a decade, and David for almost the same," says Peter Bernstein. "The system was streamlined and he knew what he could rely on us for. He would usually sketch on four lines, whereas a score will have maybe 30. He could [write] very complete sketches where we didn't have to do much aside from translate what he wanted onto a full score page. At other times he would sketch something very bare and say, 'You know what to do, make it sound like this, make it sound big, use all octaves.' There would be a lot of shorthand involved, but after 10 years we knew pretty much what he was expecting."

STRANGE SOUNDS

Elmer Bernstein incorporated a couple of unusual instruments into his score. Firstly, there was the ondes Martenot, an early electronic instrument that resembled a cross between a keyboard and a Theremin and suited the spooky elements of the movie (as heard in tracks such as 'Library and Title' and 'Dana's Theme').

While Bernstein had used the ondes Martenot on his earlier scores for the Reitman-produced *Heavy Metal* and *Spacehunter: Adventures in the Forbidden Zone*, *Ghostbusters* also saw him use another (soon-to-be-ubiquitous) instrument for the first time. "There was a new Yamaha digital synthesiser on the market called a DX7, which was extremely sought after and hard to get," Peter Bernstein remembers. "My father happened to be friends with the Yamaha importer for the Los Angeles area. Even though there was a vast waiting list for these things, I showed up at his shop and literally snuck one out the back so that no one would see! I drove up to Santa Barbara where my dad lived, and we started going through the factory sounds. We chose about 10 or 15 of them to use. In fact, the very first

BELOW A collector's edition of Elmer Bernstein's *Ghostbusters* score was released in 2006 by Varese Sarabande. It was limited to 3,000 copies.

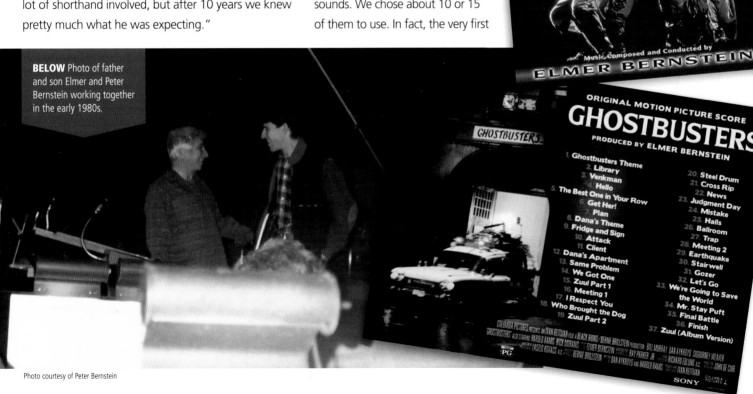

BELOW Photo of father and son Elmer and Peter Bernstein working together in the early 1980s.

Photo courtesy of Peter Bernstein

RIGHT The otherwordly sound of the ondes Martenot can be heard in Elmer Bernstein's composition 'Library and Title' early on in the movie.

note that you hear in the score is a factory programme from a DX7. We had three of them on the scoring sessions. At the time it felt rather leading edge."

DOWN TO THE WIRE

The score was recorded at the famed Village Studios in West Los Angeles and performed by the Hollywood Studio Symphony Orchestra. However, the music continually evolved during the recording sessions, not least because much of the score had been composed for footage without special effects in place. "Once we got to the recording sessions, you'd see the special effects, and things would have to be changed to accommodate the fact that things were funnier or scarier than you might have thought," Bernstein remembers. "Plus, the special effects didn't always come in at the same length that we thought they would, so you'd have to adjust the length of the music as well…. There was constant fine-tuning during the recording sessions."

The tight schedule, combined with the fact that the

score was being refined as the effects were finished, meant that its recording and mixing went right down to the wire. "They were mixing the film down the hall, so – if it didn't need to be remixed – as soon as a piece was recorded, the music editor would snip that piece out of the recording and run it down to the mixing stage. It was all going on at the same time, and it was very stressful. Usually in a good way, but not always!"

Amazingly, Peter Bernstein says that the score to the climax and end titles were still to be written the day before the final recording session. "After the recording finished [on the day before the final recording session], my father set out all his scores on a piano in the studio and stayed there for a couple of hours constructing the end titles and some of the climactic cues out of previously recorded bits. Then he would write material to connect one piece to another. As orchestrators, David and I got things like, 'Copy bars 5 through 27 of this cue but transpose it up a half step' or 'Here's 10 bars of some connecting material I've just written, and after that copy bars 43 through 60 of this other cue but

RIGHT Elmer Bernstein only wrote the music that accompanies the climax of the movie the day before the final recording session.

Photo courtesy of Peter Bernstein

LEFT Photo of Elmer Bernstein (left) and Peter Bernstein (right), taken in Hawaii in 1999. The two worked together on many projects.

transpose it down a whole step.' To do something like that the day before the final recording session not only speaks to how tight the schedule was, but also his level of self-confidence. To know that whatever happened, he'd be able to fix it the next day while recording. David and I gathered up the road maps and sketches he gave us – and this was at least eight at night – and went over to my house and stayed up all night orchestrating it. It was picked up by the copyist I believe at five in the morning, and the first piece was ready to go at nine."

Of course, elements of Elmer Bernstein's score were replaced with pop music in the final edit, including Ray Parker Jr.'s theme song and Air Supply's 'I Can Wait Forever.' Peter Bernstein says they had a fairly good idea of which pieces were likely to be substituted during the recording sessions. Did his father mind some of his music being swapped out for pop songs? "He would have rather scored it all himself, but he understood what was going on in the market place and who this movie was for. I liked it as I was in the rock and roll business myself, but it was not where he came from."

Impossibly tight schedule or not, Elmer Bernstein's score complimented the movie perfectly, eerie one minute, jazzily upbeat the next, and often hauntingly beautiful. Today it endures as one of the best scores of the 1980s. "We had so much fun in those days," Peter Bernstein recalls. "This was in my father's comedy career phase. The movies made us laugh, they were tremendously successful and it was great to work under those conditions. It was kind of perfect."

THE LIVE ORCHESTRA

In recent years Peter Bernstein – who went on to compose the scores for everything from the two 1980s Ewoks TV movies to *21 Jump Street* and *Chicago Hope* – has found himself appreciating the nuances of the score all over again while conducting a live orchestra for screenings of the film. "I forgot about a lot in 35 years!" he says. "It's a constant reminder of how skilled and creative my father really was. The score sounds like it couldn't have been any other way. But that's not true at all. It was the result of many, many small decisions that he made. That's always a great lesson at any stage of someone's career."

Photo: Peterbernstein.com

ORIGINAL SOUNDTRACK ALBUM

GHOSTBUSTERS

CHARTBUSTERS!

The soundtrack to *Ghostbusters* featured several pop hits – including Ray Parker Jr.'s impossibly catchy theme song.

A **LONGSIDE ELMER BERNSTEIN'S SCORE,** various pop acts were brought into contribute songs to *Ghostbusters*' soundtrack to broaden its appeal. Under the watch of the late music supervisor Gary LeMel, the soundtrack featured such heavy-hitters of the time as Air Supply ('I Can Wait Forever'), Alessi ('Savin' the Day'), Thompson Twins ('In the Name of Love') and, for the movie's conclusion, The Bus Boys ('Cleanin' Up the Town') . The original soundtrack also featured Elmer Bernstein's 'Main Title Theme' and 'Dana's Theme' – the full orchestral score only became available years later.

Of course, the best remembered song on the soundtrack will always be Ray Parker Jr.'s 'Ghostbusters,' which appears in both

Extended Version
Ray Parker Jr.
GHOSTBUSTERS

The Blockbusting Theme from the Ghostbusting Movie

RIGHT The music video to Ray Parker Jr.'s impossibly catchy 'Ghostbusters,' directed by Ivan Reitman. The extended version was over two minutes longer than the original single.

vocal and instrumental versions. Huey Lewis & The News (whose song 'I Want the Drug' was used as a temp score for screenings, according to Ivan Reitman) was originally asked to write the theme tune but was already tied up writing the theme to *Back to the Future*. Other artists were considered, including Fleetwood Mac's Lindsay Buckingham, before 28-year-old Parker Jr. was approached by LeMel to record a demo in three days.

THE TOP SPOT

According to Parker Jr., he was told to include two things: a saxophone line and the word 'Ghostbusters' in the lyrics. "It sounds stupid when you just sing it ['Ghostbusters']. I mean, there's no way you can say this word," he told the website *Professor of Rock*. "Then it occurred to me… No wonder he [Reitman] got 60 songs and no winners! This is a helluva job."

While Parker Jr. came up with the music fairly quickly, he initially struggled with the lyrics – until he stumbled across a commercial for a pesticide spray that asked viewers to call a number to get rid of pests. It immediately reminded him of the Ghostbusters. "I realized I had to say, "Who ya gonna call?" If I do that, it allows me to never say

the word 'Ghostbusters'. Then I'm gonna have the crowd answer 'Ghostbusters,'" Parker Jr. said.

While Reitman was certain the song would be a hit, the head of Arista Records, Clive Davis, took a little more convincing. But everyone knows what happened next: the song – accompanied by a Reitman-directed music video that featured the stars of the film, alongside cameos from the likes of Danny DeVito, Chevy Chase and John Candy – became a number one on the US Billboard Hot 100 chart. It remained there for three weeks. The song went on to secure an Oscar® nomination for Best Original Song, and has enjoyed regular airplay ever since.

The song was remixed by Run DMC for *Ghostbusters II*, while Fall Out Boy and Missy Elliot recorded a cover for 2016's *Ghostbusters*.

CHAPTER 5
THE MAKING OF
GHOSTBUSTERS II

GHOSTBUSTERS **HAD BEEN A RUNAWAY HIT,** while the popularity of the animated series *The Real Ghostbusters*, which launched in 1986, further cemented the franchise's credentials, especially with a younger audience. A sequel was inevitable – the only surprise was that it took five years to arrive.

The delay was due in part to the fact that the in-demand cast were keen not to rush into making a sequel. "Everyone was concerned that we wanted to get it right, especially Billy," says Aykroyd. "But there was such demand for it and we had such fun doing the first one…"

Momentum gathered when Dawn Steel took over as head of Columbia Studios in 1987. For Steel, *Ghostbusters II* was a priority. "It was one of the first things we talked about when I was being interviewed for the job," she told *Empire* magazine in 1989. Super-agent Michael Ovitz – who represented the core team of Murray, Aykroyd, Ramis and Reitman – convened a meeting of his clients to discuss a sequel, and eventually Columbia negotiated a deal with the film's principal players.

Finally, Aykroyd and Ramis began developing script ideas. Their central story was inspired by the negative atmosphere in New York City in the late '80s. "Once we came up with the story we felt more confident," Aykroyd says. "There was so much bad energy in the city at that point – in the world, really. What if you could quantify and qualify that energy? Would it manifest as a river of slime running under the city? It was that premise that we were operating on, and how we would deal with it as Ghostbusters." This concept was combined with another plot element: the re-emergence of a 16th century sorcerer named Vigo the Carpathian.

Though *Ghostbusters II* was inspired by the negative energy Ackroyd and Ramis felt emanated from New York City, the city itself embraced the sequel. "People saw the first film was a hit and how good it was for the city," Aykroyd says. "We got our permits without having to pay, we got co-operation from various entities without having to pay. It was much smoother; people were glad to have us there."

As well as the core Ghostbusters actors (Murray, Aykroyd, Ramis, and Ernie Hudson), Sigourney Weaver, Rick Moranis, Annie Potts, and David Margulies all returned. They were joined by *Dragonslayer*'s Peter MacNicol as the hapless Janosz, Harris Yulin as Judge Wexler, Kurt Fuller as the smarmy Hardmeyer, and former boxer Wilhelm von Homburg as Vigo (though the character was voiced by Max von Sydow). Behind the scenes, ILM, under the supervision of the Oscar®-winning Dennis Muren, was hired to create the ambitious effects. This time the score was composed by Randy Edelman (*Twins*), while the movie also boasted the hit single 'On Our Own' by Bobby Brown (who cameoed as a doorman) and Run DMC's new take on the theme song.

Like the first film, pre-production, filming, and post-production was completed on a breakneck schedule, largely so it could meet a release date of June 16 1989 – one week before Tim Burton's *Batman*. While its $215 million box office didn't equal the $282 million of the first film, it was still the eighth-highest grossing film of 1989. Today it is regarded with much affection by *Ghostbusters* fans worldwide.

GHOSTBUSTERS II
LOCATION GUIDE

Ghostbusters II's art director Tom Duffield guides us through the movie's key sets, from Peter Venkman's loft apartment to Judge Wexler's courtroom and the Museum of Art.

GHOSTBUSTERS II MARKED THE FOURTH TIME THAT ART director Tom Duffield and production designer Bo Welch had worked together. "We had a really good shorthand, and it made our lives much easier," says Duffield. It was Welch who devised the key set design concepts, while Duffield was in charge of realizing those concepts by overseeing a battalion of concept artists, set builders, and decorators. "The first thing you do when you read a script is break it down into sets," Duffield explains. "Then you go scout and pick the exterior locations, and that leads you into building sets that match the exteriors."

Photo courtesy of Tom Duffield

PETER'S LOFT APARTMENT

"That was one of my favorite sets in the movie. We wanted to give Peter something that was interesting and open, and Bo came up with the idea of it being a converted warehouse loft. We spent a fortune on the floor as we wanted to make it look like it had been beaten-up. So we had carpenters in there grinding the wood floor, then we sealed it – and it looked like an old warehouse floor! The cool thing was we had different day and night translites [illuminated film backings used as backdrops], which we could slide in and out on a shower track, depending on whether it was a day or night scene. It worked great! The set was built on a ten-foot platform, because we needed to build the ledge [that Oscar crawls out onto] on the outside of it. You had to shoot from way down below to see the baby on that ledge. We picked a really cool building in New York for the exterior that had good detail around the windows and thick brickwork."

DANA'S APARTMENT

"We had a lot of discussion about how we wanted the set design to differ from the original film. John DeCuir had a much more fantastical look to the design of the first film. We were trying to give a more realistic feel to Dana's apartment so it didn't feel like a movie set. We wanted the backings of the windows to look as real and as believable as possible, whereas if you look through the glass [in Dana's apartment] in the first film it appears more like a set. I remember Sigourney said that her apartment in *Ghostbusters II* looked like a real New York apartment this time!"

JUDGE WEXLER'S COURTOOM

"At the beginning, everyone was professing that we didn't have much money. We found that the set from *Legal Eagles* was available, so we put it back together. We did spend a lot of money on the ceiling as we put up these big corniced panels. We wanted to have something interesting up there because we knew we were going to see the Scoleris flying around. Unfortunately, we didn't see the ceiling as much as we thought! The set was on a platform as they needed to fit effects people beneath it. They put in compressed air charges to blow the chairs into the air. We also made multiple wall pieces. After they burned through a wall, [the effects team] replaced the panel with a new one to film from another angle."

RESTORATION ROOM

"After we picked the US Custom House for the exterior, Bo had the idea of what he called 'the Cathedral of Art.' We made it like a basilica, with apses at the end. The hardest thing for me was trying to come up with the finish. We wanted it to be like cut stone; it was difficult to get that effect! We also spent a lot of money on that marble-like floor. I read recently that after they struck the set, they had to reassemble it for a couple of effects shots later! That was probably the single most expensive set in the movie."

Photo courtesy of Tom Duffield

Photo Wikimedia Commons

MAYOR'S HOUSE

"That was Greystone Mansion. It's a big estate house that a rich person owned many years ago and donated to the city. There's this big diamond black-and-white floor pattern by the stairs, and as I recall we used several of the rooms there. Several hundred movies have been shot in that place. I recognize it straight away when I see it in a movie!"

RAY'S OCCULT BOOKS

"We wanted to make it feel weird and strange – like something in the [Greenwich] Village downtown. It wasn't some nice, glitzy bookstore. You walk into these sorts of shops in New York, and there are not big open spaces inside. Real estate is very expensive, so everything's packed right up next to you. We just wanted to make it cramped like a real New York boutique bookstore."

FIREHOUSE

"We used the same firehouse in downtown LA for the interiors but added a couple of things to it. The party scene at the beginning of the movie, with all those obnoxious kids, was shot in the Captain's residence on the third floor. We did the experiment with the toaster on the second floor, and shot on the first floor for the actual firehouse scenes. Movie companies like to shoot as many sets in one location as possible! We used the same New York firehouse for the exteriors."

THE SUBWAY

"We researched old New York subways and came across a guy [Alfred Ely Beach] who invented this pneumatic subway that ran on compressed air. That influenced our image of Van Horne subway station, though it wasn't nearly as elaborate as the pneumatic tube. Bo wanted to do a kind of checkerboard tile pattern, so we two-toned thousands of pieces of Masonite and cut them to the size of tiles. Then we softened the edges to be like tiles and painted them with a brown-and-yellow basket weave, and built the big roof on top. The effects guys added the River of Slime in post-production."

Photo courtesy of Tom Duffield

THE WORLD OF THE PSYCHIC

"Bo wanted it to look really cheesy. It was this stupid, one-camera talk show, like an old UHF show – the cheaply made public interest shows that used to be on when we were kids. It was such a goofball, simple set. We made a curved wall and put some planets behind it. You have this huge movie, and then this crappy little set! It made me laugh."

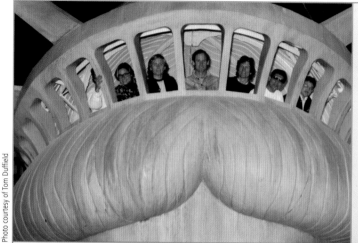

Photo courtesy of Tom Duffield

STATUE OF LIBERTY

"This was actually kind of hard for me because we didn't scout it – we didn't measure and photograph it as we would typically do. I was told we've got to create the crown so we can put the Ghostbusters up there, along with the stairs inside the Statue of Liberty. So I had to find historical photos of it, and then duplicate things like the copper sheets and strapping on the inside. We scaled it based on a few measurements we could find, including the average size of person's size head – which is about nine inches! I was happy with how it all looked considering that we had to extrapolate from photographs!"

THE MANHOLE

"The scene where they are digging a hole on First Avenue in New York was shot in downtown LA. We had to rent the corner and change the signs, so I went to the UPM [unit production manager] and asked him if he wanted me to give him a quote for how much it would cost. The UPM told me, "It costs what it costs." That is the first and only time I have heard that in this business. It worked for me!"

PSYCHIATRIC HOSPITAL

"That was the VA veterans' hospital in Westwood. We always try to add something to a public space – so if we're trying to sell that it's a psychiatric hospital, we'll put medical signs on the wall, stuff like that. Two things I always do are paint the walls dark – DPs hate white-colored walls – and give them a bit of a sheen. I hate flat walls and I'm amazed when I see flat walls in other movies. But what you don't want to do is add too much, or it looks over art directed."

ARMAND'S RESTAURANT

"That was a real restaurant called Val's in [LA neighbourhood] Toluca Lake. It was trying to be a really classy restaurant. To me it didn't look like a New York restaurant, but it was available and they were willing to shut down for the night for us. And it was only six blocks from the studio! It was a little messy with all the goo, but we shot it quickly. The restaurant isn't there anymore."

KURT FULLER

Kurt Fuller's breakout role as Jack Hardemeyer in *Ghostbusters II* allowed him to quit his day job. But, as he recalls, it was accompanied by high anxiety and some ill-fated improv.

BY 1988, KURT FULLER HAD MADE FLEETING appearances in two Schwarzenegger actioners (*The Running Man*, *Red Heat*) as well as popping up in everything from *Cagney & Lacey* to *Elvira: Mistress of the Dark*. Yet, by then in his late thirties, he still wasn't able to quit his day job selling real estate. Until, that is, *Ghostbusters II* came along.

"Those earlier roles didn't pay – they were not career builders," says Fuller. "But once I was in *Ghostbusters II*… A role like that confers on you that you're OK and that because people who are very successful have said 'yes' to you, other people who were previously afraid to say 'yes' to you can now say 'yes' to you. That's how it works!"

Fuller landed the role after Harold Ramis's then-wife saw him in the hit Steven Berkoff play *Fetch* and recommended that Ramis come down and see it. Ramis was equally impressed. "Harold recommended me to Ivan Reitman, so I went down and read for a part. Harold and I stayed friends for the rest of his life after the film. He's the reason I'm not selling real estate."

The actor initially read for a different part: the probably-not-career-building role of "guy whose desk catches on fire." But then the Mayor's assistant, Jack Hardemeyer, came his way. "I think they were negotiating with William Atherton but he couldn't do it," says Fuller. "So it came to me. I was shocked to get that role in the second movie."

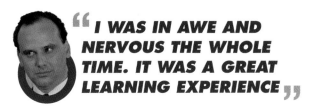

> " I WAS IN AWE AND NERVOUS THE WHOLE TIME. IT WAS A GREAT LEARNING EXPERIENCE "

As a fan of both the first film and *Saturday Night Live*, Fuller spent a large amount of time on set in a "fog," not quite able to believe where he was. "The first film had been a complete revelation. That scene where they were passing the bottle around outside the university really spoke to me – there was something about their chemistry and how relaxed

and improvisational it seemed. I don't know how many times I'd seen it. These people were giants from *Saturday Night Live*, people I never thought I would meet in my entire life – and yet here I was. I was in awe and nervous the whole time. These were people who had to disguise themselves to walk down the streets of New York – and yet they were very normal, you know? Very open, very nice. Harold took me under his wing, and Bill [Murray] and I got along great because we're both golfers. They had an ease with each other, they were like brothers. They really knew what they were doing. It was a great learning experience for me."

THE ART OF DROWNING

Despite the welcoming nature of his co-stars, Fuller is candid about just how anxious he was working on the movie. "I was petrified. *Petrified!* I barely knew what I was doing. I was lucky they didn't fire me. That's really how I feel. I was drowning every day and I actually can't believe I didn't completely have a breakdown."

BELOW Hardemeyer has his first run-in with Venkman. Fuller was a long-time fan of *Saturday Night Live* and was shocked to suddenly find himself starring alongside the show's cast.

That anxiety hardly eased when, in the scene in the Mayor's office just before Hardemeyer has the Ghostbusters committed to the insane asylum, Fuller was given the dreaded instructions from Ivan Reitman to "improvise part of the scene." Fuller laughs at the memory. "I had never improvised in my life! I had no idea what I was doing. I just started making things up. These guys were brilliant world-class improvisational actors, world class sketch artists – and *me* trying to be the leader of this improv? I

don't think it was very good!"

Fuller didn't have to look far for influences on his character: selling real estate proved to be the perfect training ground. "It's really a middle manager kind of job. You put on a suit, agree with everyone that you're supposed to agree with, and try to fool everybody that you're supposed to fool. And that's sort of what this guy did. My daily job did actually inform this role." He chuckles. "It's sort of the way I was at the time – you know, just a little asshole. In many ways I was playing myself!"

Fuller remembers receiving some sage advice from Reitman about playing an antagonist that proved essential to his performance: "He said – because I was sort of twirling my moustache, I'm sure – 'Do less than you ever thought was possible to.' I'd mostly done theater at the time, and I didn't tap into how you don't need to overact because the camera is doing so much. I still think I overdid it after that [Reitman's advice], but much less."

 " *MY DAY JOB ACTUALLY INFORMED THE ROLE. IN MANY WAYS I WAS JUST PLAYING MYSELF!* "

Despite Fuller's reservations about his performance, *Ghostbusters II* made him a recognizable face and showed his flair for playing bad guys – something he would return to again and again in the following years, in everything from *Wayne's World* to *Alias* and *Supernatural*. "I became the go-to funny asshole, which was a fairly good living," Fuller says. "It kept me working for years and years – until my agent showed me things that said, 'We want a Kurt Fuller type, but not Kurt Fuller.' They'd seen enough of me!

So I went from bad guys to detectives to lawyers to fathers to grandfathers – that was the journey I took. When I had kids, I think it softened me a little bit and I played things differently. For longevity, you've got to have a lot of bullets in your gun."

However, Fuller makes clear that he enjoyed his years as a bad guy for hire. "Being typecast is not a bad thing," he points out. "It's better to be known for something than being known for nothing. And *Ghostbusters II* started me on that road."

ABOVE The weaselly bureaucrat in the Mayor's office. Fuller remembers Reitman's advice was to 'do less than you've ever done before'.

THE HARD WAY

Despite the potential for puns in the name 'Jack Hardemeyer,' Fuller says that the cast deliberately avoided rude jokes at his expense. "Bill Murray said to me he wasn't going to call my character 'hard-on' because it would be a very tough five or six years for me afterwards. He said that when he'd said that line ["This man has no dick"] to Atherton, it tortured him, with people yelling it out of cars and buses. Bill Murray said he wasn't going to do that to me. I appreciated it!"

Fuller actually worked alongside Atherton six years later in the 1995 TV movie *Virus*. Did the two of them exchange stories of playing weaselly bureaucrats? "No, we never talked about *Ghostbusters*. I'm sure we both thought about it but figured, 'You know, we both did it.' He played that character so well in *Ghostbusters*. I just picked up his crumbs really!"

RIGHT One of Montalbano's unused monster designs for *Ghostbusters II*.

OPPOSITE PAGE Clockwise: Early Vigo sketch; Scoleri brothers storyboard panel; two more 'general monster' concept designs for the film.

GARY MONTALBANO
CONCEPT ART

Artist Gary Montalbano recalls his time creating effects storyboards and concept art for *Ghostbusters II* — and says why the experience fulfilled a childhood dream.

CHICAGO-BORN ARTIST GARY MONTALBANO wanted to work at ILM ever since he was a teenager. "Seeing what Ralph McQuarrie and Joe Johnson did made me pursue my dream of working for the company," he says. Montalbano went on to work as a layout artist on TV series such as *GI Joe* and *ALF Tales*, before finally getting the chance to work for ILM when he "took a risk" and called the company's art director Steve Beck to see if they had work. Impressed, Beck hired Montalbano as an effects storyboard artist on *Ghostbusters II*. "At first, I was working from a brief special effects outline, but afterwards a rough script," he says. "Initially, Steve and Dennis [Muren] wanted to see what I could come up, so I played with some ideas. Then the collected ideas were focused to conform to the script."

VISUAL MAPS

Montalbano storyboarded effects sequences for the Scoleri brothers and the Statue of Liberty, and recalls working all night in his hotel room to complete sequences for meetings the following morning. "Visual effects storyboards tend to be more focused on the quick visual mapping out of what the director needs to see to plan out the finished sequence," he explains. "Because of this, the board drawings I did were not that detail-oriented. They were more of a placeholder of what would be developed for the final special effects, way before what the audience would see. Dennis Muren told me not to worry that much about the design aspect of the subject matter depicted in storyboards, but to focus more on the scene's action."

After the storyboard work was completed, Montalbano was commissioned to create more fleshed-out concept art of "general ghosts and demons," as well as Vigo, whose look at that point was undecided. "It was all pretty open-ended and fun; they left me to generate some designs that would possibly spark some new visual ideas," he says.

In more recent years, Montalbano has storyboarded Marvel and DC animation, *Trolls* and *Curious George* amongst others, but the experience of working on *Ghostbusters II* remains a high point. "The original film was great, and it was really a dream come true to work on the sequel," he says. "It was very satisfying to see some of my work utilized in the final movie."

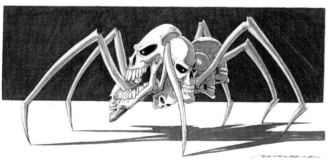

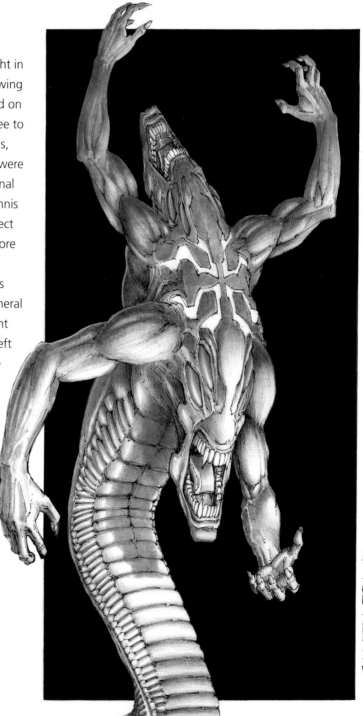

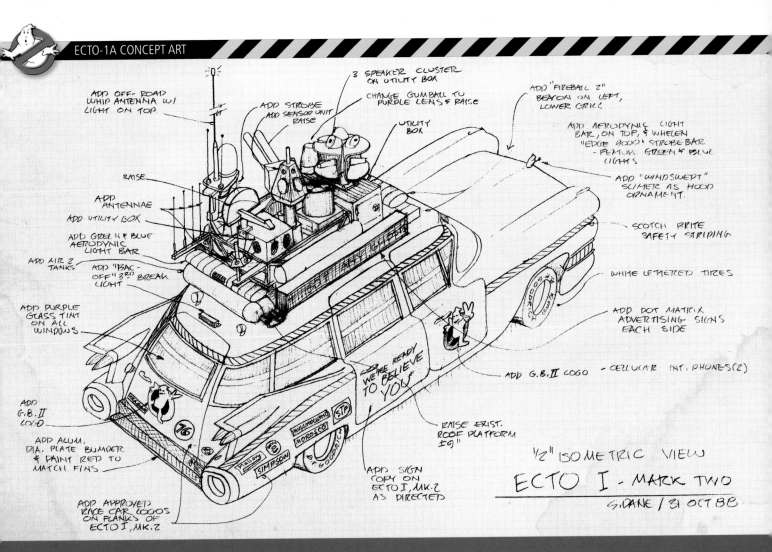

Labels on the concept art:

ADD OFF-ROAD WHIP ANTENNA W/ LIGHT ON TOP.

3 SPEAKER CLUSTER ON UTILITY BOX

CHANGE GUMBALL TO PURPLE LENS & RAISE

ADD "FIREBALL 2" BEACON ON LEFT, LOWER GRILL

ADD STROBE ADD SENSOR UNIT RAISE

UTILITY BOX

ADD AERODYNIC LIGHT BAR, ON TOP, & WHELEN "EDGE 9000" STROBE BAR - FEATURE GREEN & BLUE LIGHTS

RAISE

ADD ANTENNAE

ADD UTILITY BOX

ADD "WINDSWEPT" SLIMER AS HOOD ORNAMENT.

ADD GREEN & BLUE AERODYNIC LIGHT BAR

SCOTCH BRITE SAFETY STRIPING

ADD AIR 2 TANKS

ADD "BAC-OFF" 3RD BRAKE LIGHT

WHITE LETTERED TIRES

ADD PURPLE GLASS TINT ON ALL WINDOWS

ADD DOT MATRIX ADVERTISING SIGNS EACH SIDE

ADD G.B.II LOGO - CELLULAR INT. PHONES(2)

ADD G.B.II LOGO

WE'RE READY TO BELIEVE YOU

ADD ALUM. DIA. PLATE BUMPER & PAINT RED TO MATCH FINS

RAISE EXIST. ROOF PLATFORM ±9"

ADD SIGN COPY ON ECTO I, MK.2 AS DIRECTED

½" ISOMETRIC VIEW

ECTO I - MARK TWO

S. DANE / 31 OCT 88

ADD APPROVED RACE CAR LOGOS ON FLANKS OF ECTO I, MK.2

ECTO-1A CONCEPT ART

Concept artists Stephen Dane, John Bell, and Benton Jew were brought in to redesign the Ectomobile for *Ghostbusters II*.

ABOVE Stephen Dane, who created concept designs of the original Ecto-1, updated his old drawings with new details.

THE COOLEST CAR IN MOVIE HISTORY returns in *Ghostbusters II*, complete with some stylish new embellishments. The car's roof rack boasts the addition of a satellite uplink, while digital signs attached to its side flash advertisements to passers-by, including 'Ghostbusters for hire' and 'We are ready to believe you.' The *Ghostbusters II* logo now adorns the hood, front doors, and back of the vehicle, and the license plate has become 'Ecto-1A' – though in the scene outside Peter's apartment it is clearly seen as 'Ecto-2' (a holdover from the name of the car in earlier scripts). Other additions include the team's phone number, black and orange reflective tape strips, and a red aluminum step replacing the rear bumper.

FRANKENSTEIN VARIATIONS

Various concept artists were brought in to brainstorm ideas for the updated Ectomobile. John Bell created several variations that saw the vehicle become a limo retrofitted with intriguing new tech. "They just said come up with something that fits the franchise," Bell recalls. "I figured that the Ghostbusters team was becoming more and more successful and their budgets were bigger, so the car should reflect that."

"John Bell would create a bare-bones car sketch and make Xeroxes to use as a base, then add the bells and whistles with markers," adds fellow artist Benton Jew. "I took a few stabs at it, some from his base sketch and some from my own. We were just trying to crank out as many variations as we could. We had lots of car reference around and Frankensteined as many crazy ideas as we could."

Stephen Dane, concept designer and hardware consultant on the original movie, also returned to update his original designs. "I basically took my old drawings off the heap and added more detail to them," he said in the 2015 book *Ghostbusters: The Visual History.* "With the second vehicle you could see how much more complex it was, but it has that off-the-shelf hardware look which is what we were going for."

BELOW One of Benton Jew's designs for Ecto-1A, complete with the new logo and additional tech.

BELOW Two of John Bell's designs for the revised Ectomobile, based on a retrofitted limo.

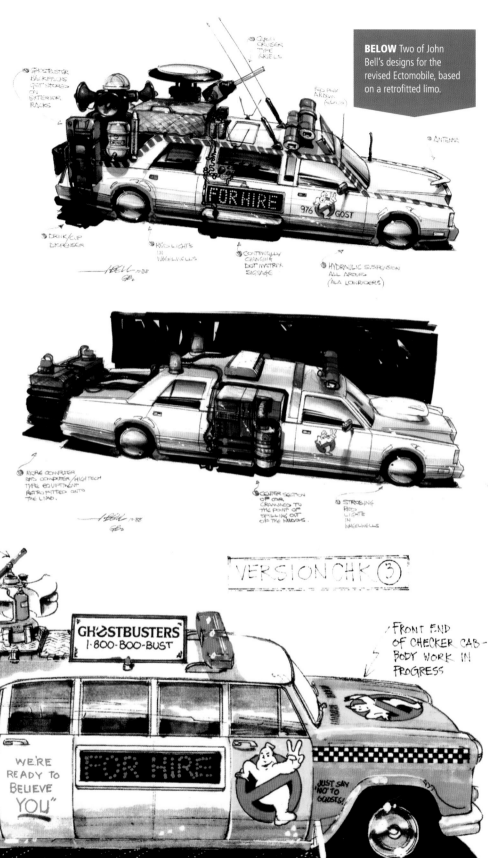

CHAPTER 6
VISUAL EFFECTS OF
GHOSTBUSTERS II

The cutting-edge Industrial Light and Magic (ILM) was tasked with developing the visual effects for the sequel — and what a task it was. The studio needed to develop a vast array of new ghosts and creatures, including the Scoleri brothers, Vigo and the street-stomping Statue of Liberty, all within a schedule just as unremitting as the first. Luckily the studio, led by visual effects supervisor Dennis Muren, had plenty of inventive solutions to the film's challenges.

RIGHT Robin Shelby in the Slimer costume with head of the creature shop, Tim Lawrence. Shelby had previously worked with Ned Gorman on *Willow*.

THE MAGIC FACTORY

ILM's visual effects co-ordinator Ned Gorman looks back on one of the last – and most challenging – movies of the pre-digital era.

WHILE AUDIENCES AND CRITICS WERE WOWED by the groundbreaking work that Boss Film Studios did on the original *Ghostbusters*, the visual effects for the sequel were commissioned out to a larger facility – Industrial Light and Magic (ILM). The visual effects supervisor on the movie was the much in demand Dennis Muren (who by this time had won five Academy Awards® for movies including *The Empire Strikes Back* and *ET*), and he headed up a talented team of mold-makers, sculptors, puppeteers, production managers, optical technicians, and make-up artists who would try to make the near-180 effects shots a reality.

ABOVE Two of ILM's key FX sequences: the ghost train careers towards Winston, while behind the scenes Danny Wagner works on the mold for the Statue of Liberty costume.

Visual effects co-ordinator Ned Gorman was one of ILM's key players on the movie. At the start of the process he worked with Muren, Ivan Reitman, and Harold Ramis to figure out exactly how many effects shots were required and how ILM was going to achieve them. It soon became clear that the schedule would be just as challenging as it had been for Boss Film on the original. "It was done on a breakneck schedule," remembers Gorman. "There was nowhere near the amount of pre-production time that was required. And this was all old-school, practical effects – it was the last film I worked on with no digital components whatsoever."

Gorman recalls how he and Muren had just finished working on another challenging shoot, *Willow*, prior to *Ghostbusters II*. "I thought *Willow* would be the toughest thing we'd ever do. How wrong I was! I think the final tally of special effects shots in *Ghostbusters II* is untouched by any movie in the photochemical era. It was huge. But we developed a plan to realize Ivan's vision."

ILM's work began in the late spring of 1988, and the company's art director Harley Jessup hired a team of talented storyboard and concept artists to visualize the effects shots. "I disseminated information so we could get everything from Dan and Harold's brains onto a concept artist's storyboard," says Gorman.

Soon ILM was furiously building maquettes, models, and mock-ups for key sequences such as the Scoleri brothers, the Statue of Liberty, and the River of Slime. "We had the not inconsiderable task of differentiating it from the first movie but hanging onto all the stuff that fans loved," recalls Gorman. This was not always an easy balance to strike. "Ivan wanted the proton beams to look the same as they had done in the first movie. We thought, 'Oh, we know how to do effects animation!' We even had a few animators working with us who had worked on the first movie. But it turns out that matching something exactly is not as easy as it looks. And even though Ivan believed he wanted the same things, he didn't really. We managed to match the look of the proton beams exactly as it had been in the ballroom scene in the first movie, but Ivan said, 'Those are too skinny!' So we added some elements to them and they wound up being a little wider."

CHANGING TIMES
One of the central challenges for ILM was that the script kept changing, with fresh pages – often containing new ghosts – arriving all the time. "I've never worked on a film that was so amorphous and not nailed down by day one!" Gorman laughs. "Every film is always changing,

Photo: Kerry Nordquist

RIGHT Sculptor Mark Siegel and Tim Lawrence discuss Slimer's lip attachments. The two men worked on both *Ghostbusters* movies.

but here we would get pages that we never talked about in pre-production."

Most of the effects sequences went through multiple iterations, from Slimer, who was cut and then reintegrated into the script, to Vigo, who – with the aid of the Pageant of the Masters' 'tableaux vivant' technique – was originally meant to step out of the painting during the third act. The evolution of the latter sequence was one that Gorman remembers being particularly tough for the ILM team. "Unfortunately, Ivan saw a test that wasn't quite there yet," he says. "Ivan said, 'It's probably my fault for not giving you enough time, but this is never going to

work.' We told him, 'This is one of those situations where we're doing a 100-mile marathon and we're on mile 99! We might stumble over the finish line, but by God, we'll get there.' But he told us to stop work on it, and came up with the idea of the giant face over the River of Slime. Frankly, I think it was the right decision, but it was disappointing to us at the time."

The process may have been "nerve-wracking and knuckle-biting," but Gorman – like most of those involved in the effects work on the movie – talks about his time on *Ghostbusters II* with real affection. Part of this was down to the collaborative process that Reitman (along with Ramis, Aykroyd, and producers Gross and

RIGHT The Scoleri brothers was one of the film's biggest effects sequences. In addition to creating the brothers, it took time to perfect the proton beams.

ABOVE Vigo (played in this shot by Howie Weed) is zapped by proton beams and positively charged slime. The Vigo effects went through many changes during the process.

Medjuck) encouraged. "We were more involved in the production and embraced in the creative process of that film than anything I've done before or since," he says. "It was a film where they wanted our ideas and responded to them. If we came up with a wacky storyboard and Harold and Michael liked it, it would get written into the next draft of the script. It was a symbiotic process, and that doesn't always happen."

ILM managed to complete their 180 effects shots within the punishing schedule, allowing the movie to make its all-important box office opening one week before Tim Burton's *Batman*. While *Ghostbusters II* was one of the last films of the pre-digital era, the other movie that the company was working on simultaneously, *The Abyss*, would revolutionize digital effects and change the industry forever.

PARTY LIKE IT'S 1989!

A vast amount of the visual effects ideas that were discussed (and, in the case of the exorcised Slimer/Louis sequences, even filmed) never made it into the final movie. Gorman recalls the New Year's Eve montage as being one particular sequence where ILM's artists devised many wild concepts. "There were a lot more cutaways of all hell breaking loose. We created concept art of what looked like the ghost of Jimi Hendrix appearing on a bandstand, laying down licks and setting his guitar on fire. But someone raised the issue that the estate of Mr. Hendrix is notoriously litigious. We thought of just *suggesting* so as not to invite any lawsuits. We had other wacky ideas like that too. But Ivan wanted

it to be a little less specific. And at that point, it was pretty late in the schedule and all hands on deck, which is why we farmed stuff out to Phil Tippett [who created the Washington Square Ghost] and Pete Kuran [at Visual Concept Engineering] for that montage sequence."

ABOVE Nunzio's larger than life (and very heavy) latex head.

RIGHT Henry Mayo's Scoleri brothers artwork, created for a trading card set.

THE SCOLERI BROTHERS

The team behind the Scoleri brothers reveal how the chuckling criminals were brought to the screen with the aid of wires, animatronics, Mylar, and a Gumby doll.

THE SCOLERI BROTHERS WERE LOOSELY based on a pair of criminals who once robbed a store belonging to Harold Ramis's father. However, the script was light on character detail, stating simply that they were "big in life, bigger in death" and "seem[ingly] ten feet tall." The initial character design instead came from the darkly humorous concept art of Henry Mayo, who worked closely with executive producer (and former graphic designer) Michael C. Gross.

"They were kind of a tribute to Archie Goodwin, who was the [writer] of *Uncle Creepy* and *Cousin Eerie* from Warren comics," says Mayo. "At the time Archie was sick with cancer, so I was thinking about him when I came up with those designs. Jack Davis designed *Uncle Creepy* and *Cousin Eerie*, and you can definitely see those characters in the Scoleris… Michael – who was a big driver all the way through the process – loved it because it was right up his alley. The contrast between them was part of his sense of irony."

Mayo remembers that the Scoleris looked more like Italian gangsters in the original designs. "Michael rightly felt that we didn't want to attack Sicilians just for a comedy act, so we moved rapidly away from that and moved to the uniforms they wore. Michael had some very real ideas about how the Scoleri brothers were going to move and how he wanted

electricity coming off them."

For ILM's creature shop supervisor Tim Lawrence, the Scoleris instantly reminded him of another set of (more benevolent) brothers. "The first thing that occurred to me was *The Blues Brothers*," he says. "Dan and John working together – that size and shape differential, with the tall and thin one and the short and round one."

HEAVY HEADS

While Gross liked his concept art to resemble something out of EC Comics, Mayo says he always knew that the characters would become less cartoon-like during the sculpting stage. "The sculptors brought it back to a more physical reality," he says.

Once the designs had been approved, Lawrence assembled a talented team to work on the sculpts and costumes, including Bob Cooper, Bill Forsch, Mike Smithson, Buzz Neidig and Howie Weed. The latter sculpted 12-inch clay character studies, which were sent to Production for feedback before the full-size versions were made. Lawrence also asked specialty costume designer Camilla Henneman to create a fat suit for Nunzio that would resemble the one she'd designed for Weird Al Yankovic's uproarious *Fat* video, and her costume was fitted with bean-bag style fat pouches that moved with the character.

Lawrence himself played Nunzio, while the role of Tony went to Jim Fye. Fye had originally been hired to play the Statue of Liberty but found he had extra time on his hands. "Tim said, 'Come here, I want to try something on you,'" Fye remembers. "He had this very crude mock-up of the Tony Scoleri costume, and he wanted to take pictures of it to see what it was going to look like. It was a paper mâché mask with pieces that were made of construction paper. The little lightning bolts that came out of his head were pipe cleaners. I said to Tim, 'If you haven't cast it yet, I'm here and I'm happy to play it.'"

Fye remembers the costume being much less claustrophobic than his Statue of Liberty costume, if not entirely comfortable. "Underneath it all there

BELOW One of Henry Mayo's vivid concept illustrations for the Scoleri brothers.

LEFT TO RIGHT Howie Weed works on Nunzio's foam head; Tim Lawrence dons the Nunzio fat suit; Jim Fye in his skeletal Tony costume; the airborne brothers on wires.

was a one-piece unitard that had been painted to look like Tony's skin. It had the variegated blues and greens to make him look ghost-like. On top of that was torn-up jeans and a torn-up, open prison shirt. Then there were Tony's emaciated ribs, which were stuck onto my chest, and gloves for the hands. The great thing about the costume was the head, of course…"

The larger-than-life latex heads were particularly heavy, especially as complex animatronics had been built into them. "They unitard was pulled up over my head so my head was actually [inside] Tony's neck," Fye remembers. "It was animatronic in that there were a couple of guys with joysticks controlling his facial expressions. So he could smile, open and close his eyes, and his eyes lit up…. I couldn't get out of the costume for breaks, though I could take the head off at lunchtime, thank God!"

Lawrence's fat suit ensured that his costume was even heavier than Fye's. However, both men – who were filmed separately – agree that the greatest challenge was the fact that the shoot took place suspended above ground. "I was hooked up at my sides and at least ten feet off the ground," Fye remembers. "They said, 'Turn your head this way,' and I would do it. I did all of the arm and leg and hand movements up there. The harness that went underneath the costume – which was attached to the wires at about waist level – was made out of something very soft called moleskin. It was like German lederhosen – pants with braces. I thought, 'Well this is nice, it's very soft and comfortable.' But when you're up in the air, gravity is a law of nature. As I was up in the air, my body wanted to be down

on the ground. I was pushing against whatever clothing I had on, so I needed something soft and malleable to stop everything from hurting."

Fye says that the suit took its toll on his body. "On the last day, we took everything off and I was pretty bruised where the moleskin harness had been. It looked like somebody had taken a baton and beaten me!"

Lawrence, meanwhile, had one particularly close shave while filming his airborne footage. "Day two, we were shooting reactive lighting from the sky. As soon as I start a backward roll, I heard this 'PING!' and felt the left cable snap. Then, almost immediately, there was a second 'PING!' as the other cable snapped. Everything went into slow motion at that point, and my vision was just through the wide mouth. I was still moving backward when I lost the cable support and started to fall. I fell

Photo (composite): Kerry Nordquist

LEFT The final costumes, which were created in deathly shades of blue and green.

ABOVE The brothers are back: Tony and Nunzio return to haunt Judge Wexler's courtroom in *Ghostbusters II*.

BELOW Photo showing the detailed mechanics underneath the Scoleri brothers costumes, allowing puppeteers to control their movements.

straight down and landed flat on my back on a pad. All the breath left me. I couldn't breathe, couldn't move. The stage was silent. Finally, I got my breath back and went, 'Huh!' As soon as I did that, everyone on the stage exhaled at the same time. I was fine. The next day I went to the dailies room and that shot came up... I asked [VFX supervisor] Dennis [Muren] afterwards, 'Any chance I could get a copy of that?' Dennis said, 'Nobody's ever going to see that!'"

Still, it could have been worse – Lawrence remembers that the first day of filming had involved being even higher up with no pad underneath him – "just sharp, spiky things."

TORNADO LEGS

The footage of the Scoleri brothers on wires was shot against a blue screen, projected on a rear-projector screen and reflected into a very thin piece of stretched polyester film called Mylar. Visual effects camera operator Peter Daulton then used a Vista Cruiser motion control camera to rephotograph the image off the Mylar.

Rephotographing the rear-projection footage in Mylar – an idea that came from experiments Dennis Muren had undertaken for an earlier aborted project – allowed Daulton to create several neat effects. "It allowed us to distort the image, almost like a funhouse mirror in an amusement park," he explains. "We had the thin piece of Mylar in a wooden frame to keep it upright. We found if we took off a side-edge of the frame, the Mylar stayed upright but had enough flexibility for us to manipulate it from the back. We put a little metal ball on a rod on the back of the screen, which you could just push in slightly using programmable motion control movers. It allowed you to distort the image and come up with some very cool effects."

One of these effects was appropriately dubbed 'tornado legs.' "You could distort from the hips down to the feet of either of the Scoleri brothers, and make their legs get thinner like the base of a tornado,"

Daulton says. "Something else we could do with the distortion effect was squash and stretch the image – if the ghost was rising up and coming to a stop, we could have it stretch up on the rise and then, when it got to the top of the rise, we could squash it down a little bit. As I recall, we added a little jiggle to Nunzio Scoleri's belly with the distortion effect as well." Daulton adds that the motion control camera also gave the characters additional motion beyond what would have been possible for performers on wires.

Lawrence points out that Daulton was responsible for another vital – if unconventional – tool in the development of the Scoleri brothers. "Every morning when we started, we'd stand around the storyboard and talk about the shots we were going to do. Pete had to turn the shots into something that could be used. In order to explain what he needed out of the shot, he had a bendy Gumby doll – the American animation icon from the '60s. Pete would bend the Gumby into the correct position and say, 'OK, we need to start vertical and we need to go to this position and then we need to turn and do this.' He had these specific things that he wanted out of the action, and this little bendy figure of this character was how he got that across. The Gumby was very important to making the Scoleri brothers work!"

THEY MIGHT BE GIANTS!

According to Tim Lawrence, at one point the Scoleris were going to be much larger, less airborne apparitions. "The original idea was that they were these giants stomping around the courtroom and cursing in Italian. I was thinking, as they're electrical beings, they probably need an electrical grounding for full power. The courtroom floor is not on the ground, so [I thought] their feet should go through the floor to seek the ground as they're stomping. And whenever their feet are not in contact with the ground, it should turn into lightning bolts and electricity until it gets to ground again." While Lawrence says that the action and dialogue of the Scoleri brothers sequence barely changed from the script, the concept of the ghosts did evolve. "They became more airborne, more distorted and more covered with electrical effects. By the time we got to the set, they were fully airborne, they were never on the ground and they were on wires all the time."

Photo: Kerry Nordquist

SCOLERI BROTHERS
EARLY CONCEPT ART

During pre-production on *Ghostbusters II*, Benton Jew drew various concepts for the Scoleri brothers. Here he reveals some of those early designs.

WHILE THE LOOK OF THE SCOLERI BROTHERS in *Ghostbusters II* was largely shaped by Henry Mayo's concept art, other artists were commissioned with drawing various designs for the characters during pre-production.

ILM concept designer Benton Jew was one of those tasked with devising different takes on the Scoleris. In some of his designs, the characters appear to be twins with electricity shooting out of their heads; another illustration sees them as

huge, sharply-dressed skull-headed gangsters; in another they are skeletal, wild-eyed and terrifying. One illustration sees a porcine Nunzio (as the character would be named) dressed in a more traditional mobster outfit. All are very different to the eventual design, but prove a fascinating glimpse into what the Scoleris could have turned out like.

"One of the most challenging parts of the project that was especially fun was during the bid phase," explains Jew. "We were coming up with crazy ideas and just riffing off of each other's ideas. Nothing was solidified script-wise [at this stage]... We were just trying to come up with as many ghost gags as we could."

BOTH PAGES Benton Jew's early illustrations for the Scoleris. Ideas included making the brothers giant skeletons and seeing them as more traditional mobsters.

ABOVE The final treated photograph as seen in *Ghostbusters II*.

OPPOSITE, TOP LEFT
Lou Police's painting, used as reference for the photograph.

OPPOSITE, BOTTOM RIGHT
Reference picture from the initial acetate composition.

THE LIVING
PAINTING

Glen Eytchison, the authority on living pictures, talks about the design process behind the portrait of Vigo and reveals how the Scourge of Carpathia was originally meant to manifest in the real world.

WHEN ILM WERE TASKED WITH TURNING Vigo into a living painting, there was only one person to call: Glen Eytchison. As director and producer of the Laguna Beach show *Pageant of the Masters* since 1979, Eytchison was the ultimate authority on living pictures. An eyepopping show in which performers step out of famous artworks to the sound of a live orchestra and narration, the *Pageant* had been wowing theater-goers since its curtains opened in 1932. Now ILM hoped to recreate the same 'tableaux viveux' artform with Vigo.

Yet Eytchison initially needed convincing that a big FX house like ILM needed his skills. "I flew up to San Rafael to meet with Dennis Muren," Eytchison remembers. "I'd idolized Dennis for years and felt compelled to tell him, 'You guys can figure this out. You don't really need me!' And he said, 'Yeah, we *could* figure this out but you do such a great job, so why waste our time?' It turns out it *is* tricky to do properly!"

Before he started work on the live action effect of Vigo stepping out of the painting, Eytchison and his team first needed to create the painting itself. This was no easy task. Eytchison recalls how on his first day on the picture, ILM handed him a big folder stuffed with 30 or so illustrations. It turned out to be reference on what *not* to do. "They told me Ivan had rejected every one of them for various reasons. Too *Conan the Barbarian*, too cartoonish… he just hated everything!"

Eytchison spent a day in his studio with two of his costume designers and an ILM illustrator researching what a Carpathian warlord would wear into battle and examining paintings from the period. Knowing that Reitman would want a say in the final composition, he decided to place the various elements of the picture on individual cells of acetate before starting work on the final version. These cells could easily be swapped around as necessary. "I placed the cells together in a cell composition that I felt was appropriate, then I showed Ivan the composition," he recalls. "It was very

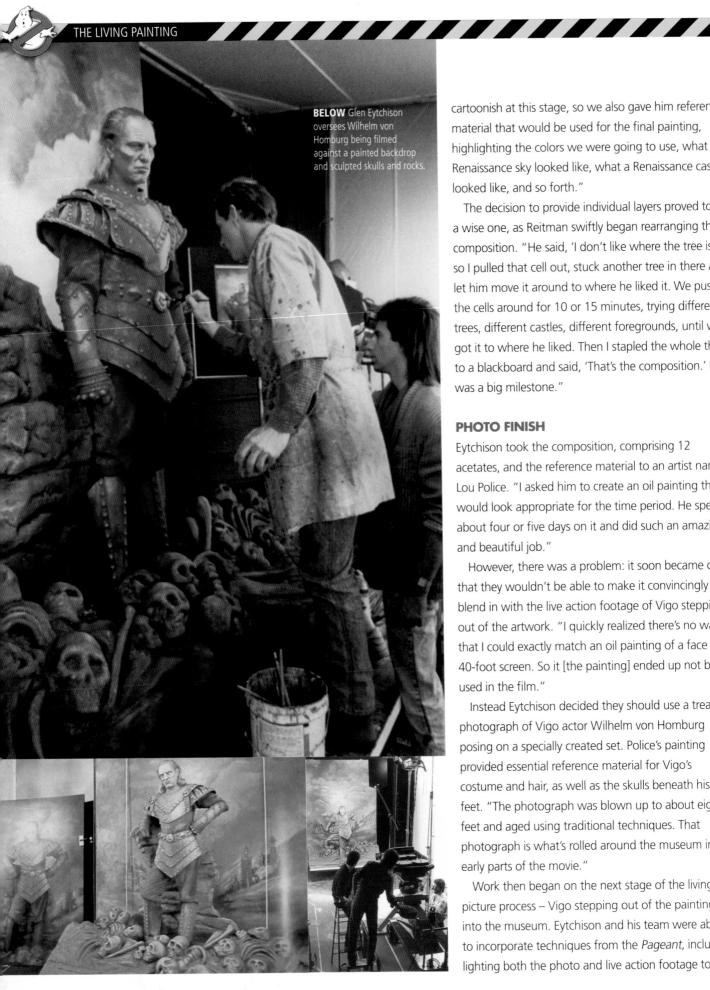

BELOW Glen Eytchison oversees Wilhelm von Homburg being filmed against a painted backdrop and sculpted skulls and rocks.

cartoonish at this stage, so we also gave him reference material that would be used for the final painting, highlighting the colors we were going to use, what a Renaissance sky looked like, what a Renaissance castle looked like, and so forth."

The decision to provide individual layers proved to be a wise one, as Reitman swiftly began rearranging the composition. "He said, 'I don't like where the tree is!', so I pulled that cell out, stuck another tree in there and let him move it around to where he liked it. We pushed the cells around for 10 or 15 minutes, trying different trees, different castles, different foregrounds, until we got it to where he liked. Then I stapled the whole thing to a blackboard and said, 'That's the composition.' It was a big milestone."

PHOTO FINISH

Eytchison took the composition, comprising 12 acetates, and the reference material to an artist named Lou Police. "I asked him to create an oil painting that would look appropriate for the time period. He spent about four or five days on it and did such an amazing and beautiful job."

However, there was a problem: it soon became clear that they wouldn't be able to make it convincingly blend in with the live action footage of Vigo stepping out of the artwork. "I quickly realized there's no way that I could exactly match an oil painting of a face on a 40-foot screen. So it [the painting] ended up not being used in the film."

Instead Eytchison decided they should use a treated photograph of Vigo actor Wilhelm von Homburg posing on a specially created set. Police's painting provided essential reference material for Vigo's costume and hair, as well as the skulls beneath his feet. "The photograph was blown up to about eight feet and aged using traditional techniques. That photograph is what's rolled around the museum in the early parts of the movie."

Work then began on the next stage of the living picture process – Vigo stepping out of the painting into the museum. Eytchison and his team were able to incorporate techniques from the *Pageant*, including lighting both the photo and live action footage to appear flat. Reitman wasn't satisfied with the first attempt, so Eytchison continued to show him different test footage. "Ivan would look at it and then we would get notes and try something else. We did that for a couple of days. We shot a bunch of different versions of Vigo stepping out, saying his lines."

There was one other difficulty. "The cast member [Homburg] was supposed to stay perfectly still and deliver his lines, then come to life and step out. But he had difficulty standing still… At one point we got a note from Production saying, 'Bolt him to the set!'"

Despite these issues, Eytchison says shooting the sequence went fairly smoothly. "We would do 40 pieces a year at the *Pageant*, so for us this was just another challenge."

After three-months of pre-production and a week of

shooting, Eytchison and ILM had footage everyone was happy with. Yet as fans will remember, *Ghostbusters II* does not actually end with Vigo stepping out of the painting. After the footage had been shot, Reitman decided to alter the sequence, with Vigo becoming a disembodied head who disappears from the painting before reappearing in the museum. For Eytchison, it was an unwelcome surprise. "The end of the movie was disappointing to us, because we'd worked really hard on Vigo stepping out of the painting," he admits.

Yet Eytchison remains sanguine about his time on the movie. "I've done other really big movies like *Devil's Advocate* and *Wild Wild West* and Broadway shows – and no one asks me about them. But Vigo the Carpathian is huge! People still want to talk about it. So I can't complain. Vigo has been very good to me."

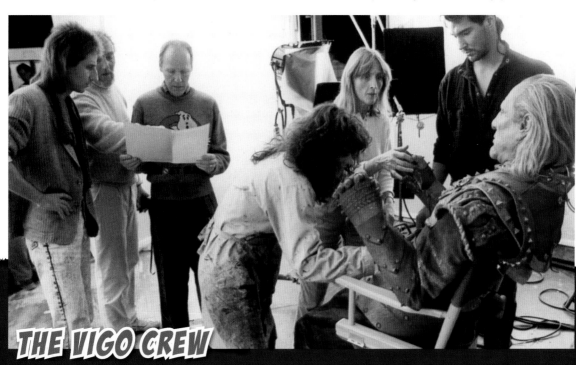

LEFT Glen Eytchison (far left) discusses Vigo with camera operator Terry Chostner and producer Michael C. Gross, while Mike Smithson, sculptor Judy Parker, and scenic artist Leslie Turnbull perfect Wilhelm von Homburg's costume and makeup.

THE VIGO CREW

Eytchison is keen to point out that many people were involved in creating the iconic image of Vigo we know today. In fact, he says at least a hundred people should take some credit, including his team, ILM and the production crew. "There's no one person who can take credit for Vigo. But a huge part of Vigo was Mike Smithson, who did the makeup and hair… Without Mike, it's a completely different film, a completely different

Vigo." He also stresses the importance of the "brilliant Pageant crew" (including set designer Richard Hill, costume designers Skipper Skeoch and Marci O'Malley, and sculptor Judy Parker), as well as key players at ILM such as Dennis Muren and Ned Gorman, and producer Michael C. Gross. "Though Michael, being an artist, kept picking up a brush and touching up the background… that was a bit problematic for us!"

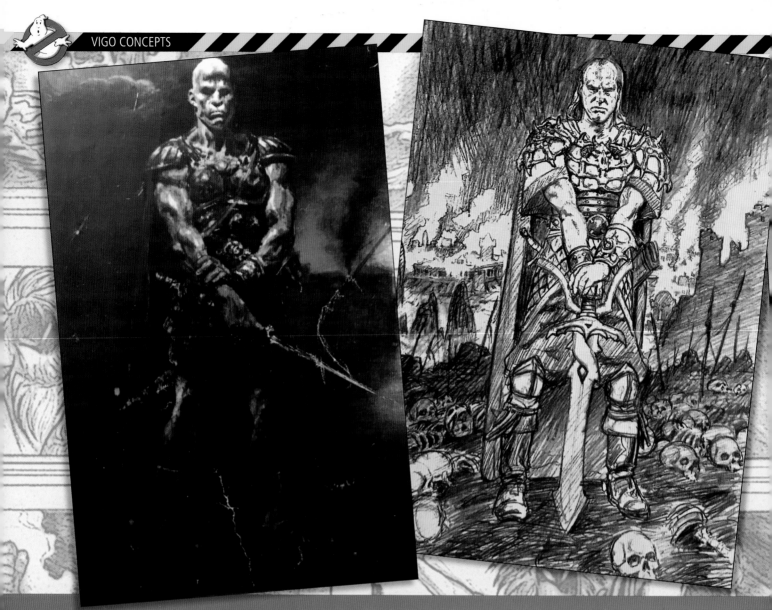

VIGO CONCEPT ART

Before ILM decided to use a treated photograph as Vigo's portrait, several top concept artists created some stunning illustrations. Three artists share their artwork and memories.

▲ **SEAN JOYCE:** "ILM called me up and said, 'There's this thing we want you to help us out with.' I had created matte paintings at ILM but I'm also a classical painter, sculptor and fantasy artist. I was [initially] thinking of something like Frazetta's *Conan*, but ILM said, 'We're looking for something sort of like Velázquez, something sort of Rembrandt-ish.' Figurative artists from the Renaissance. I did three or four little color illustrations, then I went down to the studio and the actor [Wilhelm von Homburg] posed for me so I could get his likeness. Then I did my drawing of the Vigo painting, which was also a costume design."

▼ BENTON JEW:

"This picture is of Vigo as the Statue of Liberty from very early during the bidding phase. The full script may not have been finalized at that point. I don't think people realize how fluid some shows can be script-wise, especially during the early phases. They can ask us to brainstorm and contribute our own ideas to see if something different works. I don't remember how solid this idea was, but there were hundreds of ideas and gags that were played with and discarded. There's a lot more stuff that didn't make it on screen than did. Most of the big FX films are like that. Only a tiny percentage makes it on screen."

OPPOSITE PAGE Sean Joyce's design and costume illustrations for Vigo.

LEFT Two of Henry Mayo's designs for Vigo. The larger image shows Vigo throwing aside 'Justin' (Janosz in the final movie).

BELOW In an early draft of the *Ghostbusters II* script, Vigo takes over the Statue of Liberty, as seen in Benton Jew's concept sketch.

▲ HENRY MAYO: "I did a lot of effects storyboards of Vigo, where his head comes out of the painting. They were a lot of fun. I think it was Dennis Muren who came up with the idea of having Vigo lean out of the painting because they wanted to do that effect. At one point I had Vigo turn his head inside out, and when he was blasted [by the Ghostbusters] he would transform into weird things. My storyboards were effects storyboards not conventional 'story' storyboards – I had to show them how the transformation would work. When they wanted to do the final painting, Dennis Muren came up with the idea that he wanted Vigo to look something like a Frazetta painting. I did a bunch of little sketches of the giant Vigo painting. At one point they were going to have me to do the painting of Vigo at the end, but I was leaving ILM at that point. At the time I had so much to do I didn't care, but I regret that – it would have been really great to do that painting."

VIGO

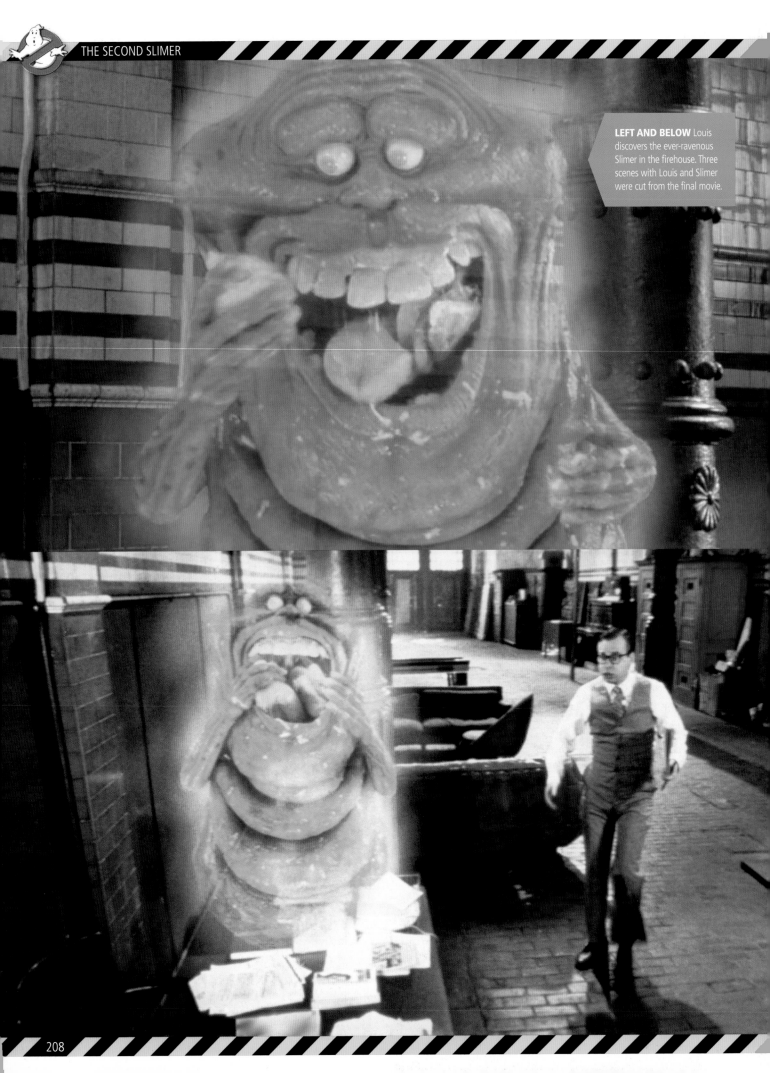

LEFT AND BELOW Louis discovers the ever-ravenous Slimer in the firehouse. Three scenes with Louis and Slimer were cut from the final movie.

THE SECOND
SLIMER

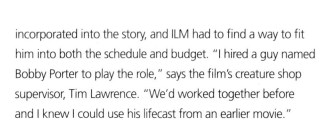

The stinking green ghoul was back for the sequel, but in the early days, his return was far from certain. Actress Robin Shelby and creature shop supervisor Tim Lawrence reveal more.

BY THE TIME PRE-PRODUCTION BEGAN on *Ghostbusters II*, Slimer was a wildly popular character thanks to his scene-stealing role in *The Real Ghostbusters* cartoon show. Yet he drifted in and out of early drafts of the story. In the original script, the green ghoul – as with other characters, from Dana to Janosz – was nowhere to be found. But by September 1988, he had been

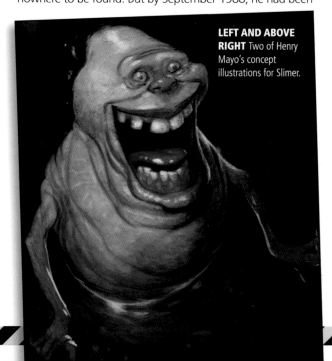

LEFT AND ABOVE RIGHT Two of Henry Mayo's concept illustrations for Slimer.

incorporated into the story, and ILM had to find a way to fit him into both the schedule and budget. "I hired a guy named Bobby Porter to play the role," says the film's creature shop supervisor, Tim Lawrence. "We'd worked together before and I knew I could use his lifecast from an earlier movie."

Both Henry Mayo and Thom Enriquez (who had created a wealth of concept art for the original Slimer) drew a series of updated designs for the character. Lawrence remembers being told that the new puppet needed to have "a little of the monster ghost from the original movie, a little bit of the Saturday morning TV show, and a lot of the great expressions from Enriquez's storyboard designs."

With that in mind, Lawrence and his team developed an initial maquette with "a big cartoon grin, little monster claws, and a flying torso." After this was approved, they began work on the suit itself, with 'Team Slimer' including Mark Siegel (returning from the first movie), who sculpted the head; Bob Cooper on arm-sculpting duties; Howie Weed, who did the finishing work; and speciality costumer supervisor Camilla Henneman, who supervised construction of the foam body.

ABOVE Tim Lawrence directs Robin Shelby in the Slimer costume against blue screen. Days during the six-week shoot could last up to 15 hours.

BELOW RIGHT Another of Henry Mayo's sketches.

The creature shop was almost done with the Slimer suit when it received some unwelcome news: Slimer had been cut from the script. Bobby Porter was let go, and work on the character stopped. But just two weeks later, Slimer was back in, now in an expanded role which saw him develop a burgeoning friendship with Tully. "They told me, 'Get Bobby back!'" Lawrence recalls. "But Bobby was on another show. So we had an open call to see if we could find someone who was his height and could wear his suit. [Visual effects coordinator] Ned Gorman suggested Robin Shelby, who he had worked with on *Willow*."

Shelby was swiftly hired for the role. While the main body shell fitted her, Lawrence says the creature shop needed to re-engineer the fingercaps, make a new headcast, and refit the head mechanics. An already tight schedule had just got tighter. "We went to work right away," says Shelby. "Because Slimer was added so late in the game, they had a lot to do in a very short period of time. It was pretty crazy!"

THE SLIMER FAMILY

Shelby recalls that days during the six-week shoot could last up to 15 hours, with the greatest challenge being the sheer weight of the head, which was packed with servos, wires and tubes. The face also featured complex animatronics that Lawrence says included "eyes that could stick all the way out of his skull and fully rotate for shock value," though these features were never fully seen in the final film.

Shelby emphasizes how the supportive atmosphere on set made wearing the heavy suit much easier. "Everybody felt like family," she says. "They kept checking I was OK, and they made sure that we took breaks every hour so I could take the head off and get a sip of water."

Shelby's scenes – which were directed by Lawrence – were shot against blue screen and, like most of the effects work, intercut with the first-unit footage later. Shelby controlled the body and arm movements, while other puppeteers operated the facial movements, something that required a large degree of co-

LEFT All aboard: Louis is surprised to see Slimer commanding a bus in one of *Ghostbusters II*'s memorable sequences.

ordination. "Six puppeteers controlled everything from the sniffing of the nose to the movements of the eyes," Shelby says. "We all had to know what everybody else was doing to create the right expression at the right time."

While Slimer survived into the final cut, not all of the character's scenes did, after preview audiences – along with Reitman – felt they didn't fit seamlessly into the story. Exorcised footage included two sequences in which Louis tries to apprehend Slimer in the firehouse and another in which Slimer catches up with Louis after he disembarks from a bus. "That guy really stinks…" says Louis to himself. "I got a lot of

friends that smell, I guess it's not that bad."

"That scene after they get off the bus worked out so well that I was bummed it was cut, but it's part of the business," says Shelby. "I'd love to see it [the first unit and effects footage] cut together at some point."

Twenty-seven years later, Shelby returned as a different gelatinous apparition in 2016's *Ghostbusters: Answer the Call*. This time she wasn't required to wear a 50-pound costume, instead providing the voice of Lady Slimer. "I think I'm the only actor who has played my own love interest!" she laughs. "Gosh, aren't I the luckiest girl in the world to have played both those roles?"

MESSY EATER!

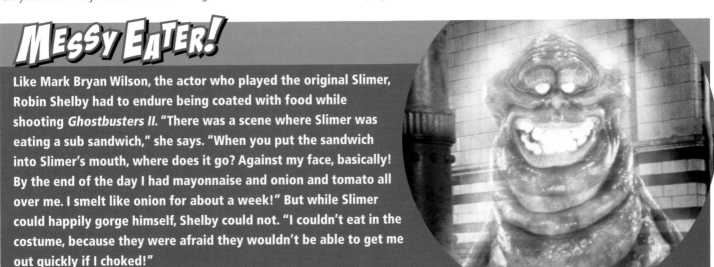

Like Mark Bryan Wilson, the actor who played the original Slimer, Robin Shelby had to endure being coated with food while shooting *Ghostbusters II*. "There was a scene where Slimer was eating a sub sandwich," she says. "When you put the sandwich into Slimer's mouth, where does it go? Against my face, basically! By the end of the day I had mayonnaise and onion and tomato all over me. I smelt like onion for about a week!" But while Slimer could happily gorge himself, Shelby could not. "I couldn't eat in the costume, because they were afraid they wouldn't be able to get me out quickly if I choked!"

THE GHOST NANNY

The demonic nanny that grabs baby Oscar was realized with a mixture of blue screen work and puppetry, as Don Bies and Bob Cooper explain.

VARIOUS OPTIONS WERE CONSIDERED FOR the entity that kidnaps baby Oscar from Dana's apartment in *Ghostbusters II*. Concept artists such as Thom Enriquez and Benton Jew worked up diverse designs, including a double-headed bird and a bat monster, that were ultimately rejected in favor of an evil nanny.

Once it was decided that Janosz, under Vigo's influence, would snatch Oscar, Peter MacNicol dressed up in the nanny outfit and was shot holding the pram, suspended on a platform against blue screen. A full-size extended arm was attached to MacNichol for the moment in which the nanny reaches out to grab the baby.

Part of the sequence also utilized a puppet version of Janosz, which was supervised by the late stop motion animator Dave Allen. Effects artists Bob Cooper and Don Bies were amongst those who built and puppeteered it.

"We built up a body in soft foam directly on an armature, and

sculptor Mike Smithson sculpted heads and hands in the likeness of the actor," recalls Bies. "A miniature replica costume was also created by [specialty costumer] Camilla Henneman. Because the stages were so busy, we acted as a night crew. We worked into the early morning to shoot all the angles required over the course of two to three nights."

NANNY FROM HELL

Cooper adds that clever camerawork helped give the puppet an appearance of movement. "The puppet was mounted and stationary – it looked like the puppet was moving, but actually the camera was moving," he says.

The main challenge that the Ghost Nanny crew faced was getting the cape to flow in the right way. "Whenever you miniaturize something – in this case, cloth – you need it to flow like the full-size article," Bies explains. "Getting the Ghost Nanny's clothing to flap in the wind realistically was remedied by using a thin, flowing fabric. We had to augment its movements by attaching fish-line to the corners of the cape to help billow it out."

The result was an effective horror sequence that acted as a segue into the third act showdown at the Museum of Art.

ABOVE Blue screen footage of actor Peter MacNicol was composited in with the miniature puppet version of the Ghost Nanny and the New York City skyline.

LEFT MacNicol as the Ghost Nanny incarnation of Janosz is filmed on a suspended platform against a blue screen.

GHOST STORIES

The creators of two memorable sequences in *Ghostbusters* II's 'mood slime chaos' montage discuss raising the *Titanic* and assembling the theater ghost.

"**B**ETTER LATE THAN NEVER," SAYS CHEECH MARIN'S understandably surprised dock worker as he observes the spirits of passengers who died on the *Titanic* disembarking the ship. The gag shot in *Ghostbusters* II's 'mood slime chaos' montage was achieved using a 12-foot miniature *Titanic*. Special effects co-ordinator Ned Gorman, remembers how he narrowly saved the production making a major blooper. "I was fascinated with the *Titanic*. My mother's old college friend Walter Lord wrote the seminal book on the topic, *A Night to Remember*, and he used to tell me stories of visiting the survivors. So I was the one appointed to tell Ivan that the storyboard he'd approved had the hole in the ship in the wrong place. The iceberg hit the starboard side of the ship not the port, and they had it the other way. So we flipped it around."

GHOSTBUSTERS II
FINAL THEATER GHOST DESIGN
COLUMBIA PICTURES

ABOVE LEFT TO RIGHT
Henry Mayo's original
concept art; Rick Lazzarini
and his monster puppet;
John Blake, sculptor of the
ghost's head. Lazzarini
used a custom 'waldo' to
manipulate the theater
ghost's expressions.

It was effects artist Howie Weed who was charged with devising the make-up design for the actors playing the ghosts of the passengers (which included several ILM employees). "Because it was a real-life event, we didn't want to make anything too depressing or ghoulish, so it was more of a fantasy work up," he says. "We did multi-coloured death characters with the hair plastered down."

Gorman remembers having the unenviable job of having to tell several child actors that they would no longer be playing ghosts in the film. "Just as we were getting ready to shoot it, the head of the studio was visiting with Ivan. She looked at the concept art and said, 'Oh, are you sure you want to have children in there?' So at the 11th hour we had to break the heart of several children who were cast. There are no pets there either – we couldn't have ghost dogs!"

THEATER GHOST

A sequence with a ghost freaking out cinema-goers was originally due to appear in the first *Ghostbusters*, but was cut for being too expensive and time-consuming. In the original script the screening was described simply as "an all-night horror marathon," but by the sequel it had become *Cannibal Girls*, Ivan Reitman's sophomore movie.

Ghostbusters II's theater ghost was largely based on one of Henry Mayo's concept designs. "I think [producer] Michael Gross mentioned the movie *Night of the Demon* and said he wanted something scary like that," Mayo says. "Michael wanted something really out-there. I did a ton of drawings and they'd feed them to Aykroyd and Ramis, who would laugh and come up with more crazy ideas. I probably did 30 or 40 ideas. They settled on one design, which was

handed to Rick Lazzarini. They told him to go crazy."

The ghost – a winged creature with four arms, fangs and six eyes – was added to the film late in the process, and Lazzarini had just three weeks to create the sculpt, mold, and rubber skin for the puppet. "The skins had internal armatures for the arms and they were rod-operated," he says. "The wings were also rod-operated."

Lazzarini incorporated a custom animatronic 'facial waldo' system into the lightweight foam head, allowing it to rotate, move up and down, and move its jaws. The waldo could also manipulate all six eyebrows into a sinister 'V' shape. "Rather than having a joystick to make those things move, I wore a cap and vest, so if I tilted my head it pulled a string which turned a control which in turn sent a wireless signal to tell the puppet to do the same thing," Lazzarini explains. "If I opened my jaw, the puppet opened its jaw, and so on. That way you get a very seamless connection between performance and result."

The sequence was filmed at the visual effects studio Apogee as ILM was at capacity.

BELOW The theater ghost
terrifies attendees of the
1973 film *Cannibal Girls* in
the *Ghostbusters II* montage
sequence. *Cannibal Girls* was
the second film that Ivan
Reitman had directed.

"THE COAT COMES ALIVE"
GHOSTBUSTERS II
I.L.M. 1988

MAYO

LEFT Henry Mayo's concept art for *Ghostbusters II* shows the mink coat coming to life.

THE MINK COAT

The mink coat that springs to life in *Ghostbusters II* was originally designed to operate in a different manner, explains creature shop supervisor Tim Lawrence.

IT'S A BRIEF BUT UNFORGETTABLY BONKERS sequence: as the mood slime oozes into the streets of New York, a wealthy woman (played by Louise Troy) wrapped in a mink coat unwittingly steps in the goo. Moments later the yapping spirits of the dead minks spring out from the coat. After the woman hurls the coat to the ground in horror, the coat scurries off down the street.

The concept of a monstrous mink coat featured in an early draft script of the original *Ghostbusters*, where it sprang into life at a fashion show. Though the scene was storyboarded, it was never filmed. The idea was resurrected for the sequel, with illustrator Henry Mayo drawing the concept art.

After that, it was the responsibility of ILM's creature shop to construct the coat. Creature shop supervisor Tim Lawrence remembers how his team originally constructed the multi-headed monster. "Loren Soman built this really neat little runaway toy gag, and Eben Stromquist made these wonderful radio-controlled minks that came up from under the coat," he says. "The hair-work on their faces was also wonderful. It felt very alive."

Lawrence and his team believed that their design was signed off and ready to go – but they were in for a surprise. "We'd done a test with white fur that had been sent down and approved. We had milled a special fur with a flex back. A week before we were supposed to get on a plane with it and meet Ivan for the night shoot [outside] the hotel, we got this big box of pelt and a note saying, '*This* is what the coat needs to look like.' We were looking at each other saying, 'What are you talking about? The coat's done!' But, nope, that's what they wanted. Everything had to be re-covered."

THE FINAL DESIGN

It soon became clear that the mechanisms inside the coat also needed to be rapidly amended. "Because it's stiff pelt, the wonderful mink that Evan built just didn't work as well and the hip motor would not raise the minks up out of the coat anymore. They had to be replaced with foot-controlled pedal cables. So now you've got four pedal cables attached to the coat instead of it being completely wireless."

Though today the mink coat holds up as one *Ghostbusters II*'s many highlights, Lawrence admits that at the time he felt a little disappointed in the new version of the coat compared to the original. Nevertheless, he says he loved the shot of it running off down the sidewalk. "That's a totally mechanical, practical effect that I still think looks good. Way down the end of the sidewalk there was a little pulley and a string going around the corner. Alan Coulter – who was the supervisor of animatronics on *Ghostbusters II* – then ran off down the sidewalk in the other direction [with the string] to make the thing tear off."

This wasn't quite the last anyone saw of the coat – it popped up in two issues of IDW's comic in 2012.

LEFT AND BELOW
The final sequence of the minks snapping at the coat's wealthy owner (Louise Troy). The design changed a week before filming.

WASHINGTON SQUARE GHOST

Animators Randal Dutra and Harry Walton recall how they helped Phil Tippett bring the hulking monstrosity to life.

HE MAY NOT BE CREDITED ON THE MOVIE, but revered stop-motion animator Phil Tippett was instrumental in bringing to life the Washington Square ghost, the hulking monstrosity that terrifies New Year's Eve revellers in the Greenwich Village park in *Ghostbusters II*. Before founding his own studio, Tippett had created groundbreaking work for ILM (including animating the chess sequence in *Star Wars* and the AT-ATs and Tauntauns in *The Empire Strikes Back*), and he maintained an excellent relationship with the studio. So when a stretched ILM wanted to ensure they hit their deadline by outsourcing certain effects work late in the day, it made sense to approach Tippett.

ABOVE Photographs of the Washington Square Ghost puppet, courtesy of Prop Store.

OPPOSITE PAGE The monster as seen in the mood slime montage in *Ghostbusters II*.

Tippett tasked fellow animator Randal Dutra (who would later be nominated for Academy Awards® for his work on *The Lost World: Jurassic Park* and *War of the Worlds*) with creating the initial sculpt in clay. "It was a two to three-day project," remembers Dutra. "My recollection is that it was a bit of a Production afterthought/insertion. The design then went through some additional permutations that I believe were requested by Ivan Reitman and addressed accordingly by Phil."

MOOD SLIME MONTAGE

With time tight, Tippett incorporated existing stop-motion armatures into the puppet as he finalized the design. It was then handed to another experienced animator, Harry Walton. "Phil built it up with foam and painted it, and then I animated it," says Walton, who in that period was dividing his time between creating optical effects for ILM and shooting stop-motion for Tippett Studios. "It was a really quick stop-motion shot."

Walton says he spent one day setting up and shooting exposure tests at Tippett Studio and then animated it on the second day. "First of all I had a plate of the [location] shot from Production, which I put in the animation camera. I then rotoscoped it out and built a little mock-up model of the arch so the puppet could react to it when it was shot in stop-motion. As it was double-exposed into the shot, everything behind the creature was black."

Walton took on multiple tasks during the quick shoot. "I set up the camera, rotoscoped it, lit the creature and animated it. I think I may have composited it too as I was doing a lot of optical work for ILM!"

The stop-motion shot was composited into the location footage, which had been shot in the early hours at Washington Square by another effects company, John Dykstra's Apogee. The sequence was then incorporated into the movie's mood-slime montage. "The screen time was fleeting but it served its purpose!" says Dutra.

LEFT TO RIGHT Benton Jew's concept art, which influenced the look of the ghost jogger; Jim Fye in his pale white makeup; Howie Weed sprays Streaks 'N Tips on the actor.

GHOST JOGGER

Performer Jim Fye and effects artist Howard Weed remember the chill-inducing experience of shooting the ghost jogger sequence.

H E'S THE FASTEST SPOOK IN NEW YORK CITY – although still not fast enough to outrun Peter and Ray's ghost trap. The pale, lanky ghost jogger seen zipping through Central Park in *Ghostbusters II*'s montage sequence was not described in detail in the script, and the look largely came from one of artist Benton Jew's concept illustrations.

The jogger was played by Jim Fye. Originally brought on board to play the Statue of Liberty, the actor found he had enough downtime to take on other roles – in addition to playing the ghost jogger, he also wound up being cast as Tony Scoleri. The ghost jogger was the first of Fye's three roles to be filmed, with the sequence shot against blue screen at an ILM soundstage on a chilly day in January 1989. Fye remembers the

sequence as being his most straightforward role on the picture, largely consisting of running down a long, elevated ramp and checking his pulse. "It was pretty intimate – there weren't many people involved in the shoot and we did it all in one day," he says.

However, one of Fye's over-riding memories of shooting the sequence is just how cold it was, with the jogger's outfit of white shoes and socks, yellow running shorts, and a white tank top offering scant protection. "I didn't have a dressing room, it was just the corner of the soundstage, and I was cold enough to begin with," he says. "Then Howie Weed sprayed me with liquid makeup. It was freezing!"

"I felt really bad," insists effects artist Weed. "I actually went cheap and quick with that rather than using an airbrush. He was due to be brought backstage 20 minutes before the shoot in his costume, and I just had to get white pancake makeup on him. I quickly realized that it takes a long time to put on white makeup and make it all even. There's a lot of stippling and fussing, and I knew there was no time. So I went

out and bought an entire case of white Streaks 'N Tips – that's what you use at Halloween to make your hair different colours. I spray-painted him completely with it! It was seven o'clock in the morning, and I'd spray up his back, knowing it was freezing. I'd say, 'Sorry!' as I sprayed around the top of his body, his eyes, his legs... He'd hold his breath as it smelt just like hairspray."

Still, Weed points out it was an effective method for creating the effect. "It was quick and easy to touch up after lunch. I'd just say, 'Close your eyes!' and WHOOSH! he's ready for the shot. It worked great. It was very even-looking and only took a fraction of the time that stippling makeup would have taken." The only thing left was to add a glow effect around the jogger before the health-freak was composited into the first-unit footage at Central Park.

The scene was slightly longer in the original script, with Stantz checking his timer and commenting how the ghost jogger had run his last lap in under six minutes. "If he wasn't dead, he'd be an Olympic prospect," deadpans Venkman.

ABOVE Stills from *Ghostbusters II* show Jim Fye's ghost jogger running around Central Park and repeatedly checking his time – shortly before being sucked into a ghost trap.

BELOW A chilly Jim Fye prepares himself for filming, and the ghost jogger sequence is shot on an elevated ramp against a blue screen. The outfit provided little protection from the cold.

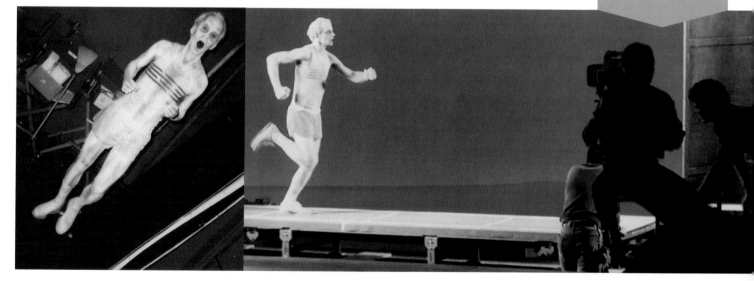

FROG GHOST

Concept artist Henry Mayo and monster maker Rick Lazzarini look back on the unseen frog ghost that almost hopped its way into *Ghostbusters II*.

NOT ALL OF THE SPOOKS DESIGNED FOR THE *Ghostbusters* movies made it to the screen. Many creatures never made it beyond the concept stage, while others were actually built but cut late in the day. One of the most intriguing entries in the latter category is the frog ghost, which very nearly appeared in the subway sequence in *Ghostbusters II*.

The origins of the frog ghost lay in a stroll that concept artist Henry Mayo took around the Warner Bros lot. "I was walking outside when I saw this frog on the ground," he recalls ."When I came back in I drew a frog attacking somebody on the subway – and [producer] Michael Gross fell in love with it. He said, 'This is going to be our great monster sequence!' It was funny because it was just a throwaway idea."

FROG-THING EMERGES FROM TUNNEL INTO PLATFORM AREA   9/28

The picture was sent to animatronics expert Rick Lazzarini – who took it in an even more insanely monstrous direction. Lazzarini was given the go-ahead to run with his idea and sculpt the creature, which was to appear after the ghost train vanished in the subway.

"I went over to Rick's shop down the street while it was in process and looked at the creature," Mayo remembers. "It had changed. It no longer looked so much like a frog as some kind of monstrous thing... it was horrific to see in person! It was just so horrible-looking in a wonderful way. Rick had developed this great mechanical system, and it moved in the creepiest way."

Lazzarini, who constructed a fully animatronic latex puppet of the frog ghost, also has fond memories of his creation. "It was kind of chubby with big bug eyes, a mouthful of fangs, and a big tongue lashing out," he laughs. "We actually had a performer, Jon Price, with his arms inside the creature's arms as if it was crawling,

and his head actuated the tongue. He had a helmet on with a rod – sort of like a dildo-hat! – that went inside the tongue. He could make the tongue slobber from left to right and up and down as he moved his head. It had animatronic eyes which blinked, and brows, which I operated off-screen."

While footage of the frog ghost was shot, it never made it into the final film. Lazzarini says that Ivan Reitman felt it was just a little too comical. "To me it fits right in with the *Ghostbusters* oeuvre, but Ivan said he didn't think it was scary enough, so it ended up on the cutting room floor," he says with a touch of sadness. "Bye bye frog ghost."

Lazzarini's latex puppet has long since deteriorated – or, in his words, "shipped upstairs to the old creature farm to chase Saturn Awards for all eternity" – leaving Mayo's illustrations and a handful of on-set photos all that remains of the amphibian behemoth's legacy.

BELOW Monster maker Rick Lazzarini and his outlandish frog ghost creation. The puppet featured an intricate mechanical system and was able to blink, slobber and crawl.

BATHTUB MONSTER

Former ILM effects wizards Ned Gorman, Tim Lawrence, Howie Weed, and Danny Wagner discuss the creation of *Ghostbuters II*'s bathtime beast.

LIKE MANY OF THE DESIGNS IN THE *Ghostbusters* movies, the bathtub monster went through dozens of iterations during pre-production. Concept artists including Henry Mayo, Thom Enriquez, and Benton Jew drew up different takes on the creature, while alternative attack monsters – including toys and teddy bears brought to life by Vigo – were also considered.

ILM's practical effects team ran experiments during the development stage too. "For every creature gag, we did 30 or 40 different workouts," says effects artist Howie Weed. "There was a bubble monster at one point that [consisted of] foam with giant bubbles coming out of it, and there was a slime creature that was going to stand up. All kinds of crazy stuff."

Creature effects supervisor Tim Lawrence also has vivid memories of the different ideas that were worked up. "I remember making a tiny miniature rubber model and hooking it up like a little marionette. It could move and [develop] a great big porcelain mouth. That was popular, but they just wanted something simple and easy. So we went with a glove puppet covered in slime."

Before ILM could recreate the miniature bathtub and slime puppet, they needed to know exactly what the bath would

LEFT TO RIGHT Concept
art by Henry Mayo; an early
bathtub monster sculpt;
molds and plastics artist
Danny Wagner and 'bathtub
wrangler' Wim Van Thillo
with the bathtime beast.

look like. "We pushed Ivan towards an old-fashioned, claw-footed bathtub because it's menacing by its very nature," says visual effects co-ordinator Ned Gorman.

Gorman attended the first-unit shoot in Dana's apartment set. "For the bathtub sequence, they pulled out the wall behind Sigourney and the baby and had her react in front of the blue screen. They gave us that footage quickly, and it said, 'insert monster here.'"

The quarter-scale miniature bath was constructed from silicone enabling it to flex easily. The creature itself was designed and built by Thom Floutz, while the sequence was directed by stop-motion legend Dave Allen. Effects artist Danny Wagner assisted on set. "Thom was the lead puppeteer, and I was underneath the tub, helping to hold up a silicone blanket that covered a fiberglass mandrel," he says. "In that way we puppeteered the creature's body and mouth. It was a quick sequence but effective."

Gorman says they shot the monster lunging in a few alternative ways so Ivan Reitman would have more options to choose from. However, after seeing the initial dailies Gorman wasn't entirely convinced about the sequence. "I remember thinking it didn't look so much menacing as silly," he admits. Thankfully, when he saw the footage intercut with Weaver's performance and with added sound effects, Gorman was reassured. "By the time they put it all together – and once Ivan made a tight cut of it – the sequence worked rather well," he says. "I'm sure today it would be 100% CGI and the animation would be a little more elegant. But while we can do effects like this cleaner and faster now, I'm not sure we can necessarily do them better."

The effect may have been relatively simple, but the result was perhaps the greatest bathtime fright since Freddy Krueger's hand emerged from the water in *A Nightmare on Elm Street*.

LEFT The bathtub monster puppet was created using a silicone blanket covering a fiberglass mandrel, while the bathtub was also silicone to allow it to flex easily.

RIGHT In the movie's opening scene, the wheel of Dana's pram runs through a pool of mood slime oozing through a crack in the street.

MOOD SLIME

The psychomagnotheric slime was a key plot point of *Ghostbusters II*. ILM's visual effects co-ordinator Ned Gorman and effects artist Howie Weed share their slime experiences.

SLIME WAS BACK FOR *GHOSTBUSTERS II.* In fact, according to the movie's publicist Stuart Fink, 100,000 gallons of the stuff was concocted for the sequel.

This time, the substance acts as an important plot point, with the psychomagnotheric slime (or 'mood slime') responding to the mood of surrounding humans, whether that is positive vibes (the sound of Jackie Wilson's 'Higher and Higher') or negative (the default position of the vast majority of New Yorkers). The slime is also appropriated by Vigo to attack both Dana and her baby in the form of the bathtub monster, and later used by the Ghostbusters – with the aid of their slime blowers – to bring the Statue of Liberty to life.

Like the first film, the slime was largely made from methylcellulose, but this time it was mixed with pink food coloring – not that it was always going to be pink. "We weren't sure what color the slime was going to be," says the film's visual effects co-ordinator Ned Gorman. "Ivan knew he didn't want it to be green or like the clear gloop from the first movie, but he wanted to keep his options open. But Michael Chapman, the DP, needed to know what color the slime was; he was going to be up against it as there are a lot of reflective surfaces in the museum. And we needed to know what to match in post. We didn't have the digital toolbox we do now."

Gorman remembers how ILM experimented with many different colors of slime, from red ("too *Fangoria*") to yellow

("too gross"). They eventually settled on a shade of "grotesque pink" that they used to create a test for the River of Slime a few days before the first-unit footage was due to shoot. "Ivan liked it, and Michael [Chapman] and the grips said, 'We can work with that,'" says Gorman.

The final River of Slime effect – which was composited into on-set footage with Dan Aykroyd dangling on a rope – was spearheaded by Ralph Miller (credited as "River Rat"), who oversaw a team of slime-mixers and tentacle puppeteers.

NIGHT AT THE MUSEUM

The other big slime effect was the gloop-encased museum. Howie Weed was one of those involved in sculpting, casting, and coating the replica museum used in the sequence. "We made a black silicone box, which we coated with crystalline pink glaze," he explains. "Once the glaze cooled, it became like thin glass."

For the shot in which the slime falls away from the museum following the Ghostbusters' victory over Vigo, Weed and his colleagues headed down to ILM's parking lot at night armed with hammers. "We slowly turned the pink box upside down, hoping it wouldn't start to come apart, and [suspended it] on a pipe-rig," he says. "Then we crawled up on top of this thing. When someone said 'Action!', we would hit it with mallets as hard as we could. It would cause the pink crystalline stuff to shatter and fall to the ground. But sometimes a piece wouldn't come off the silicone box, it would just hang there – so we'd have to do it again. We did that three times a night until two in the morning for over a week."

For Weed, the experience sums up the thrill of working in an era of practical effects. "In visual effects now, you'd just say, 'Oh, we did it in a computer with fluid simulation software.' But we were smashing up crystalline goop the middle of the night with mallets!"

ABOVE Firefighters look on at the slime-covered Museum of Art; a specimen of mood slime bubbles in the Ghostbusters' lab.

THE STATUE OF LIBERTY

Performer Jim Fye and effects supervisors Ned Gorman and
Tim Lawrence reveal how they helped Lady Liberty save the world.

THE FACT THAT THE STATUE OF LIBERTY existed in real life did not make it any easier to bring to the screen than *Ghostbusters II*'s assorted imaginary creatures. In fact, it posed several logistical problems right from the start. "We thought it was going to be one of the easier effects, but we ran into all kind of strange challenges," says the film's visual effects co-ordinator Ned Gorman. "We all know that metal doesn't bend without ripping apart – so how were we going to have our big-hearted audience believe that she could walk down Fifth Avenue without ripping apart? And just trying to build a suit that we could put a human being into without breaking their neck or limbs was no mean feat."

The human being in this potentially limb-breaking suit was Jim Fye (who went on to play Tony Scoleri and the ghost jogger too). After securing the role, Fye studied Ken Burn's acclaimed 1985 documentary *The Statue of Liberty*, which had 360-degree images of Lady Liberty, and he tried to imagine how the statue might move. Yet moving inside the suit was easier said than done.

The costume Fye had to wear was constructed from polyfoam 1014, an expanding flexible polyurethane foam, and a lifecast of the actor was used for the mold as it needed to form-fit. Getting into the costume was not a simple

BELOW A sculpted Statue of Liberty bust, complete with miniature Ghostbusters in the crown, was used in some shots in the sequence.

process. "It took three hours, maybe more to get into that costume," Fye remembers. "That was the longest part of the day. It was [lead finisher and painter] Buzz Neigid's job to get me in and out of the costume and keep it in a good state of repair, because it tore every time I moved. He put the neck piece on, then the feet and gloves, and then the skirt – the body of the costume – would be put on last as that was the heaviest. I remember the pieces would be glued on and held until they set. At the end of the day, they had to use solvent to peel the costume off. The glue wouldn't shower off. I was pretty funky for a couple of weeks!"

The other key pieces of the costume, says Fye, were the plastic mask, the hair and the crown that contained lights and little plastic recreations of the Ghostbusters. "There was no part of my body showing," he says.

BANGING THE SHOVEL

If getting the suit on and off was difficult, filming the sequence was hardly any less arduous. "The costume was heavy and as it was form-fitting, I'd sweat buckets – and it only got heavier with the sweat!" Fye continues. "I couldn't take the costume off during breaks, so they had this slate leaning board for me. There was mesh over the eyes, so I couldn't really see either. It was very uncomfortable, and you would not have liked it if you were claustrophobic as it was completely black in there!"

As well as not being able to see, Fye couldn't hear much either, and was reliant on others for direction.

Stage manager Ed Hirsh would stand underneath him translating stage directions from the other side of the room, while creature shop supervisor Tim Lawrence developed his own method of communicating with Fye inside the suit. "We'd talk about what direction he would be going and what the beat would be, and when they started filming, I would be on the edge of the stage with a shovel and a wrench," Lawrence says. "I would pound out the beat so that Jim could hear me and keep his feet in time!"

Yet another challenge for Fye was keeping his arm raised straight for hours on end. "That was a real challenge," the actor admits. "There are some shots where it wasn't quite right... but then you can't [replicate] the way that the Statue of Liberty's arm is so straight and close to her head with a human being. It's not really anatomically correct!"

The majority of the footage was shot against an illuminated blue screen so it could be intercut with second-unit footage, but one sequence was shot against a miniature stretch of New York City. "There's a wonderful close-up where a foot crushes a model police car," Lawrence remembers. "They used a wax car. There was a guy underneath there blowing margarita salt through a little tube so it looked like shattered glass coming out around it. These details wind up being important."

"That shot of the Statue of Liberty crushing the police car flat was going to be in the first movie, except with the Marshmallow Man, but they ran out of time,"

Gorman adds. "Ivan was determined to get it in this movie, so we started working on that straight away."

OFF THE PEDESTAL

At the time, the effects teams had various concerns about how they were going to make the Statue of Liberty march to the Manhattan Museum of Art without impacting upon her iconic appearance. "[The sequence with the Statue of Liberty walking] is designed to be seen from a ground perspective," says Lawrence. "But the Statue of Liberty has a very long neck, and as soon as you have that costume on a miniature set and you have the head [turn], the neck disappears. It affects the look of the character."

For Gorman, one of the central challenges was how to believably show the Statue of Liberty climbing down from its 89-foot pedestal. "How would an iron and copper statue climb down from that? Does the slime give elastic properties to the metal? If so, how are we going to show it? Ultimately Ivan wisely decided, 'Guys, let's just solve the problem by not showing it [climbing down from the pedestal]. Let's show the torch igniting it, cut away to the foot separating, and then show her wading through New York harbor.' If we were asking people to believe that New York was over-run by ghosts, they'd give us a break!"

Gorman adds that he's just glad that the sequence was made before the age of social media. "In the age of the Twitter-sphere, we'd probably be eviscerated with people saying 'metal can't bend like that!'" he laughs. "Thankfully, no one at the time questioned it."

BEST FOOT FORWARD

The construction of the Statue of Liberty's foot, seen ripping away from the pedestal in close-up, fell to effects artist Howie Weed. "The audience can see these beams and mechanisms pulling out of the ground as she's taking her first step out," Weed recalls. "We took the casting that we already had from the Statue of Liberty costume and just built this special rig that had girders glued to the bottom of the foot. They added the sounds of grinding metal as the foot pulled up from the base. That was a fun one to work on!"

POSSESSED!

While playing the possessed version of Ray, Howie Weed was deprived of his senses and blasted by slime. He also had to endure a *Clockwork Orange*-style eye procedure...

DURING THE FINAL ACT OF *GHOSTBUSTERS II*, when Ray takes on a monstrous form as he is possessed by Vigo, it is neither Dan Aykroyd nor Wilhelm von Homburg under the makeup. Instead it is effects artist Howie Weed. "The sequence was added at the 11th hour, but they couldn't get Dan Aykroyd back to do it," he remembers. "Everyone turned to me and said, 'Well he looks a bit like Dan Aykroyd...' Weed readily agreed – but he didn't know what he was letting himself in for.

After some design experiments that saw ILM frantically trying to figure out what the possessed Ray should look like, Weed made a green clay mold based on a lifecast of Von Homburg – and promptly took a blow-torch to it. "I knew Roma-Plastilina clay would bubble up and become

this diseased zombie-looking thing," he explains. After the clay had cooled down, Weed showed it to art director Harley Jessup. "Harley grabbed it, took it over into the spray booth and did this extenuated, almost drag queen-type makeup on it with rouge eyebrows. That was the genesis of the final design!"

Once Reitman had given his seal of approval to the design, it was passed to makeup artist Mike Smithson to sculpt the prosthetic pieces that Weed would wear. These pieces consisted of a chin piece, an upper mouth piece, and forehead piece, all of which would be glued on, as well as a big cowl that covered the top of Weed's head and neck. The makeup took around three hours to apply and left Weed unable to hear. Or see. Or barely talk. "I had dentures and they made me swirl grape Cool Aid so my mouth would look black!" he laughs.

Perhaps the strangest aspect of the role was having a cast of his eyeballs made. "They used these big, custom-made glass things that covered the whites of the eye. I sat in the doctor's seat and he took a cup and stretched my eyelids over it, *Clockwork Orange* style. Then he mixed up this stuff called alginate, a molding material like powdered seaweed. When you mix it with water it solidifies real fast. He put it into a tube coming off the back of the cup and – *boom!* – my eye went black and cold. Then he started wiggling the cup, which went all the way back to my optic nerve. I had to have the other eye done after that. Later we got these black contacts back for me to wear."

Just when it seemed like the costume couldn't get any more inhibiting, a 30-pound Slime Blower tank was strapped to his back, throwing him off balance.

When Weed eventually got to the stage for filming, he found he had yet another challenge: despite his limited ability to talk, he had to lip-sync to several lines of dialogue. "They had Wilhelm on playback saying, 'I,

Vigo, shall rule the Earth… blah, blah, blah.' The director said, 'You got it?' I was like, 'No I haven't!' So they played it over and over while we were setting up. Then they told me I'd have to lip-sync to it at double speed!"

Having memorized the lines, Weed stood on his platform – at which point he noticed a tent in front of him containing a pipe pointing at his head. "I was a little concerned," he says.

Filming began. Just after Weed launched into his lip-synched lines, he was hit by a high-speed jet of slime. "It hit me with such force that I staggered back! It was thick, like butter. My mouth was filled with slime, and we shot it five or six times. I would keep some slime in my mouth and spit it out at the end of each shot for dramatic effect!"

Weed remembers his vision was so impaired that visual effects supervisor Dennis Muren brandished a torch to indicate the direction in which he should look. "That was kind of bizarre – having this eight-time Academy Award winner running around the stage with a flashlight." When Weed saw the final footage, he was pleased to see the way his disembodied head detonated. "It exploded like the Death Star!"

Despite the challenges, Weed had a ball playing the role. However, he remains unsure as to whether he could have had a permanent career as Dan Aykroyd's double. "I remember one of the effects guys asked Dan Aykroyd's wife [actress Donna Dixon] what she thought of the film. She said, 'I really enjoyed it but who the hell was playing Dan at the end? That's the worst performance I've ever seen!' One day maybe I'll get the chance to explain. I could have been better without that slime shooting in my face!"

ABOVE LEFT TO RIGHT Weed in Vigo/Ray prosthetics; a near-blind Weed in between prosthetic makeup supervisor Mike Smithson and creature shop supervisor Tim Lawrence; the performer's custom-made eye contacts are inserted.

BELOW Howie Weed's near-final design maquette based on art direction notes.

OPPOSITE PAGE Weed in final makeup, about to be blasted with slime!

INDEX

CREDITS

Writer: Matt McAllister

Art Editor: Dan Rachael

Sound Design Feature: Daniel Wallace

Project Manager: Jo Bourne

Head of Development: Ben Robinson

Cover Illustration: Brian Williamson

Thanks to John Ainsworth, John Alberti, Brandon Allinger at Prop Store, Lance Anderson, William Atherton, Dan Aykroyd, Richard Beggs, John Bell, Peter Bernstein, Don Bies, John Bruno, Bill Bryan, Tony Cecere, Randy Cook, Bob Cooper, Ron Croci, Peter Daulton, John DeCuir Jr., Tom Duffield, Randal Dutra, Richard Edlund, Leslie Ekker, Michael Ensign, Glen Eytchison, Thom Enriquez, Jim Fye, Kurt Fuller, Bruno George, Adam Gelbart, George Giordano, Ned Gorman, Greg Grusby, Ernie Hudson, Simon Hugo, Benton Jew, Steve Johnson, Sean Joyce, Virginia King, Gene Kozicki, Tim Lawrence, Rick Lazzarini, Henry Mayo, Michael McWillie, Joe Medjuck, Dennis Michelson, Gary Montalbano, Ronald B. Moore, Thaine Morris, Steve Neill, Kerry Nordquist, Melody Pena, Zach Pogemiller at Profiles in History, Annie Potts, John Rothman, Kevin Stern at Beyond the Marquee, Chris Prince at Insight Editions, Violet Ramis Stiel, Eric Reich, Ivan Reitman, Jennifer Runyon, Michael J. Schwartz, Aleksander U. Serigstad, Robin Shelby, Bob Shelley, Mike Smithson, Mark Stetson, Danny Wagner, Harry Walton, Howie Weed, Mark Bryan Wilson, Stuart Ziff

Published by **Hero Collector Books**, a division of Eaglemoss Ltd. 2020
1st Floor, Kensington Village, Avonmore Road, W14 8TS, London, UK.
All rights reserved.

BOSS Film photos by Virgil Mirano;
courtesy of Richard Edlund

ILM photos © Industrial Light
& Magic. Used with permission.

www.herocollector.com